Table of Content

Table of Content..1
Chapter 1: Introduction 3
Chapter 2: The Jewish Roots of Faith 22
Chapter 3: Messianic Identity and Beliefs............................41
Chapter 4: Connecting with Jewish Culture 56
Chapter 5: Encountering the Hebrew Language 79
Chapter 6: Navigating Religious Differences 91
Chapter 7: Embracing the Messianic Jewish Community 111
Chapter 8: The Power of Worship and Prayer 130
Chapter 9: Living Out Faith in Daily Life 147
Chapter 10: The Role of Social Justice................................. 168
Chapter 11: Exploring the Arts and Culture......................... 187
Chapter 12: Facing Challenges and Questions 212
Chapter 13: The Importance of Family and Community 231
Chapter 14: Sharing the Message of Messiah 247
Chapter 15: Building a Legacy of Faith................................. 266
Chapter 16: The Future of Messianic Judaism..................... 282
Chapter 17: Personal Reflections and Testimonies 299
Chapter 18: Engaging with Technology and the Digital World
.... 316
Chapter 19: Finding a Place to Belong 333
Chapter 20: Conclusion 348

Chapter 1: Introduction

The Rise of Messianic Judaism

From the Shadows to the Spotlight: Origins and Early Development

The origins of Messianic Judaism can be traced back to the early centuries of Christianity, when the nascent faith attracted followers from diverse backgrounds, including Jews. While the relationship between early Christians and Jews was initially marked by shared roots and a sense of commonality, theological differences concerning Jesus' identity and the nature of salvation soon emerged, leading to growing tensions.

The first significant wave of Jewish Christians, often referred to as "Jewish Messianic believers," emerged in the 19th century, particularly in the United States. This early movement was largely influenced by the writings of prominent figures like Isaac Mayer Wise, a prominent Reform rabbi, who believed in a spiritual interpretation of the Messiah that reconciled Jewish tradition with the figure of Jesus. These early Messianic Jewish congregations, often referred to as "Hebrew Christians," aimed to retain their Jewish identity while embracing Jesus as the Messiah, drawing upon both Jewish and Christian scriptures for their theological framework.

The 20th Century Shift: A Resurgence and New Perspectives

The 20th century witnessed a significant resurgence in Messianic Judaism, fueled by several key factors. The rise of Zionism and the establishment of the State of Israel in 1948 instilled a renewed sense of Jewish identity among many Jewish Christians, prompting them to explore their roots and reclaim their Jewish heritage. The growing popularity of evangelical Christianity, particularly in the United States, further contributed to the movement's growth, as evangelical churches increasingly sought to engage with the Jewish community.

This renewed interest in Messianic Judaism coincided with the emergence of new perspectives and theological interpretations. While early Messianic Jewish communities often embraced a more Christian-centric approach, emphasizing the importance of Jesus as the central figure in salvation, a growing number of groups began to emphasize the continuity of their Jewish identity, drawing heavily upon traditional Jewish practices and interpretations. This shift reflected a deeper understanding of Jewish tradition and a desire to navigate the complex relationship between Messianic faith and Jewish cultural identity.

The Contemporary Landscape: Growth, Diversity, and Challenges

Today, Messianic Judaism thrives as a diverse and growing movement, encompassing a spectrum of viewpoints and practices. While some communities maintain strong ties to evangelical Christianity, others have developed their own unique liturgical and theological frameworks, drawing upon both Jewish and Christian traditions. This diversity is reflected in the wide range of practices observed in Messianic Jewish congregations, from observing traditional Shabbat rituals to incorporating elements of Christian worship like hymns and prayer meetings.

Despite its growth and diversity, Messianic Judaism continues to face challenges. One significant point of contention lies in its relationship with mainstream Judaism, which often views Messianic Judaism as a form of proselytism and a rejection of core Jewish tenets. This tension has led to ongoing debates and discussions, with both sides seeking to understand and navigate the complexities of their shared history and evolving identities.

Another challenge facing Messianic Judaism is the question of theological coherence. The movement's embrace of both Jewish and Christian traditions raises questions about the interpretation of scripture, the nature of salvation, and the role of Jesus within the broader Jewish theological framework. While some Messianic Jews emphasize a seamless synthesis of Jewish and Christian beliefs, others acknowledge the inherent tensions and complexities, seeking to navigate a path that respects the integrity of both traditions.

The Future of Messianic Judaism: Dialogue, Integration, and Continuity

The future of Messianic Judaism remains an open question, shaped by the ongoing dialogue and interaction between the movement and both Jewish and Christian communities. While the movement has undoubtedly contributed to a deeper understanding of Jewish identity and the evolving nature of faith, it also continues to challenge existing religious boundaries and provoke critical reflections on the role of tradition, interpretation, and the complex interplay between faith and culture.

One potential future trajectory for Messianic Judaism lies in fostering deeper dialogue with mainstream Judaism, seeking to bridge theological divides and establish a more respectful and collaborative relationship. This dialogue could focus on exploring commonalities between Jewish and Messianic Jewish beliefs, promoting mutual understanding, and finding ways to address the concerns and anxieties that have often fueled conflict and misunderstanding.

Another avenue for Messianic Judaism lies in seeking greater integration within the broader spectrum of Jewish life, actively participating in interfaith dialogues, and contributing to the vibrant intellectual and cultural landscape of the Jewish world. This integration could involve engaging with Jewish social justice movements, advocating for shared values, and contributing to the ongoing conversation about Jewish identity and the future of Jewish life in a rapidly changing world.

Ultimately, the future of Messianic Judaism will be determined by its ability to navigate the complex terrain of theological innovation, cultural adaptation, and interfaith dialogue. Its success will depend on its capacity to maintain its unique identity while fostering meaningful connections with other religious communities, contributing to a more inclusive and understanding world where diverse faith traditions can coexist and thrive.

Exploring Key Concepts and Debates

The rise of Messianic Judaism presents a rich and multifaceted topic, inviting of key concepts and debates:

Theological Framework: Examining the unique theological framework of Messianic Judaism, exploring its interpretation of scripture, its understanding of Jesus' role in salvation, and its engagement with traditional Jewish theology.
Jewish Identity: Analyzing the complex relationship between Messianic Judaism and Jewish identity, examining the ways in which Messianic Jews navigate their dual identity and engage with traditional Jewish practices and beliefs.
Interfaith Dialogue: Investigating the ongoing dialogue between Messianic Judaism and both Jewish and Christian communities, exploring the challenges and opportunities for understanding, reconciliation, and collaboration.
Social and Cultural Impact: Exploring the social and cultural impact of Messianic Judaism, analyzing its role in shaping the contemporary Jewish and Christian landscapes, and its engagement with issues of social justice, equality, and interfaith understanding.

This deeper exploration of these key concepts and debates offers a valuable opportunity to understand the dynamic nature of religious identity, the evolving landscape of faith, and the potential for dialogue and collaboration in fostering a more inclusive and understanding world.

Millennials and Faith: A Unique Perspective

The Millennial Landscape: A Crossroads of Influence

Millennials are often characterized by their strong sense of individualism, their comfort with technology, and their diverse backgrounds. These factors have a profound impact on their religious landscape, fostering a dynamic interplay between tradition and innovation.

1. Individualism and the Quest for Meaning: Millennials are known for their independent spirit and their desire for authenticity. They are less likely to blindly accept traditional doctrines or institutional pronouncements, preferring to explore their own personal understanding of faith. This pursuit of personal meaning and individual truth often leads them to seek spiritual fulfillment outside of traditional religious institutions, exploring alternative spiritual paths, or even rejecting organized religion altogether.

2. The Digital Age and the Rise of Online Communities: The digital age has significantly influenced Millennial's approach to faith. They have grown up in a world where information is readily accessible, and they are adept at navigating online communities and accessing diverse perspectives on faith. This has fostered a new level of engagement with religion, where online platforms serve as spaces for spiritual exploration, dialogue, and community building. However, it has also exposed them to a constant barrage of conflicting information and opinions, creating challenges in discerning authentic faith from superficial trends.

3. Diversity and Inclusion: Millennials are the most racially and ethnically diverse generation in American history, reflecting the changing demographics of the country. This diversity brings a multitude of perspectives and experiences to the table, challenging traditional religious frameworks and demanding greater inclusivity and understanding. Millennials are increasingly questioning rigid interpretations of scripture and seeking a more nuanced understanding of faith that embraces diversity and promotes social justice.

4. The Legacy of Secularization: Millennials are coming of age in a world increasingly influenced by secularism, where religious institutions have lost some of their traditional authority. The rise of secular values, coupled with the perceived failings of religious institutions in addressing social issues, has led some Millennials to question the relevance of faith in their lives. However, this does not necessarily translate to a complete rejection of spirituality. Instead, it fosters a search for new expressions of faith that are more relevant to their contemporary realities.

Understanding the Millennial Perspective: Key Trends and Challenges

Millennials' unique perspectives on faith are reflected in several key trends:

1. Spiritual Seeking: Many Millennials, while not necessarily subscribing to traditional religious institutions, are actively seeking spiritual meaning and purpose. This quest for spirituality often manifests in eclectic practices, incorporating elements from various traditions and philosophies, such as mindfulness, meditation, yoga, and environmentalism.

2. Shifting Boundaries: The lines between religion and spirituality are blurring for Millennials. They are more likely to identify as "spiritual

but not religious" or to blend their faith with other aspects of their lives, integrating spiritual practices into their everyday routines and seeking spiritual growth in areas like social justice activism or artistic expression.

3. Embracing Social Justice: Millennials are deeply concerned with social justice issues, and their faith often informs their commitment to these causes. They are more likely to see faith as a call to action, demanding a more just and compassionate world.

4. Questioning Authority: Millennials are more critical of traditional religious authority than previous generations. They are less likely to blindly accept pronouncements from religious leaders, preferring to engage in critical dialogue and independent research. This critical engagement can lead to a more nuanced and informed understanding of faith but can also contribute to a sense of disillusionment or apathy towards traditional institutions.

5. The Rise of New Expressions of Faith: The Millennial generation is fostering new expressions of faith that are more aligned with their values and experiences. This includes the emergence of online faith communities, "spiritual entrepreneurship" where individuals offer alternative spiritual guidance, and faith-based organizations focusing on social justice and environmental stewardship.

Challenges Facing Millennials in their Engagement with Faith:

Despite their unique perspective on faith, Millennials face several challenges in navigating their spiritual journey:

1. Navigating a Pluralistic World: The abundance of information and perspectives available in the digital age can be overwhelming, making it difficult for Millennials to discern truth and find a coherent path. This information overload can lead to confusion, uncertainty, and even a sense of spiritual exhaustion.

2. Bridging the Generational Divide: Millennials often find themselves navigating a generational divide within religious institutions, facing resistance from older generations who may be less receptive to their perspectives and approach to faith. This can create a sense of isolation and discouragement for Millennials seeking to engage with traditional religious communities.

3. Addressing Institutional Challenges: Millennials are increasingly critical of the perceived failings of religious institutions, including issues of sexual abuse, political involvement, and social inequality. This criticism can lead to a loss of trust and a reluctance to engage with established religious organizations.

4. Finding Meaning in a Secular World: The increasing influence of secular values can make it challenging for Millennials to integrate their faith into a society that often prioritizes material success and individual achievement. This disconnect can lead to a sense of alienation and a struggle to find meaning and purpose in their lives.

Looking Forward: The Future of Faith for Millennials

The future of faith for Millennials remains uncertain, but it is likely to be characterized by continued exploration, innovation, and a search for meaning in a rapidly changing world. The following factors will likely play a significant role in shaping their religious journey:

1. Continued Digital Engagement: Technology will continue to play a crucial role in Millennial's engagement with faith. Online communities, faith-based apps, and digital resources will continue to offer avenues for spiritual exploration, connection, and community building.

2. The Rise of Interfaith Dialogue: The growing diversity of the Millennial generation will likely encourage greater interfaith dialogue and collaboration. Millennials are more likely to be open to learning from different faith traditions and finding common ground for

understanding and cooperation.

3. Faith-Based Social Activism: Millennial's strong commitment to social justice will likely continue to drive faith-based activism, as they seek to address issues like climate change, poverty, and racial inequality through the lens of their faith.

4. The Emergence of New Religious Movements: The unique perspectives and experiences of Millennials are likely to foster the emergence of new religious movements and spiritual practices. These movements may focus on environmental stewardship, social justice, or personal empowerment, offering a more relevant and engaging approach to faith for the current generation. Their unique perspectives, shaped by the digital age, diversity, and a growing sense of individualism, offer both challenges and opportunities for the future of faith. As Millennials continue to explore, adapt, and shape their understanding of faith, their journey will undoubtedly continue to inform the evolution of religious institutions and the expression of spirituality in the years to come.

The Need for a Fresh Approach

Let's explore why a fresh approach is crucial in various areas, examining the pitfalls of clinging to outdated methods and highlighting the potential benefits of embracing new perspectives.

The Stagnation of Tradition:

The allure of tradition can be powerful. It offers a sense of stability and security, providing familiar frameworks for understanding and navigating the world. However, clinging to tradition for the sake of it can stifle progress and lead to stagnation. Many societal institutions, practices, and beliefs have evolved over time, often in response to specific historical and social contexts. Yet, clinging to these traditions, even when they no longer serve their original purpose or are demonstrably outdated, can hinder adaptation and innovation.

Consider, for example, the field of education. Traditional classroom structures, centered around rote memorization and standardized testing, have been criticized for failing to adequately prepare students for the challenges of the 21st century. The emphasis on standardized assessments often neglects the development of critical thinking, creativity, and collaboration skills, crucial for navigating a rapidly changing world. This approach to education often leaves students ill-equipped to adapt to new technologies, solve complex problems, and engage effectively in a globalized society.

Similarly, in the field of medicine, traditional practices that have served us well for generations are being challenged by new scientific discoveries and technological advancements. While the foundation of medical knowledge remains essential, adhering rigidly to established practices can lead to missed opportunities for innovation and impede progress in treating diseases and improving health outcomes.

The Power of Reimagining:

Instead of clinging to outdated frameworks, a fresh approach calls for a critical examination of existing paradigms and a willingness to reimagine them. This requires a shift in mindset, embracing a spirit of inquiry and a willingness to question assumptions. It involves recognizing that even the most deeply ingrained practices and beliefs may need reassessment in the light of evolving circumstances.

Reimagining doesn't necessarily mean discarding everything from the past. Instead, it entails building upon existing knowledge and insights while recognizing the need for adaptation and evolution. This process requires critical thinking, creativity, and a willingness to challenge conventional wisdom. It involves seeking out diverse perspectives, embracing new technologies, and experimenting with novel approaches.

The Benefits of Innovation:

The potential benefits of adopting a fresh approach are vast and multifaceted. It allows us to break free from the shackles of tradition, embrace new possibilities, and address pressing challenges more effectively.

In scientific research, a fresh approach can lead to breakthroughs that were previously unimaginable. By challenging existing theories and exploring novel research methodologies, scientists can unlock new frontiers of knowledge, paving the way for transformative innovations in medicine, technology, and other fields. For example, the development of CRISPR technology, a revolutionary gene-editing tool, emerged from a fresh perspective on gene manipulation, leading to new possibilities for treating genetic diseases and advancing scientific understanding.

In technological development, a fresh approach can lead to the creation of disruptive innovations that reshape entire industries. By embracing unconventional ideas and challenging traditional business models, entrepreneurs and innovators can develop solutions to existing problems and create new opportunities for growth and progress. The rise of artificial intelligence, for instance, represents a paradigm shift in computing, opening up new avenues for automation, data analysis, and problem-solving, while also posing significant ethical and societal challenges that require a fresh perspective to navigate.

In social policy, a fresh approach can lead to the development of more equitable and just societies. By critically examining existing systems and structures, policymakers can identify areas of inequality and inequity and implement policies that address these issues. For example, the shift from traditional welfare models to universal basic income programs represents a fresh approach to social safety nets, aiming to provide a more secure and empowering foundation for individuals in a rapidly changing economy.

The Role of Interdisciplinarity:

A fresh approach often necessitates collaboration across disciplines. The complex challenges facing our world often require insights and solutions from multiple fields of study. Bringing together experts from different backgrounds can lead to synergistic innovation and cross-pollination of ideas.

Consider, for example, the field of climate change. Addressing this complex issue requires a multifaceted approach, drawing upon expertise in environmental science, economics, political science, engineering, and social psychology. By fostering collaboration across these disciplines, we can develop more comprehensive and effective solutions for mitigating climate change and adapting to its impacts.

Personal Growth and Development:

The need for a fresh approach is not limited to large-scale societal challenges. It also applies to individual growth and development. Embracing a fresh perspective can help us overcome limiting beliefs, challenge our assumptions, and expand our horizons. It encourages us to learn new skills, explore different perspectives, and engage in self-reflection. By stepping outside of our comfort zones and embracing new experiences, we can foster personal growth, expand our capacity for empathy and understanding, and navigate the challenges of an increasingly complex world with greater resilience and adaptability.

The Importance of Critical Thinking:

A critical approach is essential for fostering a fresh perspective. It involves questioning assumptions, examining evidence, and considering alternative viewpoints. Critical thinking allows us to identify biases, evaluate information objectively, and make informed decisions. By cultivating critical thinking skills, we can navigate the flood of information in the digital age, discern truth from misinformation, and make more informed choices.

Cultivating a Fresh Approach:

Developing a fresh approach is an ongoing process that requires ongoing self-reflection, continuous learning, and a willingness to embrace change. It involves:

Challenging assumptions: Questioning established beliefs and practices, even those we hold dear.
Seeking out diverse perspectives: Engaging with people from different backgrounds, cultures, and experiences.
Embracing new technologies: Learning new tools and technologies that can enhance our understanding and problem-solving abilities.
Experimenting with novel approaches: Trying new things, even if it means stepping outside of our comfort zones.
Staying informed: Keeping up with the latest developments in our field of interest and beyond.
Cultivating curiosity: Maintaining a childlike sense of wonder and a thirst for knowledge. It is the key to progress, innovation, and a better future for all. By embracing a spirit of inquiry, challenging assumptions, and seeking out new possibilities, we can unlock the potential for transformative change and create a world that is more just, equitable, and sustainable.

The need for a fresh approach is not a call to abandon the past. Instead, it is a call to build upon the knowledge and insights we have inherited while recognizing the need for adaptation and evolution. It is a call to embrace the dynamism of the world around us and to actively participate in shaping a better future.

Navigating the Landscape of Jewish and Christian Identity

To embark on this exploration, we must first acknowledge the historical context that forms the bedrock of this relationship. Judaism, the older of the two faiths, arose in ancient Israel and Palestine, its foundational texts – the Hebrew Bible – serving as a cornerstone of religious and cultural identity for the Jewish people. The emergence of Christianity, however, is intimately intertwined with Judaism. Christianity emerged from within the Jewish world, with its origins traced to the life, teachings, and death of Jesus of Nazareth, a Jewish preacher and religious leader who, according to Christian belief, was the promised Messiah. This inherent connection forged a deep historical and theological link between the two faiths, a connection that has shaped both their individual trajectories and their interactions throughout centuries.

The early centuries of Christianity were marked by a complex and often tumultuous relationship with Judaism. As Christianity gained momentum and expanded beyond its Jewish roots, the relationship evolved, punctuated by periods of coexistence, theological debate, and even persecution. This evolution was driven by a combination of factors, including the nascent Christian theology's attempt to establish itself as distinct from Judaism, the growing political and social power of the Roman Empire, and the development of differing interpretations of religious texts and practices.

Despite the complexities, the shared heritage of Judaism and Christianity remains undeniable. The foundational texts of the Hebrew Bible – recognized as the Old Testament by Christians – stand as a testament to this shared legacy, providing common ground for theological reflection and understanding. From the narratives of creation and the patriarchs to the pronouncements of the prophets, these texts echo through the scriptures and traditions of both faiths, shaping their worldview, moral compass, and understanding of God and humanity. This shared legacy is further reflected in the commonalities found in their moral codes and ethical teachings, often rooted in principles of justice, compassion, and respect for human life.

However, the divergent paths taken by Judaism and Christianity have resulted in significant theological and cultural differences. Central to these differences is the figure of Jesus Christ. Christians recognize Jesus as the Messiah, the Son of God, and the embodiment of God's love and salvation. Judaism, however, does not acknowledge Jesus as the Messiah, viewing him as a prophet or religious leader who did not fulfill the Messianic prophecies. This theological divergence, central to each faith's core beliefs, has shaped distinct interpretations of salvation, the role of ritual and law, and the understanding of God's relationship with humanity.

The diverging paths of Judaism and Christianity have also manifested in the development of distinct cultural identities. While Judaism has historically maintained a strong sense of community and cultural continuity, often characterized by shared customs, traditions, and communal practices, Christianity has branched into diverse denominations and traditions, each with its own unique cultural expressions and interpretations of faith. This diversity, while enriching the Christian landscape, has also contributed to the complex and evolving relationship between Judaism and Christianity.

Despite their differences, the relationship between Judaism and Christianity continues to evolve, influenced by historical events, theological advancements, and changing social dynamics. The 20th century witnessed a growing movement toward interfaith dialogue and understanding, driven by a recognition of the shared humanity and common values that unite these two faiths. This dialogue has fostered greater appreciation for each other's traditions, encouraging respectful engagement and fostering a more inclusive and harmonious relationship.

In the present day, navigating the landscape of Jewish and Christian identity requires sensitivity, understanding, and a commitment to respectful dialogue. Recognizing both the shared roots and the divergent paths of these faiths is crucial for fostering a climate of mutual respect and appreciation. This journey requires an open mind, a willingness to listen, and a commitment to building bridges of understanding and cooperation. By engaging in meaningful dialogue and seeking common ground, we can move towards a future where the relationship between Judaism and Christianity is one of mutual respect, collaboration, and shared commitment to a more just and peaceful world.

A Deeper Dive into Shared Roots and Divergent Paths

To delve deeper into the complexities of the relationship between Jewish and Christian identity, we can explore specific areas of convergence and divergence, highlighting the nuances that shape their unique perspectives.

1. The Role of Scripture:

While both faiths acknowledge the Hebrew Bible as foundational, their interpretations and applications differ significantly. Christians see the Hebrew Bible as part of a larger narrative, culminating in the New Testament, which introduces the figure of Jesus Christ. This interpretation views the Hebrew Bible as prophetically foreshadowing the coming of Jesus, highlighting the Messiah's role in fulfilling God's plan. Judaism, however, maintains a distinct approach to scripture, focusing on the Hebrew Bible as a complete and authoritative text, with no need for additional revelation. The differences in interpretation highlight the distinct understandings of God's will, the role of Messiah, and the nature of divine revelation.

2. The Understanding of God:

While both traditions affirm the existence of one God, their conceptions of the divine differ. Christianity's concept of the Trinity, with God existing as Father, Son (Jesus Christ), and Holy Spirit, distinguishes its theological understanding from Judaism. Jewish tradition emphasizes the singularity and indivisibility of God, rejecting the notion of a triune deity. This divergence in understanding of God's nature impacts their respective understandings of the divine attributes, the relationship between God and humanity, and the nature of salvation.

3. The Role of Law and Ritual:

Jewish practice places a significant emphasis on the observance of the Torah, a set of laws and commandments viewed as divinely given and binding for all Jews. These laws govern aspects of daily life, including dietary restrictions, Sabbath observance, and rituals of prayer and worship. While Christianity recognizes the importance of the Old Testament laws, its interpretation emphasizes the fulfillment of the law in the person of Jesus Christ. This theological understanding emphasizes the importance of faith and grace over strict adherence to legalistic practices. The diverging approaches to law and ritual reflect differing conceptions of salvation, the relationship between human action and divine favor, and the role of religious practice in daily life.

4. The Notion of Salvation:

Salvation, the state of being delivered from sin and death and achieving eternal life, is a central concept in both Judaism and Christianity. However, their understandings of salvation differ significantly. Christianity emphasizes salvation through faith in Jesus Christ, recognizing him as the atonement for sin and the path to redemption. Judaism, however, emphasizes righteousness and ethical conduct as the means of achieving salvation, focusing on fulfilling God's will and adhering to divine commandments. The diverging perspectives on salvation highlight distinct conceptions of sin, redemption, and the nature of the relationship between humanity and the divine.

5. The History of Interfaith Relations:

The relationship between Judaism and Christianity has been marked by periods of coexistence, conflict, and evolving understanding. Early Christianity's emergence from within Judaism set the stage for a complex relationship, characterized by theological debate, cultural clashes, and periods of persecution. The rise of the Catholic Church in the Roman Empire further impacted the relationship, leading to centuries of theological disputes and occasionally violent conflict. The Reformation in the 16th century introduced new challenges and opportunities, with Protestant denominations evolving their own theological interpretations and engaging in diverse forms of interaction with Judaism.

The 20th century witnessed a growing movement toward interfaith dialogue and understanding, fostered by a shared recognition of the common humanity and values that unite these two faiths. This movement has paved the way for more respectful interactions and collaboration, fostering a more inclusive and harmonious relationship in the present day.

Navigating the Landscape: Building Bridges of Understanding

Understanding the complexities of Jewish and Christian identity requires a commitment to open-mindedness, respectful dialogue, and a willingness to engage with diverse perspectives. By recognizing both the shared roots and the divergent paths of these faiths, we can cultivate a more inclusive and harmonious relationship, fostering a future where mutual respect, understanding, and collaboration thrive.

This journey requires active engagement with the rich history, diverse interpretations, and evolving dynamics of both Judaism and Christianity. By listening attentively, asking questions, and seeking common ground, we can build bridges of understanding, fostering a more peaceful and harmonious world where differences are embraced and shared values are celebrated.

Chapter 2: The Jewish Roots of Faith

Exploring the Hebrew Scriptures

This exploration is not merely an academic exercise, but a journey into the heart of a living tradition. The Hebrew Scriptures are not static relics of the past, but a dynamic tapestry woven through centuries of interpretation and reinterpretation. They resonate with contemporary readers, offering insights into human nature, the nature of God, and the meaning of existence. This journey invites us to understand the Scriptures not as a dusty collection of ancient texts, but as a vibrant source of wisdom, inspiration, and spiritual guidance.

Understanding the Context: A Mosaic of History and Culture

The Hebrew Scriptures are not a monolithic entity, but a collection of diverse texts written over a span of approximately 1,000 years, from the 10th century BCE to the 2nd century BCE. Each text emerged from a specific historical moment, reflecting the cultural, social, and political realities of its time. Understanding this context is crucial for comprehending the meaning and message of the Scriptures.

For instance, the Pentateuch, the first five books of the Hebrew Bible, offers a narrative of the origins of the Israelites, their journey through the wilderness, and the establishment of the covenant with God. These stories are deeply rooted in the historical context of the early Israelite monarchy, a period marked by political upheaval, social change, and the emergence of a distinct national identity.

Similarly, the prophetic books, like Isaiah and Jeremiah, speak to the social injustices, political corruption, and religious apathy prevalent in their respective times. They offer a powerful critique of the status quo, challenging both the people and their leaders to live in accordance with God's will.

The diverse historical contexts that shaped the Hebrew Scriptures offer a unique lens for understanding the development of religious thought, social values, and ethical principles. They illustrate the human struggle for justice, peace, and meaning, a struggle that resonates across cultures and generations.

A Literary Tapestry: Exploring Genres and Themes

Beyond their historical context, the Hebrew Scriptures are also remarkable for their diverse literary forms. The Bible encompasses poetry, prose, law, history, prophecy, and wisdom literature. Each genre employs its own unique language, style, and structure to convey its message.

Poetry: From the majestic Psalms to the haunting Song of Songs, Hebrew poetry offers a profound exploration of the human condition. It uses parallelism, imagery, and metaphor to evoke emotions, reveal truths, and inspire awe. The Psalms, for example, provide a powerful expression of human emotions, ranging from praise and gratitude to lament and despair.

Prose: Narrative, law, and history are primarily conveyed through prose. The books of Genesis, Exodus, and Numbers, for example, tell the story of creation, the covenant with God, and the journey to the Promised Land. The laws in Deuteronomy offer insights into ancient Israelite society and their moral framework. The historical books, such as Kings and Chronicles, provide an account of the Israelite monarchy, highlighting their triumphs and failures.

Law: The books of Torah (Genesis, Exodus, Leviticus, Numbers, and

Deuteronomy) contain a collection of laws that formed the basis of Israelite society. These laws cover a wide range of topics, including religious practices, social justice, and personal conduct. They offer a glimpse into the values and priorities of the ancient Israelites.

Wisdom Literature: Proverbs, Job, and Ecclesiastes are examples of wisdom literature that explore the nature of wisdom, justice, and suffering. They offer reflections on life's complexities and provide insights into living a meaningful and fulfilling life.

The diverse literary forms present in the Hebrew Scriptures offer a multifaceted approach to exploring the meaning of life, the nature of God, and the human condition. They challenge readers to engage with different perspectives, explore diverse emotions, and consider the complexities of the human experience.

Theology and Interpretation: A Dialogue Across Time

The Hebrew Scriptures are not simply a collection of stories and laws; they are a source of theological reflection and spiritual inspiration. They offer profound insights into the nature of God, the relationship between humanity and divinity, and the meaning of existence.

God in the Hebrew Scriptures: The Hebrew Scriptures portray a God who is both transcendent and immanent, powerful and merciful, just and compassionate. This God is revealed through actions, covenants, and laws, and is experienced through personal encounters and historical events.

The Covenant: The concept of covenant is central to the Hebrew Scriptures. It represents a binding agreement between God and humanity, signifying a relationship of mutual responsibility and faithfulness. The covenant with Abraham, for instance, promises God's blessing and protection to his descendants, in exchange for their faithfulness and obedience.

Ethical Principles: The Hebrew Scriptures are rich in ethical teachings. They emphasize justice, compassion, and righteousness. They condemn oppression, exploitation, and social injustice. These ethical principles provide a framework for living a life of integrity and contributing to a just and compassionate society.

However, the Hebrew Scriptures are not a closed book. They have been interpreted and reinterpreted throughout history, with each generation drawing its own meaning from these texts. This ongoing dialogue, spanning centuries and cultures, has enriched the understanding of the Scriptures and their relevance to contemporary life.

The Relevance of the Hebrew Scriptures Today

The Hebrew Scriptures offer a wealth of insights and inspiration for contemporary readers. They address timeless themes of human existence, exploring the search for meaning, the struggle with suffering, the pursuit of justice, and the longing for peace. They challenge us to reflect on our values, question our assumptions, and strive for a more just and compassionate world.

Theological Reflections: The Hebrew Scriptures continue to inspire theological reflection, prompting discussions on God's nature, the relationship between faith and reason, and the meaning of human life.

Ethical Guidance: The ethical principles enshrined in the Hebrew Scriptures offer valuable guidance for navigating contemporary moral dilemmas. Their emphasis on justice, compassion, and righteousness provides a framework for ethical decision-making in personal, social, and global spheres.

Literary Inspiration: The literary artistry of the Hebrew Scriptures continues to inspire writers, poets, and artists. Their poetic language, vivid imagery, and timeless themes resonate with contemporary readers and inspire new creative works.

Spiritual Guidance: For many, the Hebrew Scriptures serve as a source of spiritual guidance, offering comfort, hope, and inspiration in times of need. Their stories, prayers, and wisdom teachings provide a framework for spiritual growth and personal transformation. It invites us to engage with history, literature, theology, and ethics, seeking insights that can illuminate our own lives and shape our understanding of the world. It is a journey of discovery, reflection, and inspiration, a journey that continues to inspire and guide humanity's pursuit of a more just, compassionate, and meaningful world.

Understanding the Covenant

The earliest recorded covenant, the "covenant of the pieces" in Genesis 15, sets the stage for the intricate tapestry of promises and obligations that would define the relationship between God and his chosen people. This initial agreement, established between God and Abraham, establishes a foundational principle: God's faithfulness to his promises, even in the face of human frailty. The covenant is not merely a legal document but a living testament to God's unwavering love and commitment to his chosen people.

This initial covenant, with its emphasis on land, descendants, and blessing, foreshadows the multifaceted nature of God's covenantal relationship with humanity. As the narrative unfolds, the covenant is further developed and expanded upon, culminating in the New Covenant established through Jesus Christ. The Mosaic covenant, established at Mount Sinai, introduced a comprehensive legal code, emphasizing the importance of obedience and ritual observance. This covenant, while foundational for the Israelites, also highlights the limitations of human faithfulness. It underscores the inherent tension between human sinfulness and God's desire for a right relationship.

The prophetic voice, often arising in times of societal and spiritual decline, reminds the people of the importance of covenant fidelity. Prophets like Jeremiah, Isaiah, and Amos challenged the people to return to the heart of the covenant, emphasizing justice, compassion, and faithfulness to God's commands. Their messages served as a wake-up call, urging the Israelites to remember the core principles of the covenant: love, justice, and righteous living.

The New Covenant, established through the sacrifice of Jesus Christ, stands as a radical transformation of the covenantal relationship. It transcends the limitations of the Mosaic covenant, offering salvation and reconciliation through faith in Jesus. The New Covenant, sealed by the blood of Christ, emphasizes grace, forgiveness, and the indwelling presence of the Holy Spirit. This new covenant, open to all who believe, offers hope for a restored relationship with God, free from the burden of sin and the limitations of the old covenant.

Understanding the covenant is not merely an academic exercise; it holds profound personal and societal implications. For the individual believer, it offers a framework for living a life of faith, guided by the promises and principles of God's covenant. The covenant provides a roadmap for personal growth, spiritual transformation, and a deepening relationship with God.

Furthermore, the covenant has a profound impact on society. Its principles of justice, compassion, and love provide a foundation for building a just and equitable society. Recognizing the covenant's emphasis on unity and reconciliation offers a framework for resolving conflicts and fostering understanding across cultural and religious divides.

The covenant, however, is not without its complexities. Throughout history, various interpretations and applications of the covenant have emerged, leading to theological debates and social divisions. Understanding the covenant requires a nuanced approach, acknowledging its historical context, diverse interpretations, and ongoing theological discussion. It necessitates critical engagement with the biblical texts, consideration of different theological perspectives, and a willingness to grapple with the complexities of faith.

Ultimately, the covenant is a testament to God's love for humanity, his desire for a restored relationship, and his unwavering faithfulness to his promises. It is a source of hope and strength for individuals and communities, offering a framework for living a life of faith, building a just society, and embracing a future filled with God's grace and blessings.

Exploring the Covenant: A Deeper Dive

To further understand the concept of the covenant, it is essential to delve deeper into its various dimensions, exploring its historical context, theological interpretations, and practical implications.

Historical Context:

The Covenant of the Pieces: Genesis 15 records the first covenant between God and Abraham, established through a symbolic ritual involving a sacrificial animal. This covenant, known as the "covenant of the pieces," serves as a foundation for the future relationship between God and his chosen people. It establishes the key themes of land, descendants, and blessing, which would be further developed in subsequent covenants.

The Mosaic Covenant: The covenant at Mount Sinai, recorded in Exodus 19-24, establishes a comprehensive legal code, known as the Law of Moses. This covenant, through its elaborate system of rituals and laws, emphasizes the importance of obedience and faithfulness. However, it also highlights the inherent limitations of human faithfulness, paving the way for the need for a new covenant.

The Davidic Covenant: 2 Samuel 7 records a covenant between God and King David, promising him an eternal dynasty and a lasting kingdom. This covenant, while primarily focused on David's lineage, also points towards a future King who will rule over all nations, fulfilling God's ultimate purpose for the world.

The New Covenant: The New Covenant, established through the sacrifice of Jesus Christ, stands as a transformative shift in the covenantal relationship. This covenant, described in the New Testament, emphasizes grace, forgiveness, and the indwelling presence of the Holy Spirit. It transcends the limitations of the Old Covenant, offering salvation and reconciliation through faith in Jesus.

Theological Interpretations:

The Covenant of Works: This interpretation focuses on the concept of "works righteousness," emphasizing the need for perfect obedience to God's law. It sees the covenant as a contractual agreement where God's blessings are contingent upon human performance. This view, often associated with legalistic perspectives, emphasizes the difficulty of fulfilling the requirements of the covenant.

The Covenant of Grace: This interpretation emphasizes God's unmerited favor and grace. It views the covenant as a unilateral promise from God, based solely on his love and mercy. This view, often associated with Reformed theology, highlights God's initiative in establishing the covenant and his grace in redeeming humanity.

The Covenant of Redemption: This interpretation focuses on the eternal covenant between the Father, Son, and Holy Spirit, predating the creation of the world. This covenant, focused on God's plan for salvation, emphasizes the divine purpose in establishing the covenant and the active role of Christ in fulfilling its promises.

Practical Implications:

Personal Faith: The covenant offers a framework for individual faith, guiding believers in their relationship with God. It provides a source of hope, strength, and direction in navigating the challenges of life. The promises of the covenant assure believers of God's love, forgiveness, and constant presence.

Social Justice: The covenant emphasizes justice, compassion, and love, providing a foundation for building a just and equitable society. It calls believers to advocate for the marginalized, promote peace, and work towards a world where all people are treated with dignity and respect.

Interfaith Dialogue: Understanding the covenant, particularly in its historical and theological context, can facilitate deeper dialogue with other faith communities. It can foster understanding and respect for diverse religious perspectives, promoting interfaith cooperation and harmony.

Ongoing Discussion:

The concept of the covenant remains a subject of ongoing discussion within theological and academic circles. Various interpretations and applications of the covenant continue to emerge, prompting critical reflection and debate. Understanding the covenant necessitates an ongoing engagement with the biblical texts, consideration of diverse theological perspectives, and a willingness to grapple with the complexities of faith. It requires delving into the historical context, exploring theological interpretations, and engaging in ongoing dialogue. As we explore the promises and principles of the covenant, we gain a deeper understanding of God's love for humanity, his plan for redemption, and our role in living out the covenant in our daily lives. The covenant, a testament to God's faithfulness and grace, offers hope for a future where humanity and God are united in a relationship of love, justice, and peace.

The Importance of Tradition

The importance of tradition lies in its ability to foster a shared history and collective memory, serving as a powerful tool for cultural transmission. It binds individuals together through a shared understanding of values, beliefs, and norms, creating a sense of community and belonging. From the intricate rituals of ancient cultures to the modern customs of celebrating holidays, tradition acts as a unifying force, creating a sense of continuity and stability amidst the ever-changing tides of time.

Moreover, tradition plays a crucial role in shaping our individual identities. By inheriting customs, beliefs, and practices from our ancestors, we inherit a sense of who we are, where we come from, and how we fit into the larger tapestry of our community. This sense of identity is not simply a passive inheritance; it is an active process of engagement and interpretation, where we engage with traditions, imbue them with our own meanings, and adapt them to our evolving circumstances.

However, the concept of tradition is not without its challenges and complexities. As societies evolve, adapt, and encounter new ideas and perspectives, the role of tradition in shaping our understanding of the world becomes increasingly dynamic and multifaceted. The potential for tradition to become stagnant, resistant to change, and even oppressive is a concern that requires careful consideration. Striking a balance between honoring the wisdom of the past and embracing the dynamism of the present is crucial for ensuring that tradition remains a source of strength, guidance, and inspiration, rather than a rigid and limiting force.

Navigating the Labyrinth of Tradition: A Balancing Act of Continuity and Change

In exploring the intricate relationship between tradition and change, we find ourselves at the heart of a complex and ongoing dialogue. While tradition provides a sense of continuity and shared identity, it is crucial to acknowledge the potential for stagnation and resistance to progress. This dynamic tension between preservation and adaptation lies at the core of navigating the evolving role of tradition in a constantly changing world.

One of the most significant challenges facing tradition lies in its potential to become entrenched and resistant to change. When traditions are perceived as immutable and absolute, they can stifle innovation, limit individual expression, and hinder societal progress. This rigidity can manifest in various forms, ranging from inflexible social norms and outdated practices to the exclusion of diverse perspectives and experiences.

The potential for tradition to become a source of social division and inequality is a significant concern. When traditions are used to justify discrimination, exclusion, or oppression, they become instruments of social injustice. The importance of critically examining and adapting traditions to align with evolving societal values and principles becomes paramount in ensuring that tradition remains a force for unity and inclusivity, rather than a tool for division and discrimination.

However, it is crucial to avoid the fallacy of equating tradition with stagnation. Tradition is not simply a static relic of the past; it is a living, breathing entity that evolves, adapts, and reinterprets itself in response to changing circumstances. The dynamism inherent in tradition lies in its ability to incorporate new ideas, perspectives, and experiences while preserving its core values and significance.

Embracing the Dynamic Nature of Tradition: A Process of Adaption and Innovation

The true value of tradition lies in its ability to serve as a source of guidance and inspiration, while remaining open to change and adaptation. Embracing the dynamic nature of tradition involves engaging in a constant process of critical reflection, adaptation, and innovation, ensuring that the wisdom of the past remains relevant and meaningful in the present.

This dynamic process of adapting tradition to changing times is evident in the evolution of religious practices, cultural norms, and artistic expressions across generations. The continuity of tradition is not simply about preserving rituals and beliefs in their original form; it is about reinterpreting and reinterpreting them to reflect the evolving needs and perspectives of each generation.

One striking example of this adaptive nature of tradition can be found in the evolution of music. From the traditional folk songs passed down through generations to the contemporary genres that emerged in the 20th and 21st centuries, music serves as a powerful testament to the dynamic interplay between tradition and innovation. While contemporary music often draws inspiration from its predecessors, it also incorporates new sounds, rhythms, and techniques, reflecting the evolving cultural landscape and technological advancements.

Similarly, in the realm of language, the ongoing process of evolution and adaptation ensures that communication remains relevant and effective. While core elements of language, such as grammar and vocabulary, are preserved through generations, new words, expressions, and linguistic innovations continuously emerge, reflecting the changing social and cultural contexts.

The Power of Tradition: A Source of Strength, Guidance, and Inspiration

While acknowledging the potential challenges of tradition, it is essential to recognize its enduring power as a source of strength, guidance, and inspiration. By providing a sense of continuity and shared identity, tradition creates a foundation for understanding the world and our place within it. It offers a framework for navigating the complexities of life, providing a sense of purpose and meaning.

The value of tradition lies in its ability to connect us to something larger than ourselves, reminding us of our shared history, our collective struggles, and our enduring aspirations. From the stories passed down through generations to the rituals that bind us together, tradition serves as a reminder of our interconnectedness and the importance of community.

Furthermore, tradition provides a source of resilience and hope in the face of adversity. In times of change and uncertainty, the wisdom of the past can offer guidance and inspiration, providing a sense of continuity and stability amidst the turbulence. Tradition can serve as a reminder that we are not alone in our struggles; that we have a shared history, and that we can draw strength from the experiences of those who came before us.

Tradition: A Source of Strength and Guidance in an Evolving World

As we navigate the complexities of an ever-changing world, it is crucial to recognize the enduring power of tradition and its role in shaping our understanding of ourselves, our communities, and the world around us. While tradition can serve as a source of stability and continuity, it is equally important to embrace its dynamic nature, engaging in a constant process of adaptation, innovation, and critical reflection.

The challenge of navigating the complex relationship between tradition and change is not one that can be easily resolved. It requires ongoing dialogue, critical engagement, and a willingness to embrace both the wisdom of the past and the dynamism of the present. By finding a balance between preserving the values and practices that have served us well and adapting to the evolving needs of our communities, we can ensure that tradition remains a vital source of strength, guidance, and inspiration, shaping our lives and enriching our shared human experience.

Bridging the Gap Between Judaism and Christianity

This journey towards bridging the gap begins with acknowledging the historical and theological connections. Both Judaism and Christianity trace their origins to Abraham, the patriarch who is revered as the father of both faiths. The Jewish scriptures, known as the Hebrew Bible or Tanakh, are considered foundational texts within Christianity, which incorporates them as the Old Testament. This shared scriptural heritage provides a common foundation upon which to build understanding and dialogue.

However, the divergence lies in the interpretation and understanding of these texts. While both faiths embrace the prophets, their understanding of messianic prophecies differs. Jews generally interpret these prophecies as pertaining to a future messianic age, while Christians believe that Jesus of Nazareth fulfilled these prophecies as the Messiah. This differing interpretation of messianic prophecy has been a point of contention throughout history, leading to misunderstandings and tensions between the two faiths.

Furthermore, the development of distinct theological doctrines further solidified the gap between the two faiths. Christian theology emphasizes the divinity of Jesus Christ, the importance of salvation through faith in Christ, and the role of the Holy Spirit. These doctrines, central to Christian belief, are not shared by Jewish theology, which focuses on the unity of God, the observance of the Torah, and the importance of ethical conduct.

The historical relationship between Judaism and Christianity has been marked by periods of persecution and conflict. From the early Christian era to the medieval period, Jewish communities faced discrimination and violence at the hands of Christian societies. The accusations of deicide, the belief that Jews were responsible for the death of Jesus, further fueled anti-Semitism and led to centuries of suffering for Jewish communities.

However, the 20th century brought a shift in the relationship between Judaism and Christianity. The horrors of the Holocaust, in which six million Jews were systematically murdered by the Nazi regime, served as a catalyst for introspection and dialogue within Christian communities. This event forced Christians to confront the historical legacy of anti-Semitism and the role of Christian teachings in perpetuating prejudice against Jews.

In response, a growing number of Christian theologians and scholars began engaging in interfaith dialogue, seeking to bridge the theological divide and foster understanding between the two faiths. This dialogue has been marked by a spirit of mutual respect, acknowledging the differences while seeking common ground. Focus has been placed on areas of shared values, such as the importance of ethical conduct, the call to social justice, and the pursuit of peace.

One key area of common ground is the concept of covenant. Both Judaism and Christianity understand their relationship with God through the lens of covenant. While the interpretations of the covenant differ, the underlying concept of a binding agreement between God and humanity serves as a point of connection. This shared understanding can foster dialogue on topics such as the role of faith in society, the importance of ethical behavior, and the pursuit of justice.

Furthermore, the shared historical experience of persecution and the need to fight for religious freedom has led to greater collaboration between Jewish and Christian communities. This shared struggle has fostered a sense of solidarity and a common desire to promote interfaith understanding and combat prejudice against all minorities.

However, bridging the gap between Judaism and Christianity is not without its challenges. Theological differences remain a source of contention, and historical wounds continue to linger. There are ongoing debates about the interpretation of scripture, the nature of God, and the understanding of salvation.

Despite these challenges, the movement towards dialogue and understanding is gaining momentum. Interfaith initiatives are flourishing, bringing together Jewish and Christian communities to engage in meaningful conversations, share perspectives, and build relationships. These efforts are crucial for promoting mutual respect, dispelling misunderstandings, and fostering a spirit of co-existence.

The future of the relationship between Judaism and Christianity lies in continued dialogue, mutual respect, and the willingness to engage with each other's perspectives. By fostering understanding, acknowledging the shared heritage, and recognizing the common ground, both faiths can contribute to a world marked by peace, harmony, and mutual respect.

The Importance of Shared Values:

Beyond the theological complexities, both Judaism and Christianity share fundamental values that form the bedrock of ethical behavior and social responsibility. These shared values provide a foundation for building bridges between the two faiths, promoting understanding and fostering a spirit of collaboration.

The Importance of Ethical Conduct: Both Judaism and Christianity emphasize the importance of ethical conduct in all aspects of life.

The Ten Commandments, central to both faiths, provide a framework for ethical behavior, emphasizing the sanctity of life, the importance of justice, and the need to treat others with respect. These shared values offer a common ground for dialogue on issues such as social justice, human rights, and the pursuit of peace.

The Call to Social Justice: Both Judaism and Christianity have a long history of advocating for social justice and advocating on behalf of the marginalized. From the prophets of Israel to the teachings of Jesus, both faiths emphasize the need to care for the poor, the sick, and the oppressed. This shared commitment to social justice provides a platform for interfaith collaboration, enabling Jewish and Christian communities to work together to address issues such as poverty, inequality, and discrimination.

The Pursuit of Peace: Both Judaism and Christianity hold peace as a core value. The prophets of Israel spoke of a future era of peace and justice, while Jesus emphasized the importance of forgiveness and reconciliation. These shared aspirations for peace provide a basis for interfaith dialogue on issues such as conflict resolution, non-violent resistance, and the promotion of understanding and tolerance.

The Role of Interfaith Dialogue:

Interfaith dialogue is crucial in bridging the gap between Judaism and Christianity. It provides a platform for open and respectful conversations, fostering understanding, and promoting mutual respect. Through dialogue, individuals from both faiths can share their perspectives, listen to each other's experiences, and build bridges of empathy.

Dispelling Misunderstandings: Interfaith dialogue helps dispel misunderstandings and stereotypes that have plagued the relationship between Judaism and Christianity. By engaging in open and honest conversations, individuals can challenge inaccurate perceptions and promote a more nuanced understanding of each other's faith.

Building Relationships: Dialogue fosters the development of relationships between individuals and communities. When people from different faiths come together to engage in meaningful conversations, they build bonds of trust and friendship, fostering a sense of common humanity.

Addressing Common Challenges: Interfaith dialogue provides a forum for addressing common challenges and working towards shared solutions. Both Judaism and Christianity face issues such as prejudice, discrimination, and religious intolerance. By collaborating and sharing their experiences, communities can work together to combat these challenges and advocate for a more just and equitable world.

The Future of the Relationship:

The future of the relationship between Judaism and Christianity depends on continued dialogue, mutual respect, and a commitment to building bridges of understanding. As both faiths grapple with the challenges of the modern world, collaboration and cooperation will be essential for creating a more just and peaceful society.

Embracing Shared Values: Both faiths must continue to embrace their shared values, recognizing the common ground that unites them. By emphasizing the importance of ethical conduct, social justice, and the pursuit of peace, both Judaism and Christianity can work together to build a world characterized by harmony and mutual respect.

Promoting Interfaith Education: Educational initiatives that promote understanding between Judaism and Christianity are essential. By introducing students to the history, beliefs, and practices of both faiths, we can foster a spirit of tolerance and empathy.

Supporting Interfaith Organizations: Interfaith organizations play a vital role in fostering dialogue, building relationships, and promoting interfaith cooperation. Supporting these organizations is crucial for building bridges of understanding and creating a more inclusive and tolerant society.

The relationship between Judaism and Christianity is complex and multifaceted, marked by both shared history and theological divergence. However, the movement towards dialogue and understanding is gaining momentum, offering hope for a future characterized by mutual respect, collaboration, and a shared commitment to peace and justice. By embracing the shared values, promoting interfaith education, and supporting interfaith organizations, we can work together to bridge the gap between these two great faiths.

Chapter 3: Messianic Identity and Beliefs

The Messiah: The Cornerstone of Faith

Origins and Development in Judaism

The concept of the messiah in Judaism is rooted in the Hebrew Bible, specifically in the prophetic literature. Prophets like Isaiah, Jeremiah, and Micah foretold a future era of peace and prosperity, ushering in a new age under the rule of a divinely appointed king, the Messiah. This messianic figure was envisioned as a descendant of King David, who would restore the Davidic dynasty, reunite the divided kingdom of Israel, and establish a reign of justice and righteousness.

The Jewish tradition developed a complex and nuanced understanding of the messiah over time, with various schools of thought emerging. While the majority agreed on the essential aspects of the messianic figure, interpretations differed on specific details like the nature of their arrival, their role in bringing about redemption, and the timeframe of their coming. The concept of the messiah, however, remained a constant source of hope and anticipation for the Jewish people, providing solace and inspiration during times of persecution and hardship.

The Messiah in Early Christianity

The emergence of Christianity saw a significant shift in the understanding of the messianic figure. Early Christians embraced the idea of a messiah but interpreted it through the lens of their belief in Jesus of Nazareth. They saw in Jesus the fulfillment of the Old Testament prophecies regarding the coming messiah, believing him to be the long-awaited savior who had arrived to bring redemption and reconciliation with God.

The earliest Christian communities embraced Jesus as the Christ (Greek for "Messiah"), seeing him as the fulfillment of the Old Testament promises. However, debates arose about the nature of Jesus's messianic role. Some early Christians, like the Ebionites, viewed Jesus primarily as a righteous teacher and prophet who had been raised to a divine status, while others, like the followers of Paul, emphasized Jesus's divinity and his role as the Son of God, sacrificing himself for the salvation of humanity.

The Messiah in Islam

Islam, a religion that emerged in the 7th century CE, also acknowledges the concept of a messiah, though with distinct interpretations. In Islamic theology, Jesus is recognized as a prophet of God, but not as the Son of God. Muslims believe that Jesus was born miraculously through the virgin Mary, but that he was not crucified. They believe that he will return at the end times as a sign of the approaching Day of Judgment.

The concept of the messiah in Islam, often referred to as "Isa" (Arabic for "Jesus"), is closely tied to the belief in the coming of the Mahdi, a divinely appointed leader who will usher in an era of justice and peace before the Day of Judgment. The Mahdi is believed to be a descendant of Prophet Muhammad, and his arrival is anticipated as a signal of the end times.

The Messiah in Contemporary Thought

The concept of the messiah continues to resonate in contemporary thought, though its interpretations are diverse and often influenced by individual beliefs and cultural contexts. While some see the messianic figure as a literal and historical individual, others view it as a symbolic representation of hope, redemption, and the possibility of a better future.

In modern secular thought, the concept of the messiah is often interpreted in terms of social and political movements that strive for justice and equality. This interpretation sees the messianic figure as a representation of collective hope and the potential for human progress.

Theological and Philosophical Perspectives

The concept of the messiah has been the subject of extensive theological and philosophical debate. Questions surrounding the nature of the messianic figure, the timing of their arrival, and the mechanism of their redemption have sparked countless discussions and interpretations across different religious traditions.

Some theologians and philosophers have argued that the messiah is a purely symbolic figure, representing the ultimate aspiration for human redemption and the hope for a better future. Others have interpreted the messiah in a more literal sense, seeing their arrival as a historical event that will bring about a radical transformation of the world.

The concept of the messiah has also sparked debates about the relationship between human free will and divine intervention. Some believe that the messianic figure is a chosen instrument of God, acting according to a predetermined plan, while others believe that humans have a role to play in the coming of the messiah.

The Impact on History and Culture

The concept of the messiah has had a profound impact on history and culture, shaping religious beliefs, political movements, and artistic expression. It has inspired countless works of literature, art, and music, as well as theological and philosophical treatises.

The messianic hope has fueled both revolutionary movements and peaceful social reforms, driving people to strive for a better world and a more just society. It has also been a source of division and conflict, with different interpretations of the messianic figure leading to religious and political tensions. It speaks to our longing for a better future, our desire for redemption, and our belief in the possibility of transformation. Whether interpreted literally or symbolically, the messianic figure serves as a reminder of the enduring power of hope and the potential for human progress.

While the specific details of the messiah may vary depending on one's religious or philosophical perspective, the core concept remains a powerful and enduring symbol of the human spirit's aspiration for a world of peace, justice, and love. This aspiration, rooted in the concept of the messiah, continues to guide and inspire humanity's journey towards a more fulfilling and meaningful future.

Understanding the Significance of Yeshua

From Nazareth to Jerusalem: The Historical Context of Yeshua

To understand Yeshua's significance, we must first delve into the historical context in which he lived. He was born in Nazareth, a small town in Galilee, during a time of significant upheaval in Judea. The Roman Empire held sway over the region, imposing its political and cultural dominance upon the Jewish people. This period saw a burgeoning sense of Jewish nationalism and a growing desire for liberation from Roman rule. Within this tumultuous landscape, various Jewish sects emerged, each with its own interpretation of the Torah and its own vision for the future.

Yeshua's ministry unfolded within this complex tapestry of social and religious currents. He was raised within a devout Jewish family, deeply connected to the traditions and beliefs of his people. He embraced the Jewish scriptures, drawing upon them as a source of inspiration and a foundation for his teachings. Yet, he also challenged established norms, particularly those that he perceived as hindering true devotion to God. He emphasized love, compassion, and forgiveness, setting him apart from the rigid legalism that characterized some Jewish factions of the time.

The Teachings of Yeshua: A Revolution of Love and Grace

The teachings of Yeshua, recorded in the Gospels, form the heart of Christianity. They are characterized by a profound emphasis on love, a call to radical selflessness, and a vision of a kingdom of God founded on grace and forgiveness. His parables, vivid stories that illustrate complex spiritual truths, have resonated with people across centuries and cultures, offering profound insights into human nature and the nature of faith.

Yeshua's core message centered on the love and forgiveness of God. He preached a message of radical inclusion, emphasizing that God's love extended to everyone, regardless of social status, religious affiliation, or personal history. This message challenged the prevailing social hierarchy and offered hope to the marginalized and oppressed.

He also emphasized the importance of inner transformation. He called on his followers to cultivate a spirit of humility, compassion, and generosity, to live lives of service and to extend forgiveness to others as God had extended forgiveness to them. These teachings challenged the conventional wisdom of the time and offered a radically different vision for living a truly meaningful life.

The Death and Resurrection: A Pivotal Event

Yeshua's ministry ultimately led him to Jerusalem, the heart of

Jewish religious life. Here, he faced opposition from the Jewish authorities who perceived his teachings as a threat to their established order. He was accused of blasphemy and sedition, eventually leading to his arrest, trial, and crucifixion under Roman authority.

His death, while a tragic event, marked a turning point in history. For Christians, it represents the ultimate act of love and sacrifice, a demonstration of God's love for humanity. But the story doesn't end there. The resurrection of Yeshua, documented in the Gospels, became a cornerstone of Christian belief. This event, witnessed by his disciples and later believed by millions, signified his victory over death and his claim to divine authority. It offered hope of eternal life and a promise of resurrection for all who believe in him.

The Enduring Legacy of Yeshua: A Source of Inspiration and Hope

The significance of Yeshua lies not simply in historical events but also in the enduring impact of his teachings and the transformation they have sparked in countless lives. His message of love, forgiveness, and grace has inspired generations of believers to live lives of compassion, service, and reconciliation.

The life and teachings of Yeshua have provided a framework for understanding the nature of God, the meaning of human existence, and the hope for a better future. His words continue to offer solace in times of hardship, inspiration for acts of kindness, and a call to live lives of love and service.

In a world often characterized by conflict, division, and despair, the message of Yeshua offers a powerful alternative, a vision of unity, forgiveness, and hope. It reminds us of the inherent goodness within each person and the possibility of transforming the world through acts of love and compassion.

Understanding Yeshua: A Continuous Journey

The significance of Yeshua is a complex and multifaceted topic that has been pondered by theologians, historians, and believers for centuries. There are countless interpretations and perspectives on his life, teachings, and legacy. Understanding his significance is not a destination but a continuous journey, an ongoing exploration of his message and its implications for our lives.

This exploration requires an open mind, a willingness to grapple with challenging questions, and a deep commitment to seeking truth. It involves delving into the historical context, examining the scriptures, engaging in dialogue with other perspectives, and reflecting on how Yeshua's message can guide our own lives.

The journey of understanding Yeshua is a journey of faith, history, and meaning. It is a journey that challenges us to confront our own limitations, to embrace the power of love, and to strive for a world characterized by peace, justice, and compassion.

Exploring the Messianic Jewish Community

A Historical Journey: From Ancient Roots to Modern Expression

The roots of Messianic Judaism can be traced back to the earliest days of Christianity. While the New Testament portrays Jesus as a Jewish rabbi, a shift occurred over time, with Christianity largely developing outside the Jewish community. This historical context helps explain the tension that often surrounds Messianic Judaism. The community's existence highlights a continuous thread of faith in Jesus within Jewish tradition, a thread that, while often obscured, has never truly been severed.

Early Jewish Christians, who remained deeply connected to their Jewish heritage, faced challenges from both sides. The Jewish authorities saw them as heretical, while the emerging Christian church, seeking to distinguish itself from Judaism, often marginalized them. This historical struggle continues to resonate in the contemporary experience of Messianic Jews.

The modern era witnessed a resurgence of Messianic Jewish expression. Fueled by both a renewed interest in Jewish heritage within evangelical Christianity and the rise of Jewish identity movements, new communities began to emerge in the 20th century. These communities, often drawing inspiration from the writings of early Jewish Christian leaders like Rabbi Eliezer Ben Yehuda, sought to reclaim their Jewish heritage while maintaining their faith in Jesus.

Theological Landscapes: Navigating the Labyrinth of Belief

The theological landscape of Messianic Judaism is multifaceted and dynamic, encompassing a diverse range of perspectives and interpretations. While united by a shared belief in Jesus as the Jewish Messiah, differences exist in how they approach the integration of Jewish traditions and practices within their faith.

Messianic Judaism and Jewish Law: One of the most prominent points of contention lies in the interpretation of Jewish law, specifically the observance of the Torah. Some Messianic Jews hold that Jesus fulfilled the requirements of the Law, making it no longer binding. Others emphasize the importance of continuing to observe Jewish tradition, viewing it as a reflection of their commitment to their heritage. This spectrum of views reflects the complex interplay between faith in Jesus and Jewish identity.

Messianic Judaism and the Hebrew Bible: The understanding of the Hebrew Bible, also known as the Old Testament, forms another key area of theological discussion. While all Messianic Jews acknowledge the Bible's authority, their interpretations differ regarding its application in light of Jesus' ministry and teachings. Some interpret the Bible through a lens of Messianic fulfillment, seeing Jesus' arrival as the culmination of prophecy. Others prioritize a more literal reading of the text, acknowledging the importance of its historical and cultural context.

Messianic Judaism and the Nature of Salvation: The concept of salvation, a central theme in both Judaism and Christianity, is also interpreted differently within Messianic Judaism. Some emphasize the importance of faith in Jesus for achieving salvation, aligning with traditional Christian perspectives. Others highlight the role of Jewish observance in achieving a state of righteousness before God, drawing on Jewish interpretations of the concept of "mitzvah" (commandment).

Messianic Jewish Communities: A Mosaic of Expressions

The Messianic Jewish community is far from monolithic. It comprises a diverse range of individuals, congregations, and organizations, each contributing to the rich tapestry of Messianic Jewish expression.

Congregations and Fellowships: The community's core is found in local congregations and fellowships, offering spaces for worship, fellowship, and spiritual growth. These gatherings often involve a blend of Jewish liturgical traditions, contemporary Christian music, and teachings rooted in both Jewish and Christian scripture.

Ministries and Organizations: A network of ministries and organizations support the growth and development of Messianic Jewish communities worldwide. These organizations provide resources for study and worship, offer training for leaders, and engage in outreach and advocacy.

Cultural Expressions: Messianic Jews actively engage in preserving and celebrating their Jewish heritage. They participate in traditional Jewish holidays and practices, including Shabbat observance, the celebration of Passover, and the study of Hebrew language and culture.

Theological Debates: A Dialogue of Faith and Identity

As with any vibrant religious community, Messianic Judaism is not without its internal debates and challenges. These dialogues, while sometimes difficult, contribute to the ongoing evolution and understanding of the community's identity.

The Nature of Identity: A central point of debate centers around the definition of "Jewishness." While some Messianic Jews see their faith in Jesus as a natural continuation of their Jewish identity, others find themselves navigating the complexities of reconciling their Christian beliefs with Jewish traditions and practices.

The Relationship to Judaism: The nature of the relationship between Messianic Judaism and mainstream Judaism is another point of contention. Some seek dialogue and understanding with their fellow Jews, while others emphasize the distinct nature of their faith and its unique interpretation of Jewish scriptures.

The Role of Missions: The issue of missions, specifically the approach to outreach to non-Messianic Jews, also sparks debate. Some believe in the importance of sharing their faith with other Jews, while others are more hesitant, mindful of potential misunderstandings and the historical context of Christian outreach to Jewish communities.

Moving Forward: The Future of Messianic Judaism

The future of Messianic Judaism remains a source of both hope and uncertainty. The community faces challenges in navigating the complex dynamics of faith and identity, negotiating its relationship with both Jewish and Christian communities, and responding to the changing social and political landscapes.

Building Bridges of Understanding: Despite its challenges, Messianic

Judaism offers a unique opportunity for dialogue and understanding between Jewish and Christian communities. The community's commitment to both Jewish tradition and faith in Jesus provides a potential bridge for interfaith engagement, encouraging mutual respect and learning.

Embracing Diversity: The future of Messianic Judaism lies in its ability to embrace its diversity, fostering a spirit of unity and understanding among its various expressions. By fostering open dialogue and respectful disagreement, the community can strengthen its internal cohesion and build upon its shared commitment to faith and heritage.

Sustaining Growth and Impact: The community's future success depends on its ability to nurture its next generation of leaders, empower its members to engage in social justice and community outreach, and continue to inspire a vibrant and growing spiritual movement. As the community continues to navigate its unique path, it offers a compelling reminder of the enduring human quest for meaning and belonging, a quest that often finds its expression in the tapestry of faith and tradition.

To delve deeper into the world of Messianic Judaism, readers are encouraged to engage with a wealth of resources available online and in print. A few starting points include:

Websites: Messianic Jewish Alliance of America (MJAA), Messianic Jewish Fellowship International (MJFI), Jewish Voice Ministries International (JVMI)
Books: "Messianic Jewish Theology: A Concise Introduction" by Michael L. Brown, "The Messianic Jewish Movement" by Barry Kosmin, "The Jewish Jesus: How Judaism Shaped the Life and Teachings of Jesus of Nazareth" by Michael L. Brown
Journals: "The Journal of Messianic Jewish Studies," "Jewish Review

of Books" (articles related to Messianic Judaism)

Exploring the Messianic Jewish community requires an open mind and a willingness to engage with a unique and often misunderstood expression of faith and identity. By embracing the richness and complexity of its history, theology, and cultural expressions, we can gain a deeper understanding of this vibrant and ever-evolving community.

Faith Expressions and Practices

To understand faith expressions and practices, we must first acknowledge the fundamental nature of faith itself. Faith, in its simplest definition, is a belief in something beyond empirical evidence. It involves accepting propositions based on trust, intuition, revelation, or other non-tangible sources. This belief can be directed towards deities, principles, ideologies, or even the inherent goodness of humanity. While faith often manifests as a personal conviction, it frequently finds expression within communities, shaping collective values and practices.

The Diverse Landscape of Faith Expressions:

Faith expressions take on numerous forms, encompassing a spectrum of practices, rituals, and beliefs. In religious contexts, these expressions are often defined by sacred texts, theological doctrines, and established traditions. For instance, the ritualistic practices of prayer, meditation, and fasting, common across various religious traditions, serve as expressions of devotion and connection to the divine. Similarly, the observance of religious holidays, such as Christmas, Ramadan, or Diwali, provides opportunities for communal celebration and remembrance of significant events within each faith.

Beyond organized religion, faith expressions manifest in secular contexts as well. Ethical frameworks, for example, embody a set of beliefs and practices based on moral principles. These principles, often derived from philosophical thought or personal values, guide individuals in their interactions with others and the world at large. Similarly, artistic expression, be it through music, literature, or visual arts, can act as a conduit for faith-based ideas and experiences. The creation and appreciation of these works often reflect deeply held beliefs and aspirations, serving as a powerful form of communication and connection.

The Significance of Faith Practices:

Faith practices serve as the tangible manifestations of faith, providing a framework for individuals and communities to engage with their beliefs. These practices often involve actions that are perceived as symbolically significant or spiritually empowering. Through these actions, individuals seek to cultivate a deeper connection with their faith, reinforce their values, and find meaning in their lives.

Ritual practices, for example, play a crucial role in many faith traditions. From the intricate ceremonies of religious festivals to the daily rituals of prayer and meditation, these practices serve to create a sense of order and structure within the individual's life. They also provide a means for individuals to connect with their faith community, fostering a sense of belonging and shared purpose.

Furthermore, faith practices often involve acts of service and compassion, driven by a desire to live in accordance with one's beliefs. Engaging in charitable work, supporting those in need, and promoting social justice are all examples of faith-based practices that extend beyond personal devotion and aim to positively impact the world.

The Evolution of Faith Expressions:

Faith expressions are not static but evolve over time in response to various social, cultural, and historical influences. As societies change, so too do the ways in which individuals and communities express their faith. This evolution can be observed in the development of new religious denominations, the adaptation of traditional practices to modern contexts, and the emergence of alternative spiritualities that respond to contemporary concerns.

For instance, the rise of interfaith dialogue and the growing awareness of religious pluralism have led to a greater emphasis on interfaith understanding and cooperation. This shift has encouraged individuals and communities to explore the commonalities and differences between various faith traditions, fostering dialogue and building bridges across religious divides.

Understanding and Respecting Diverse Faith Expressions:

Recognizing the diversity of faith expressions is crucial for promoting mutual understanding and respect among different communities. This understanding begins with acknowledging the inherent value of each faith tradition, regardless of its specific beliefs or practices. It also requires recognizing the potential for misunderstanding and prejudice that can arise from cultural and religious differences.

To foster a climate of respect and tolerance, it is important to engage in open and honest dialogue about faith. This dialogue should be characterized by a willingness to listen to different perspectives, challenge one's own assumptions, and seek common ground. By engaging in meaningful conversations and learning from each other, we can move beyond stereotypes and appreciate the richness and diversity of faith expressions across the globe. From the deeply personal experiences of individual faith to the shared rituals and beliefs of religious communities, faith expressions offer a powerful lens through which to understand human experience. By embracing a spirit of curiosity, respect, and open-mindedness, we can appreciate the diverse tapestry of faith expressions and foster greater understanding and harmony in our increasingly interconnected world.

Chapter 4: Connecting with Jewish Culture

Immersion in Jewish Culture and Tradition

The first step towards immersing oneself in Jewish culture and tradition often involves a deep dive into the wellspring of Jewish history. Understanding the roots of Jewish identity, tracing the journey from ancient Israel to the Diaspora, and grappling with the trials and triumphs of a people dispersed across the globe, provides a vital context for comprehending the complexities of contemporary Jewish life. This historical exploration reveals how Jewish culture has been shaped by a constant interplay between continuity and change, adaptation and resilience. It highlights the inherent dynamism of the tradition, its capacity to evolve and adapt while remaining true to its core values.

Exploring the rich tapestry of Jewish texts, from the Hebrew Bible and Talmud to the vast collection of Rabbinic literature and contemporary writings, offers a direct window into the heart of Jewish thought and practice. Engaging with these texts, delving into their intricate layers of meaning and interpretation, allows us to grapple with fundamental questions of faith, ethics, and identity. This encounter with Jewish literature provides a framework for understanding Jewish values, such as the pursuit of justice, the importance of community, and the commitment to ethical living. It also reveals the diversity of thought and opinion within Jewish tradition, showcasing the multiplicity of voices and perspectives that have shaped its evolution.

Ritual plays a central role in Jewish culture and tradition, offering a tangible and embodied way to connect with the deeper meaning of Jewish life. Whether it is the practice of Shabbat observance, the intricate rituals surrounding Jewish holidays, or the daily recitation of prayers, Jewish rituals provide a framework for living a meaningful life, fostering a sense of connection to something larger than oneself. They are not merely empty formalities but acts of remembrance, expressions of faith, and opportunities for spiritual growth. Engaging with these rituals, understanding their historical and theological significance, opens up a path to personal meaning and connection to a larger community.

The realm of Jewish culture encompasses a vibrant array of artistic expressions, ranging from the breathtaking beauty of synagogues and the emotional power of Jewish music to the richness of Jewish literature and the creative energy of Jewish cinema. These artistic expressions, born from the depths of Jewish experience, offer profound insights into the soul of Jewish culture, showcasing its dynamism, its capacity for joy and sorrow, its resilience in the face of adversity. Immersing oneself in this world of art provides a unique avenue for exploring the depths of Jewish identity, connecting with the collective memory of the Jewish people, and appreciating the richness of their cultural heritage.

Beyond the realm of texts, rituals, and art, Jewish culture is also defined by a vibrant and diverse community. Engaging with the Jewish community, participating in its social and cultural life, provides a unique opportunity for firsthand experience with Jewish tradition. Whether it is attending community events, participating in volunteer opportunities, or simply engaging in conversations with fellow Jews, these interactions offer a chance to build meaningful relationships, learn from diverse perspectives, and experience the warmth and support of a community that shares your values and heritage.

The journey of immersing oneself in Jewish culture and tradition is not a linear path, but a constant process of exploration and discovery. It requires an open mind, a willingness to engage with new ideas and perspectives, and a commitment to lifelong learning. It is a path that challenges us to confront our own preconceptions, embrace the beauty and complexity of Jewish tradition, and find our own place within its rich and evolving narrative.

This journey is ultimately a deeply personal one, shaped by individual experiences, motivations, and interpretations. It is a journey that can lead to a profound sense of belonging, a connection to a community and heritage that transcends time and space. It is a journey that invites us to rediscover the meaning of Jewish life, to engage with its timeless wisdom and to find our own unique way of contributing to its ongoing story.

Exploring Jewish Texts and Their Impact on Cultural Practices

The exploration of Jewish texts is a fundamental aspect of immersing oneself in Jewish culture and tradition. These texts, spanning millennia and encompassing diverse genres, provide a rich tapestry of teachings, stories, and interpretations that have shaped Jewish life and thought. By engaging with these texts, we gain insights into the core values, beliefs, and practices that define Jewish identity.

The Hebrew Bible, also known as the Tanakh, stands as the cornerstone of Jewish literature. It comprises three main sections: the Torah (the Five Books of Moses), the Nevi'im (the Prophets), and the Ketuvim (the Writings). The Torah, containing stories of creation, covenant, and the journey of the Jewish people, serves as the foundation of Jewish law and morality. The Nevi'im offer messages of prophecy and social justice, while the Ketuvim provide a collection of diverse texts, including poetry, wisdom literature, and historical accounts.

The Talmud, a vast collection of Rabbinic discussions and interpretations of Jewish law and tradition, represents another crucial text in Jewish intellectual history. It comprises the Mishnah, a codification of oral law, and the Gemara, a collection of discussions and debates surrounding the Mishnah. The Talmud, a testament to the dynamic and evolving nature of Jewish thought, provides a framework for understanding Jewish law, ethics, and ritual practice.

Beyond the Hebrew Bible and the Talmud, a vast collection of Rabbinic literature, including commentaries, responsa, and philosophical treatises, offers further insights into Jewish thought and practice. These texts, spanning centuries and encompassing diverse theological perspectives, reveal the richness and complexity of Jewish intellectual history. They also highlight the ongoing dialogue and debate that characterize Jewish thought, demonstrating its capacity for self-critique and continuous evolution.

The impact of these texts on Jewish cultural practices is profound. They provide the foundation for Jewish rituals, holidays, and social customs. For example, the dietary laws outlined in the Torah, known as kashrut, govern Jewish food practices and serve as a powerful symbol of Jewish identity. The laws regarding Shabbat observance, detailed in the Torah and further elaborated upon in Rabbinic literature, shape the Jewish understanding of time and the importance of rest and spiritual renewal. Similarly, the texts provide guidance for the observance of Jewish holidays, outlining their historical significance, theological meaning, and specific rituals.

The exploration of Jewish texts, therefore, goes beyond simply acquiring knowledge. It offers a pathway to understanding the core values and practices that define Jewish culture and tradition. It provides a framework for interpreting Jewish rituals and holidays, for engaging with Jewish ethical principles, and for navigating the complexities of contemporary Jewish life.

The Importance of Ritual in Jewish Culture and Tradition

Ritual occupies a central place in Jewish culture and tradition, serving as a tangible and embodied expression of faith, identity, and connection to a shared history. Jewish rituals are not merely empty formalities but acts of remembrance, expressions of belief, and opportunities for spiritual growth. They provide a framework for living a meaningful life, fostering a sense of connection to something larger than oneself.

The practice of Shabbat observance is a prime example of the profound impact of ritual on Jewish life. Shabbat, the Jewish Sabbath, is a weekly observance that begins at sunset on Friday and continues until nightfall on Saturday. During Shabbat, Jews are prohibited from engaging in certain activities, such as work, cooking, and using electricity, in order to create a space for rest, reflection, and connection with family and community.

The rituals surrounding Shabbat observance are deeply symbolic. The lighting of Shabbat candles, a tradition passed down through generations, symbolizes the welcoming of Shabbat as a time of peace and joy. The blessing of the bread, known as Kiddush, reaffirms the importance of gratitude and the blessings of creation. The sharing of a Shabbat meal, a time for gathering and conversation, fosters a sense of community and strengthens family bonds.

Jewish holidays are also marked by a rich array of rituals, each offering a unique opportunity for spiritual reflection and connection to Jewish history and tradition. Passover, the festival commemorating the exodus from Egypt, involves the consumption of matzah (unleavened bread), symbolizing the haste with which the Israelites left Egypt, and the Seder, a ritual meal featuring a series of symbolic foods and readings that tell the story of the Exodus.

Rosh Hashanah, the Jewish New Year, is marked by the blowing of the shofar (ram's horn), a sound that serves as a call to repentance and renewal. Yom Kippur, the Day of Atonement, is a day of fasting and introspection, dedicated to seeking forgiveness and making amends for past transgressions. Hanukkah, the Festival of Lights, commemorates the rededication of the Second Temple in Jerusalem and involves the lighting of eight candles on a menorah, symbolizing the triumph of light over darkness.

The rituals surrounding these holidays, imbued with historical, theological, and cultural significance, provide a framework for understanding the Jewish narrative, connecting with the collective memory of the Jewish people, and fostering a sense of belonging to a shared tradition. They serve as a reminder of the resilience of the Jewish people, their unwavering faith, and their commitment to ethical living.

Beyond the specific rituals associated with Shabbat and holidays, Jewish daily life is also shaped by a wide range of practices, including the recitation of prayers, the observance of dietary laws, and the practice of charity. These rituals, embedded in the everyday rhythms of Jewish life, provide a constant reminder of Jewish values, fostering a sense of purpose and connection to a larger spiritual framework.

The importance of ritual in Jewish culture and tradition lies in its capacity to connect us to the past, to the present, and to the future. Rituals provide a tangible and embodied way to engage with the deeper meaning of Jewish life, fostering a sense of community, shared identity, and spiritual connection. They offer a framework for living a meaningful life, guided by the wisdom and values of a tradition that has endured for millennia.

The Role of Art and Creativity in Jewish Culture

Art and creativity play a vital role in Jewish culture, offering a unique lens through which to explore the depths of Jewish identity, express the full spectrum of human emotions, and celebrate the richness of Jewish heritage. Through the mediums of architecture, music, literature, film, and visual art, Jewish artists have created works that speak to the soul of Jewish culture, reflecting its resilience, its dynamism, and its profound capacity for joy and sorrow.

Synagogue architecture, a testament to the interplay between faith and artistic expression, serves as a powerful example of the role of art in Jewish culture. From the ancient synagogues of antiquity, with their intricate mosaics and symbolic frescoes, to the modern synagogues of today, with their innovative designs and contemporary aesthetics, synagogues have always served as more than just places of worship. They are spaces of beauty, contemplation, and communal gathering, reflecting the aspirations and cultural values of the Jewish community.

Jewish music, spanning centuries and encompassing diverse genres, offers a rich tapestry of sound and emotion. From the haunting melodies of the synagogue to the vibrant rhythms of klezmer music, from the soulful vocals of Jewish folk singers to the groundbreaking compositions of contemporary Jewish composers, Jewish music provides a powerful expression of the Jewish experience. It evokes memories of home, celebrates the joys of life, and offers solace in times of hardship.

Jewish literature, encompassing a vast range of genres, from poetry and prose to drama and philosophy, offers profound insights into the Jewish soul. From the ancient Hebrew Bible, with its epic tales and timeless wisdom, to the modern novels and short stories of contemporary Jewish writers, Jewish literature explores the complexities of Jewish identity, the challenges of faith, and the enduring themes of love, loss, and redemption.

Jewish cinema, a relatively recent phenomenon, has emerged as a powerful medium for exploring the Jewish experience, challenging stereotypes, and celebrating Jewish diversity. From the iconic films of Woody Allen to the moving documentaries of Steven Spielberg, Jewish filmmakers have used the power of film to tell stories that resonate with audiences around the world, showcasing the richness and complexity of Jewish culture.

Jewish visual art, encompassing painting, sculpture, photography, and other forms of artistic expression, offers a unique window into the Jewish worldview. From the intricate illustrations of medieval manuscripts to the powerful social commentary of contemporary Jewish artists, Jewish visual art reveals the depth and diversity of Jewish artistic vision, its ability to capture the nuances of human emotion, and its capacity to challenge societal norms.

The role of art and creativity in Jewish culture is not merely to entertain or beautify. It is to provide a space for expression, reflection, and connection. It is to give voice to the hopes and dreams, the joys and sorrows, the triumphs and tribulations of the Jewish people. It is to celebrate the richness of Jewish heritage, to challenge conventional narratives, and to inspire future generations.

The Importance of Engaging with the Jewish Community

Beyond the exploration of texts, rituals, and art, immersing oneself in Jewish culture and tradition requires engaging with the Jewish community itself. This interaction, fostered through participation in community events, involvement in volunteer opportunities, and simply engaging in conversations with fellow Jews, provides a unique opportunity for firsthand experience with Jewish tradition and a chance to build meaningful connections within the community.

Jewish communities, diverse in their composition and expression, offer a kaleidoscope of experiences and perspectives. Participating in community events, whether it be religious services, cultural celebrations, or social gatherings, provides a chance to experience the vibrancy and dynamism of Jewish life firsthand. These events often offer opportunities to learn about different Jewish traditions, to engage in meaningful conversations, and to connect with people from diverse backgrounds.

Volunteer opportunities within the Jewish community offer a chance to contribute to the well-being of others, to build a sense of shared responsibility, and to strengthen the bonds of community. Whether it is assisting with synagogue programs, supporting local charities, or advocating for social justice issues, volunteering provides a tangible way to engage with the needs of the community and to make a real difference in the lives of others.

Simply engaging in conversations with fellow Jews, sharing stories and experiences, and listening to their perspectives, can be a profoundly enriching experience. These conversations offer a glimpse into the diverse ways that Jews live their faith, their cultural practices, and their personal journeys. They provide an opportunity to learn from the experiences of others, to expand our understanding of Jewish identity, and to build meaningful relationships within the Jewish community.

The importance of engaging with the Jewish community lies in its ability to foster a sense of belonging, to provide a supportive and nurturing environment, and to offer a network of relationships that can enrich our lives. It provides a space for shared experiences, mutual support, and the transmission of Jewish traditions across generations.

Engaging with the Jewish community, therefore, is not just a matter of social interaction. It is a fundamental aspect of immersing oneself in Jewish culture and tradition, of connecting with a living, breathing community that shares a common heritage and a collective story. It is a journey of discovery, connection, and belonging that can transform our understanding of ourselves and the world around us.

The Ongoing Journey of Immersion

The journey of immersing oneself in Jewish culture and tradition is not a static endpoint, but an ongoing process of exploration, discovery, and transformation. It is a journey that invites us to constantly question, to learn, and to grow. It is a journey that requires an open mind, a willingness to engage with new ideas and perspectives, and a commitment to lifelong learning.

This journey is often marked by moments of challenge and growth. We may encounter beliefs and practices that challenge our own preconceptions, or we may find ourselves navigating the complexities of Jewish history and its impact on contemporary life. These challenges, however, can provide opportunities for deeper understanding and personal growth, fostering a more nuanced and informed appreciation of Jewish culture and tradition.

The journey of immersion is also a deeply personal one, shaped by individual experiences, motivations, and interpretations. We may find ourselves drawn to certain aspects of Jewish tradition, while others may hold less appeal. This diversity of experiences and perspectives is a testament to the richness and complexity of Jewish culture, allowing each individual to find their own unique place within its tapestry.

The ongoing journey of immersion is a commitment to lifelong learning, to constantly seeking out new knowledge and perspectives, and to engaging with the evolving narrative of Jewish culture and tradition. It is a journey that requires courage, curiosity, and a willingness to embrace the challenges and opportunities that come with exploring a world of profound depth and meaning.

Ultimately, the journey of immersing oneself in Jewish culture and tradition is a journey of discovery, connection, and belonging. It is a journey that can lead us to a deeper understanding of ourselves, our heritage, and our place in the world. It is a journey that can enrich our lives, foster a sense of purpose, and inspire us to contribute to the ongoing story of the Jewish people.

Observing Shabbat and Feasts

Shabbat: A Weekly Sanctuary

Shabbat, the Jewish Sabbath, transcends a mere day of rest; it is a sacred pause, a time for spiritual renewal, and a celebration of life itself. Rooted in the biblical account of creation, where God rested on the seventh day after completing the world, Shabbat signifies the cessation of labor and the embrace of a different kind of work – the cultivation of the soul.

The observance of Shabbat begins at sundown on Friday evening and continues until nightfall on Saturday. This timeframe, known as "Tzeis," marks the transition from the secular week to the holy day. The transition is marked by the lighting of candles, the recitation of blessings, and the sharing of a special meal, known as Kiddush. This act of blessing wine or grape juice symbolizes the blessing of creation itself and sets the stage for a Shabbat experience imbued with meaning and joy.

The essence of Shabbat lies in its deliberate disengagement from the pressures of the week. It's a time for disconnecting from technology, for nurturing relationships, and for focusing on what truly matters. It's a time for families to come together, for friends to connect, and for individuals to find solace in their faith and their own company.

Beyond the rituals, Shabbat embodies the principle of "Pikuach Nefesh" – the preservation of life. This principle dictates that all activities necessary for life, such as cooking, eating, and caring for the sick, are permissible on Shabbat. This emphasis on life affirms the sacredness of human existence and the importance of care and compassion.

Shabbat Observance: A Spectrum of Practice

The observance of Shabbat spans a broad spectrum, with individuals and families tailoring their practices to their personal beliefs and circumstances. While some choose to adhere strictly to the traditional prohibitions, such as abstaining from driving and using electricity, others embrace a more relaxed approach, focusing on the core essence of Shabbat as a time for spiritual reflection and connection.

Within the realm of Shabbat observance, there are numerous practices that contribute to its unique character. These include:

Kiddush: The ritual blessing over wine or grape juice, marking the beginning of Shabbat.
Havdalah: The ceremony at the end of Shabbat, marking the transition back to the week.
Shabbat Meals: Special meals, often featuring challah bread, are enjoyed on both Friday night and Saturday afternoon.
Shabbat Activities: Families engage in various activities, such as reading Torah, singing songs, and playing games.
Shabbat Rest: The refraining from work and focusing on spiritual and personal growth.

The flexibility within Shabbat observance allows individuals to find their own path to spiritual fulfillment. It emphasizes that the essence of Shabbat lies not in rigid adherence to rules, but in the intention and the spirit with which it is observed.

The Festivals: Cycles of Celebration and Renewal

Beyond Shabbat, the Jewish calendar is adorned with a tapestry of festivals, each bearing a distinct significance and a unique narrative. These festivals, ranging from joyful celebrations to solemn observances, mark the cycles of life, the journey of the Jewish people, and their relationship with the Divine.

High Holidays: Days of Introspection and Repentance

The High Holidays, Rosh Hashanah and Yom Kippur, stand as the most significant and solemn of the Jewish festivals. These days of introspection and repentance serve as a time for deep reflection on the past year and for seeking forgiveness from God and from fellow human beings.

Rosh Hashanah, the Jewish New Year:

Marked by the blowing of the shofar, a ram's horn, Rosh Hashanah signifies the beginning of a new year and the opportunity for a fresh start. It's a time for contemplating life's purpose, for expressing gratitude for blessings received, and for setting intentions for the year ahead.

Yom Kippur, the Day of Atonement:

This day of complete fasting, prayer, and introspection is dedicated to seeking forgiveness for past transgressions. The tradition of Yom Kippur embodies the Jewish belief in repentance and the possibility of renewal. It's a day for sincere reflection, for recognizing the mistakes made, and for seeking atonement for wrongs committed.

Sukkot, the Feast of Tabernacles:

Sukkot, celebrated for seven days, commemorates the Israelites' journey through the desert after their exodus from Egypt. During this festival, families build temporary shelters called sukkahs, symbolizing the fragility of human existence and the Divine protection. The act of dwelling in the sukkah serves as a reminder of the Israelites' dependence on God for sustenance and protection.

Simchat Torah, the Rejoicing of the Torah:

Simchat Torah, the culmination of Sukkot, marks the end of the annual cycle of Torah readings and the beginning of a new cycle. It's a day of joyous celebration, filled with dancing, singing, and the parading of Torah scrolls. Simchat Torah symbolizes the eternal cycle of Torah study and the enduring connection between the Jewish people and their sacred texts.

Hanukkah, the Festival of Lights:

Hanukkah, also known as the Festival of Lights, commemorates the rededication of the Second Temple in Jerusalem after its desecration by the Syrian-Greek ruler Antiochus IV. The lighting of the menorah, a candelabrum with eight branches, symbolizes the miraculous survival of the Jewish people and the power of light over darkness.

Purim, the Festival of Lots:

Purim celebrates the deliverance of the Jewish people from the wicked plot of Haman, as recounted in the Book of Esther. The festival is marked by the reading of the Megillah, the Scroll of Esther, and by festivities that include costume parades, masquerade balls, and the giving of gifts.

Pesach, the Festival of Freedom:

Pesach, also known as Passover, commemorates the exodus of the Israelites from Egypt and their liberation from slavery. The festival is marked by a seder meal, a special ritual dinner that includes the telling of the story of the Exodus and the eating of symbolic foods, such as matzah (unleavened bread).

Shavuot, the Festival of Weeks:

Shavuot, celebrated seven weeks after Passover, commemorates the giving of the Torah at Mount Sinai. It's a time for intensive Torah study, for celebrating the spiritual connection between God and the

Jewish people, and for reaffirming the commitment to living a life guided by Torah principles.

The Significance of Festivals: A Tapestry of Meaning

The Jewish festivals, in their diversity and richness, offer a tapestry of meaning, connecting individuals and communities to their heritage, their history, and their spiritual journey. They provide opportunities for:

Historical Remembrance: Each festival commemorates a pivotal event in Jewish history, fostering a sense of continuity and connection to the past.
Spiritual Renewal: The festivals serve as occasions for spiritual reflection, introspection, and renewal, reinforcing the importance of ethical living and a close relationship with God.
Community Building: The festivals bring families and communities together, strengthening social bonds and fostering a sense of belonging.
Cultural Expression: The festivals offer a platform for the expression of Jewish culture through music, dance, food, and artistic traditions.

Observing Shabbat and the festivals is not merely a matter of adhering to rituals; it is an active engagement with the heart and soul of Judaism, a celebration of life, and a commitment to living a meaningful and connected life.

Experiencing Jewish Rituals

The Power of Ritual:

Rituals, at their core, are acts that imbue everyday life with meaning and purpose. They provide a framework for navigating life's transitions, from birth to death, and everything in between. In Jewish tradition, rituals are not static, but rather fluid expressions of a vibrant, evolving faith. They are a constant dialogue between past and present, tradition and innovation, individual and community.

A Tapestry of Traditions:

The tapestry of Jewish rituals is as diverse as the Jewish people themselves. Each tradition, from Ashkenazi to Sephardi, Mizrahi to Ethiopian, boasts unique customs and interpretations. While some rituals are universal, others are specific to particular communities, reflecting their historical experiences and cultural influences. This diversity underscores the richness of Jewish tradition and its capacity for adaptation and change.

The Language of Ritual:

Jewish rituals are often characterized by a specific set of actions, prayers, and symbols. Each element carries significance, communicating a message that transcends language itself. The lighting of Shabbat candles, for instance, symbolizes the welcoming of the Sabbath, a time for rest and spiritual renewal. The breaking of bread during Passover recalls the Israelites' liberation from slavery in Egypt, reminding us of the enduring power of hope and freedom.

The Importance of Community:

Jewish rituals are not solitary acts but rather communal experiences. They strengthen bonds between individuals and foster a sense of belonging. The act of gathering together for Shabbat dinner, for example, transcends the physical act of eating. It represents a shared commitment to tradition, a celebration of family and friendship, and a moment of collective reflection.

The Evolution of Ritual:

Jewish rituals are not static relics of the past but rather dynamic expressions of a living tradition. They evolve over time, adapting to changing social, political, and cultural contexts. The introduction of new prayers and customs, the reinterpretation of traditional practices, and the emergence of new expressions of Jewish identity all demonstrate the inherent dynamism of Jewish rituals.

Exploring the Major Rituals:

This exploration will delve into the core rituals that define Jewish life, providing insights into their history, symbolism, and contemporary practice.

Shabbat:

Shabbat, the Jewish Sabbath, is a time of rest, reflection, and spiritual renewal. It begins at sunset on Friday evening and ends at nightfall on Saturday. The core elements of Shabbat include:

Candle lighting: The lighting of Shabbat candles symbolizes the welcoming of the Sabbath and the creation of a sacred space.
Kidush: This blessing over wine, often accompanied by challah bread, sanctifies the Sabbath and celebrates its arrival.
Shabbat meals: Sharing meals with family and friends is a central part of Shabbat, offering a time for connection, conversation, and spiritual nourishment.

Holidays:

Jewish holidays are celebrations of significant events in Jewish history and tradition. They provide opportunities for spiritual reflection, communal bonding, and the transmission of Jewish values to future generations. Some key holidays include:

Passover: This eight-day festival commemorates the Israelites' exodus from Egypt. It involves a special Seder meal, the reading of the Haggadah, and the consumption of matzah (unleavened bread).
Rosh Hashanah: The Jewish New Year, Rosh Hashanah marks the

beginning of the ten days of High Holy Days. It involves sounding the shofar (ram's horn), prayer, and reflection.

Yom Kippur: The Day of Atonement, Yom Kippur is a day of fasting, prayer, and repentance. It is a time for seeking forgiveness and reconciliation with God and fellow humans.

Hanukkah: This eight-day festival celebrates the rededication of the Second Temple in Jerusalem. It involves lighting candles on a menorah, eating latkes (potato pancakes), and playing dreidel.

Life Cycle Events:

Jewish rituals mark the key stages of life, providing frameworks for navigating significant transitions. Some key life cycle events include:

Birth: The arrival of a new life is celebrated with a brit milah (circumcision) for boys and a naming ceremony for both boys and girls.

Bar. Bat Mitzvah: At the age of 13, Jewish boys and girls reach the age of religious maturity and responsibility. This milestone is marked by a special ceremony and the assumption of adult religious obligations.

Marriage: Jewish weddings are often joyous and celebratory events, blending ancient traditions with contemporary expressions of love and commitment.

Death: Jewish mourning practices, known as shiva, focus on comforting the bereaved and honoring the memory of the deceased. They involve a period of mourning, reciting prayers, and receiving visitors.

Beyond the Rituals:

While these are just a few examples of the many rituals that make up Jewish life, it is essential to remember that rituals are not ends in themselves. They are a means to an end, serving to connect us to something greater than ourselves. They offer a path to spiritual growth, community building, and the transmission of Jewish values to future generations.

Experiencing Jewish Rituals:

Ultimately, the best way to understand the meaning and significance of Jewish rituals is to experience them firsthand. Attend a Shabbat service, participate in a Passover Seder, or witness a Bar/Bat Mitzvah ceremony. Engage with the rituals, ask questions, and explore the rich tapestry of meaning that they hold. Through active participation, you can deepen your understanding of Jewish tradition and its relevance in contemporary life. They offer a window into Jewish history, culture, and values. As you embark on your journey into the world of Jewish rituals, embrace the opportunity to learn, reflect, and connect with a rich and vibrant tradition that has sustained the Jewish people for centuries.

Finding Belonging and Community

The Nature of Belonging:

Belonging is not simply about being physically present in a group or a place. It is a state of mind, a feeling of being connected to something larger than ourselves. It is the experience of being valued, respected, and accepted for who we are, flaws and all. It is the feeling of being part of something meaningful, something that gives our lives purpose and direction.

Belonging is also a dynamic process, constantly evolving and shaped by our experiences. It is not something we simply find once and then hold onto forever. Rather, it is a journey of self-discovery, of learning who we are and what we value, and of finding others who share those values and resonate with our unique perspectives.

The Importance of Community:

Community provides us with a sense of belonging, a place where we can feel accepted and supported. It offers a network of relationships that provide us with a sense of purpose, identity, and belonging. Within these communities, we find shared values, common interests, and a sense of collective identity that can provide us with a strong sense of purpose and belonging.

Communities can be found in various forms, from families and close friends to religious groups, professional organizations, and even online forums. Each offers unique opportunities for connection, support, and shared experiences.

The Benefits of Belonging:

The benefits of belonging are manifold and profound. Feeling connected to a community can significantly impact our mental, physical, and emotional well-being. It can:

Reduce stress and anxiety: Belonging provides a sense of security and support, which can help us cope with life's challenges. Knowing that we have a network of people who care about us can buffer us from the effects of stress and anxiety.
Improve physical health: Studies have shown that people who have strong social connections tend to have better physical health. This is likely due to the positive impact of belonging on our stress levels, which can have a negative impact on our immune system.
Boost self-esteem and confidence: Feeling accepted and valued by others can boost our self-esteem and confidence, helping us to feel more empowered and capable in all areas of our lives.
Foster personal growth and development: Communities provide opportunities for learning, growth, and development. Being surrounded by people who share our values and interests can encourage us to challenge ourselves, explore new ideas, and develop new skills.
Contribute to a sense of purpose and meaning: Feeling connected to something larger than ourselves can provide us with a sense of

purpose and meaning. This can help us to feel more fulfilled and motivated in life.

The Challenges of Finding Belonging:

While the desire for belonging is universal, the journey to finding it can be fraught with challenges.

Social isolation and loneliness: In an increasingly interconnected world, it can be surprisingly easy to feel isolated and alone. This can be due to factors such as geographical mobility, the breakdown of traditional communities, and the rise of social media, which can create a sense of superficial connection without real intimacy.
Finding the right community: It can be challenging to find a community that truly fits with our values and interests. We may find ourselves in groups where we don't feel comfortable or accepted, or we may struggle to find groups that share our passions or beliefs.
Fear of rejection: The fear of rejection can be a significant barrier to finding belonging. We may be afraid of putting ourselves out there, of being vulnerable, or of being judged.
Difficulties with acceptance: Some individuals may face challenges finding belonging due to factors such as race, ethnicity, gender identity, sexual orientation, or disability. These individuals may experience prejudice and discrimination, which can make it difficult to feel accepted and valued.

Navigating the Journey of Belonging:

Finding belonging is not a passive activity; it requires effort and intention. It involves actively seeking out communities that align with our values and interests, being open to new experiences, and building meaningful connections with others.

Here are some practical tips for navigating the journey of finding belonging:

Explore different communities: Don't limit yourself to one or two communities. Explore a variety of groups and organizations that might interest you. This could involve joining a book club, volunteering for a cause you care about, attending meetups for your hobbies, or exploring online forums and communities that share your interests.

Be yourself: It is important to be authentic and genuine when seeking belonging. Trying to be someone you're not will only lead to frustration and disappointment.

Be patient and persistent: Finding a community that truly feels like home can take time and effort. Don't get discouraged if you don't find it right away. Keep exploring and connecting with others, and eventually, you will find your place.

Embrace vulnerability: Being open and vulnerable with others can be scary, but it is essential for building authentic connections. Share your thoughts, feelings, and experiences with others, and be willing to listen to theirs in return.

Be proactive in building relationships: Don't wait for people to reach out to you. Take the initiative to connect with others, engage in conversations, and participate in activities that interest you.

Give back to your community: One of the best ways to feel like you belong is to contribute to the community. Volunteer your time, share your skills, and help to make a positive difference in the lives of others.

The Power of Belonging:

The quest for belonging is a fundamental human need. It is a journey of self-discovery, connection, and growth. By actively seeking out communities that align with our values and interests, being open to new experiences, and building meaningful connections with others, we can find a sense of purpose, identity, and support that enriches our lives and empowers us to thrive. It provides us with a sense of purpose, identity, and support, which are crucial for navigating the challenges of life and achieving our full potential.

By embracing the journey of finding belonging, being open to new experiences, and actively seeking out connections with others, we can create a world where everyone feels accepted, valued, and part of something larger than themselves. This is a world where we can all flourish, build strong relationships, and create a more just and compassionate society.

Chapter 5: Encountering the Hebrew Language

The Power of the Hebrew Language

From Ancient Scripts to Modern Revival: A Tapestry of Time

Hebrew's journey begins in the mists of antiquity, emerging as a Northwest Semitic language spoken by the ancient Israelites. Its earliest forms, discernible in inscriptions like the Moabite Stone and the Siloam Inscription, date back to the 9th and 8th centuries BCE. However, the language's true literary blossoming occurred during the First Temple period, with the emergence of biblical Hebrew, the language of the Hebrew Bible. This period witnessed the creation of iconic texts like the Torah, the Psalms, and the Prophets, shaping not only the literary landscape but also the theological and cultural identity of the Jewish people.

The Hebrew language, however, faced periods of decline and revival. The destruction of the Second Temple in 70 CE saw the ascendancy of Aramaic as the primary language of Jewish life. Yet, Hebrew remained a vital element of religious practice, scholarship, and community life. This period, known as the "Medieval Period," witnessed the development of the Masoretic Text, a standardized version of the Hebrew Bible, and the flourishing of Hebrew literature, including philosophical treatises, poetry, and commentaries.

The 19th century marked a pivotal turning point in the history of Hebrew. The Zionist movement, fueled by a yearning for national revival, recognized the crucial role of language in forging a shared identity. The "Hebrew Revival" became a key pillar of the movement, spearheaded by figures like Eliezer Ben-Yehuda, who dedicated his life to reviving the language for everyday use. Ben-Yehuda's tireless efforts, including the creation of new words and the promotion of Hebrew as a medium of education, paved the way for the establishment of the modern State of Israel in 1948.

The Enduring Power of Hebrew: From Ritual to Innovation

The power of the Hebrew language transcends mere linguistics; it is embedded in the fabric of Jewish culture, tradition, and faith. Its use in religious rituals, from the daily prayer service to the reading of the Torah, imbues it with a sacred quality. The Hebrew Bible, considered the most influential book in Western history, serves as the bedrock of Jewish theology and ethics, shaping countless generations of Jewish thought and practice.

Beyond the realm of religion, Hebrew holds a profound cultural significance. It is the language of Hebrew literature, encompassing a vast array of genres, from poetry and drama to fiction and philosophy. Authors like Chaim Bialik, S. Y. Agnon, and Amos Oz have enriched the literary landscape with their powerful voices, using Hebrew as a tool to explore themes of identity, history, and the human condition.

The revival of Hebrew in the 20th century brought with it an explosion of creativity and innovation. Hebrew became the language of modern Israeli literature, music, theater, and film. From the iconic works of Yehuda Amichai and David Grossman to the groundbreaking music of Ofra Haza and the cinematic brilliance of Amos Gitai, Israeli artists have leveraged the power of Hebrew to express a range of emotions and perspectives.

The Language of Identity: Past, Present, and Future

Hebrew's enduring power lies not just in its literary and cultural impact, but also in its role as a unifying force. For Jews around the world, Hebrew serves as a bridge connecting them to their shared heritage and history. Learning Hebrew is a journey of rediscovering one's roots, forging a connection with ancestors who lived centuries ago.

In the modern State of Israel, Hebrew has become the symbol of national unity, bridging diverse communities and fostering a sense of shared identity. As the language of education, government, and everyday life, Hebrew plays a crucial role in shaping the nation's cultural landscape and fostering a sense of belonging among its citizens.

Looking towards the future, Hebrew continues to evolve and adapt, reflecting the changing landscape of Israeli society. The influx of immigrants from diverse backgrounds has led to the incorporation of new words and expressions, enriching the language and demonstrating its inherent flexibility. It is a language rooted in ancient traditions, reborn through a vibrant revival, and imbued with a cultural significance that transcends borders and time. Its journey, from ancient scriptures to modern innovation, serves as a testament to its resilience, its adaptability, and its profound ability to shape both individual and collective identities. As we continue to explore the depths of this fascinating language, we gain a deeper understanding of its power, its beauty, and its enduring relevance in the 21st century and beyond.

Learning Basic Hebrew Words and Phrases

This guide aims to equip you with the necessary tools to navigate the initial stages of your Hebrew learning adventure. We'll explore the fundamentals of pronunciation, delve into essential vocabulary, and practice constructing simple sentences. Remember, language learning is a gradual process, and patience, persistence, and a dash of fun are key ingredients for success.

Pronunciation: Laying the Foundation

Hebrew pronunciation, while initially challenging for non-native speakers, is ultimately straightforward and consistent. By mastering the basic sounds and their rules, you'll unlock the key to accurately understanding and speaking Hebrew.

Vowels: Hebrew boasts five main vowels, represented by a unique set of symbols:
a: (as in "father") represented by the symbol ַ
e: (as in "bed") represented by the symbol ֶ
i: (as in "machine") represented by the symbol ִ
o: (as in "go") represented by the symbol וֹ
u: (as in "flute") represented by the symbol וּ
Consonants: The Hebrew alphabet boasts 22 consonants, each with a distinct pronunciation. Some consonants may sound unfamiliar to English speakers, so it's essential to focus on accurate articulation.
Gutturals: The consonants ע, ח, ך, and ר often present challenges for English speakers due to their guttural pronunciations. They require a slightly different airflow and positioning of the tongue.
Palatals: Hebrew also features palatal consonants, which are pronounced with the tongue near the hard palate. Examples include ש, צ, and י.
Stress: In Hebrew, word stress typically falls on the penultimate (second-to-last) syllable. However, there are exceptions, so pay attention to the written form to determine the correct stress.

Essential Vocabulary: Building Your Linguistic Toolkit

Building a robust vocabulary is fundamental to mastering any language. Here's a starting point for basic Hebrew words and phrases:

Greetings:
Shalom: (Hello. Goodbye) - שָׁלוֹם

Bo'ker Tov: (Good morning) - בֹּקֶר טוֹב
Tze'har Tov: (Good afternoon) - צָהֳרַיִם טוֹב
Erev Tov: (Good evening) - ערב טוב
Lehitra'ot: (See you later) - להתראות
Numbers:
Echad: (One) - אֶחָד
Shnayim: (Two) - שְׁנַיִם
Shalosh: (Three) - שָׁלוֹשׁ
Arba'a: (Four) - אַרְבַּע
Chamisha: (Five) - חֲמִשָּׁה
Basic Words:
Ani: (I) - אֲנִי
At: (You [female]) - אַתְּ
Hu: (He) - הוּא
Hi: (She) - הִיא
Ken: (Yes) - כֵּן
Lo: (No) - לֹא
Everyday Phrases:
Ma Koreh. (What's up.) - מָה קוֹרֶה.
Todah Rabah: (Thank you very much) - תודה רבה
Bevakasha: (Please) - בְּבַקָּשָׁה
Slicha: (Excuse me) - סְלִיחָה
Im Eshta'ot: (If you want) - אם אִשְׁתָּאוֹת

Sentence Structure: Putting Words Together

Hebrew sentence structure follows a Subject-Verb-Object order, similar to English. However, there are some key differences to be aware of:

Gender Agreement: Hebrew verbs and adjectives agree in gender with the noun they modify. For example, "the woman is tall" would be "ha-ishah gavoha", where "gavoha" (tall) agrees in gender with "ha-ishah" (the woman).
Definite Articles: Hebrew uses the definite article "ha-" (ה-) before singular nouns, and "ha-" (ה-) before plural nouns.

Prepositions: Hebrew prepositions can be tricky, as they often take different forms depending on the noun they modify. It's essential to learn the various forms and their usage.

Learning Resources: Tools for Your Hebrew Journey

With the basic groundwork laid, you'll need resources to aid your language learning journey. Numerous options are available, catering to diverse learning styles and preferences:

Language Learning Apps: Duolingo, Memrise, Babbel, and Rosetta Stone offer interactive and engaging ways to learn Hebrew vocabulary, grammar, and pronunciation.

Online Courses: Platforms like Coursera, edX, and Udemy provide comprehensive Hebrew courses, often taught by experienced instructors.

Textbooks and Workbooks: Traditional textbooks and workbooks offer structured learning materials, covering grammar, vocabulary, and practice exercises.

Language Exchange Partners: Connect with native Hebrew speakers online or in your community for conversation practice and cultural immersion.

Immersion Programs: Spend time in Israel or other Hebrew-speaking communities to fully immerse yourself in the language and culture.

By embracing the challenge, utilizing available resources, and practicing consistently, you'll unlock the door to a rich tapestry of language, history, and culture. Remember, learning a new language is a journey of discovery, growth, and personal enrichment. So, embrace the process, have fun, and enjoy the journey.

Discovering the Beauty of Scripture in its Original Language

The limitations of translation:

While translations play a crucial role in making Scripture accessible to a global audience, they inherently involve a degree of compromise. Every language has its own unique structure and nuances, and translating concepts from one language to another often necessitates subtle shifts in meaning. Consider, for instance, the Hebrew word "hesed," which embodies a multifaceted concept of steadfast love, loyalty, and covenant faithfulness. While translations may use words like "love," "kindness," or "mercy," they cannot fully capture the rich tapestry of meaning woven into "hesed." Similarly, the Greek word "agape," often translated as "love," signifies a selfless, sacrificial love that transcends mere affection. Understanding the original language allows us to appreciate the profound depth of these terms and their intricate interplay in the biblical narrative.

Unveiling the richness of the text:

Beyond individual words, the original languages reveal the artistry and precision of the biblical writers. Take, for example, the Hebrew poetic structure, characterized by parallelism and imagery. Examining the original Hebrew reveals how the writers skillfully use wordplay, rhythm, and repetition to create a powerful emotional impact on the reader. In the Psalms, for instance, we see the use of parallelism, where verses are often paired to express similar ideas in different ways, creating a sense of balance and emphasis. Similarly, the use of imagery, drawing on vivid metaphors and similes, allows the reader to experience the depth of emotion and spiritual truth conveyed in these ancient texts.

The Greek language, with its rich vocabulary and nuanced grammar, offers another layer of depth to the New Testament. Examining the original Greek helps us to appreciate the subtle shades of meaning conveyed by the authors, revealing the intricate connections between different passages and the unity of thought that flows through the entire corpus of Scripture.

The joy of personal discovery:

Learning the original languages is not just about linguistic analysis; it's about engaging in a deeply personal and enriching journey of discovery. As you begin to understand the original Hebrew or Greek, you will find yourself drawn into a deeper conversation with the biblical text, experiencing a greater sense of intimacy and connection with the words of God. This journey fosters a greater appreciation for the beauty and power of Scripture, deepening your faith and expanding your understanding of its timeless message.

Practical benefits for the reader:

Beyond the purely intellectual and spiritual rewards, understanding the original languages offers practical benefits for the reader. It can enhance your understanding of biblical texts, enabling you to interpret them with greater clarity and insight. You will be better equipped to identify and address potential issues related to translation, avoiding misinterpretations and gaining a deeper understanding of the original author's intent.

A journey of lifelong learning:

Learning the original languages of Scripture is a lifelong endeavor. It's a journey of exploration and discovery, where the more you learn, the more you realize there is still to be uncovered. However, even a basic understanding of Hebrew or Greek can open up a whole new world of meaning and depth in your reading of the Bible. It is an investment in your spiritual growth and a testament to the enduring power of God's word. It is an invitation to step into the world of the ancients, to engage in a dialogue with the biblical writers, and to experience the richness and depth of meaning that lies hidden within the original texts. This journey of discovery will enrich your faith, expand your understanding, and reveal the enduring power of God's message for generations to come.

Connecting with a Deeper Meaning

The Human Need for Meaning:

Humans are meaning-making creatures. We seek to understand the world around us, to find patterns and connections that provide us with a sense of order and purpose. This innate drive is deeply embedded in our psychology and influences our actions, choices, and overall well-being. Psychologist Viktor Frankl, who survived the horrors of the Nazi concentration camps, eloquently described the human need for meaning in his seminal work, "Man's Search for Meaning. " He argued that the absence of meaning in life can lead to a state of existential despair, while the presence of meaning, even amidst hardship, can provide resilience and strength.

The Importance of Self-Reflection:

Connecting with a deeper meaning begins with an honest and introspective examination of ourselves. This involves understanding our values, our passions, and our aspirations. What truly excites us. What are our strengths and weaknesses. What are the things we find deeply fulfilling. By engaging in self-reflection, we gain clarity on our internal compass, allowing us to navigate life with greater purpose and intention.

Exploring Our Values and Beliefs:

Our values and beliefs act as guiding principles, shaping our choices and influencing our actions. They provide a framework for understanding our place in the world and making ethical decisions. Identifying and examining our core values can be a revealing exercise. Do we prioritize compassion, justice, creativity, or knowledge. By aligning our actions with our values, we create a sense of internal coherence and integrity, contributing to a deeper sense of meaning.

Finding Meaning in Relationships:

Human beings are inherently social creatures, and our relationships play a vital role in shaping our sense of meaning. Connecting with others on a deep level, fostering genuine relationships built on mutual respect, trust, and compassion, contributes to a sense of belonging and purpose. Whether it's through intimate relationships, friendships, or communities, our interactions with others can provide a sense of purpose and fulfillment.

Pursuing Our Passions:

Engaging in activities that ignite our passion is a powerful way to connect with a deeper meaning. What excites us. What makes us lose track of time. These activities tap into our innate talents and abilities, allowing us to express ourselves authentically and contribute to the world in a unique way. Whether it's art, music, writing, or any other pursuit that ignites our soul, pursuing our passions can enrich our lives with a sense of purpose and fulfillment.

The Power of Contribution:

Another essential element in connecting with a deeper meaning is the act of contributing to something larger than ourselves. This can manifest in various forms, from volunteering in our communities to engaging in activism, from pursuing scientific research to fostering creativity and innovation. Through contributing to the greater good, we find a sense of connection to something beyond ourselves, enriching our lives with purpose and meaning.

The Role of Spirituality:

While not universally applicable, spirituality can play a significant role in connecting with a deeper meaning. For many, spirituality provides a framework for understanding the universe and their place within it. It offers a sense of connection to something larger than themselves, providing a sense of purpose, comfort, and guidance.

Embrace the Journey:

Connecting with a deeper meaning is not a destination but an ongoing journey. It involves continuous self-reflection, growth, and a willingness to adapt to life's evolving circumstances. There will be moments of clarity and moments of doubt, moments of joy and moments of challenge. The key lies in embracing the journey with an open mind and a spirit of curiosity.

The Importance of Flexibility and Openness:

Our understanding of ourselves and our purpose is constantly evolving. Life experiences, interactions with others, and new learnings can shift our perspectives and lead us to redefine our values and aspirations. Therefore, embracing flexibility and openness is crucial in connecting with a deeper meaning. We need to be willing to adapt, to learn, and to grow, allowing our understanding of ourselves and our purpose to evolve alongside our experiences.

Cultivating Meaning in Daily Life:

Connecting with a deeper meaning is not a grand, singular event but a subtle shift in our perspective. It's about finding purpose in the ordinary, in the everyday moments that make up our lives. This involves appreciating the small things, finding joy in the present, and cultivating a sense of gratitude for the blessings in our lives. By bringing intention and awareness to our daily routines, we can infuse even the simplest tasks with a sense of meaning and purpose.

The Power of Gratitude:

Gratitude plays a vital role in cultivating a sense of meaning and purpose. By focusing on what we have rather than what we lack, we shift our perspective from scarcity to abundance, opening our hearts to the joys and blessings in our lives. Gratitude allows us to appreciate the simple things, to recognize the beauty in our surroundings, and to cultivate a sense of contentment and fulfillment.

Living a Life of Purpose:

Connecting with a deeper meaning is not merely a philosophical exercise but a tangible expression of our values, our passions, and our commitment to living a purposeful life. It involves making conscious choices that align with our values, pursuing activities that ignite our passions, and contributing to the greater good. This process of self-discovery and growth ultimately leads to a life filled with meaning, fulfillment, and a deep sense of purpose. It requires self-reflection, introspection, and a willingness to explore our values, beliefs, and aspirations. It involves embracing our passions, cultivating meaningful relationships, and contributing to the world around us. By actively engaging in this process, we can tap into our innate yearning for purpose and create a life that is truly meaningful and fulfilling. The journey of connecting with a deeper meaning is not about finding the perfect answer but about continuously exploring, growing, and discovering what gives our lives true significance.

Chapter 6: Navigating Religious Differences

Understanding Jewish and Christian Perspectives

The Shared Roots: From Abraham to the Messiah

The story of Abraham, the patriarch revered by both Jews and Christians, serves as the foundational narrative for both religions. His covenant with God, promising him a vast progeny and a blessed land, forms the cornerstone of their shared history. From Abraham's lineage, both faiths trace their origins to the patriarch Jacob, renamed Israel, and his twelve sons who formed the tribes of Israel. This shared ancestral heritage binds Judaism and Christianity together in a remarkable way.

The Hebrew Bible, revered as the Torah by Jews and the Old Testament by Christians, serves as the foundation of their shared understanding of God's covenant with Israel. It narrates the history of the Israelites, their struggles for freedom, and their relationship with God through prophets like Moses and Isaiah. However, while the Hebrew Bible stands as a central text for both faiths, its interpretation and the subsequent development of their beliefs diverge significantly.

The Jewish Perspective: A Legacy of Covenant and Law

Judaism, often described as the "religion of the book," places immense emphasis on the Torah, the first five books of the Hebrew

Bible. It is believed to be a direct revelation from God, containing both laws governing daily life and theological insights. This adherence to the Torah as a divinely given blueprint for living forms the central tenet of Judaism.

The Jewish faith is characterized by its strong emphasis on ethical conduct and social justice. The Torah's commandments, known as the mitzvot, guide Jewish life, encompassing aspects ranging from dietary laws and prayer to charity and social responsibility. The concept of "Tikkun Olam," the repairing of the world, underscores the Jewish commitment to actively working towards a more just and ethical society.

Judaism encompasses a spectrum of beliefs and practices, ranging from the traditional and observant to the more liberal and reform movements. While there is diversity within the Jewish faith, the fundamental belief in one God, the importance of the covenant with Israel, and the unwavering commitment to the Torah remain central to all branches of Judaism.

The Christian Perspective: The New Covenant and the Messiah

Christianity emerged from within Judaism, evolving from the teachings of Jesus of Nazareth. Christians believe that Jesus was the Messiah prophesied in the Hebrew Bible, sent by God to redeem humanity from sin and offer eternal life through his sacrifice. This belief in Jesus as the Son of God and the savior of humanity forms the core of the Christian faith.

The Christian faith emphasizes the importance of personal faith in Jesus Christ. The New Testament, consisting of the Gospels, the Acts of the Apostles, and epistles, expands upon Jesus' teachings and the early development of the Christian church. The concept of salvation through faith in Jesus Christ is central to Christianity, offering a path to reconciliation with God and a promise of eternal life.

Christian denominations vary significantly in their interpretations of scripture, theological doctrines, and practices. From the Roman Catholic Church to Protestantism, with its diverse denominations, Christianity exhibits a rich diversity of theological perspectives and liturgical expressions.

The Bridge of Shared Values: Seeking Common Ground

Despite their theological differences, Judaism and Christianity share a profound moral foundation. Both faiths emphasize the importance of ethical living, social justice, and compassion for the vulnerable. The teachings of the Hebrew Bible and the New Testament serve as ethical guidelines for both Jews and Christians, promoting values like honesty, integrity, and love for one's neighbor.

Understanding the historical and theological roots of both faiths provides valuable insight into their respective perspectives. Recognizing the shared history and moral foundations can pave the way for dialogue and understanding between Jewish and Christian communities. This understanding fosters a deeper appreciation for the complexities and richness of both faiths and promotes a spirit of mutual respect and collaboration.

Continuing the Conversation: Exploring the Future

The journey of understanding Jewish and Christian perspectives is an ongoing one. As both faiths evolve and respond to the challenges of the modern world, dialogue and engagement remain crucial. Understanding the nuances of each other's beliefs, practices, and concerns can bridge divides and foster a spirit of mutual respect and understanding.

By engaging in open and respectful dialogue, fostering interfaith partnerships, and recognizing the shared values that bind these two great faiths, we can work towards building a future where understanding and tolerance prevail. The journey of understanding Jewish and Christian perspectives is not merely an academic exercise but a vital step towards fostering a more peaceful and just world.

This exploration of Jewish and Christian perspectives serves as a starting point, a glimpse into the vast and complex world of these two faiths. Continued engagement with the scriptures, theological discussions, and interfaith dialogues will deepen our understanding and appreciation for these enduring traditions.

Respecting Different Interpretations

Understanding the Subjectivity of Interpretation:

The human mind is a complex tapestry of experiences, values, beliefs, and biases. These elements shape our perception of the world and influence the way we interpret information. No two individuals share precisely the same life experiences, cultural background, or intellectual framework. As a result, interpretations of the same event, text, or idea will inevitably differ. Recognizing this inherent subjectivity is essential to understanding and respecting diverse viewpoints.

Consider the interpretation of a historical event. Two historians, analyzing the same set of primary sources, might arrive at different conclusions about its causes, consequences, and significance. One historian might focus on economic factors, while another might emphasize social or political influences. These divergent interpretations do not necessarily imply that one is right and the other wrong. Instead, they reflect the different lenses through which they view the past, shaped by their individual knowledge, training, and assumptions.

Similarly, the interpretation of a literary text can vary significantly between readers. An individual who has experienced personal loss might resonate with a character's grief in a way that a reader without such experience cannot fully comprehend. Their interpretations of the same text will be influenced by their unique perspectives, shaped by their personal histories and emotional landscapes.

Empathy as a Bridge to Understanding:

Empathy plays a crucial role in bridging the gap between different interpretations. It involves stepping outside of our own perspectives and attempting to understand the world from another person's point of view. This requires active listening, suspending judgment, and acknowledging the validity of others' experiences and feelings.

Empathy allows us to appreciate that different interpretations are not necessarily incompatible or inherently wrong. Rather, they are often complementary, offering different facets of a complex truth. For example, in a debate about environmental policy, one person might emphasize the importance of economic growth, while another might prioritize environmental sustainability. By practicing empathy, we can recognize the validity of both perspectives and appreciate that they are both essential components of a holistic solution.

Moreover, empathy helps us move beyond simplistic binary judgments, such as "right" or "wrong," and encourages us to engage in nuanced and thoughtful discussions. It allows us to recognize the complexity of issues and acknowledge that there are often multiple valid perspectives.

The Power of Open Dialogue:

Respecting different interpretations requires engaging in open and respectful dialogue. This involves active listening, thoughtful questioning, and a willingness to consider alternative viewpoints. It is a process of collaborative exploration where individuals share their interpretations, clarify their reasoning, and engage in constructive debate.

Open dialogue allows for the exchange of ideas, the clarification of misunderstandings, and the development of a more nuanced understanding of complex issues. It encourages individuals to challenge their own assumptions, refine their arguments, and consider new perspectives. This process can lead to personal growth, intellectual enrichment, and the development of more informed and effective solutions to societal challenges.

Building a Culture of Respect:

Building a culture of respect for different interpretations requires a conscious effort from individuals and institutions. This involves promoting critical thinking, fostering empathy, and encouraging open and respectful dialogue.

Educational institutions play a crucial role in fostering critical thinking and intellectual curiosity. By exposing students to diverse perspectives, encouraging them to challenge assumptions, and providing them with the tools to analyze information critically, schools can equip future generations with the skills necessary to navigate a complex and diverse world.

Similarly, media outlets have a responsibility to present information accurately and fairly, representing diverse viewpoints and avoiding biased or inflammatory language. By providing a platform for constructive dialogue, media organizations can contribute to a more informed and respectful public discourse.

The Benefits of Respecting Different Interpretations:

Respecting different interpretations yields numerous benefits for individuals and society as a whole. It promotes:

Greater Understanding: By acknowledging the subjective nature of interpretation and practicing empathy, we can develop a deeper understanding of diverse perspectives, fostering tolerance and reducing prejudice.

Enhanced Critical Thinking: Engaging in respectful dialogue and considering alternative viewpoints encourages us to challenge our own assumptions and refine our thinking, leading to more nuanced and sophisticated understanding of complex issues.

Improved Decision-Making: Incorporating diverse perspectives into decision-making processes leads to more comprehensive and informed solutions, as individuals consider a wider range of factors and potential outcomes.

Increased Creativity and Innovation: Exposure to different ideas and perspectives stimulates creativity and innovation, as individuals are challenged to think outside the box and develop novel solutions.

A More Inclusive and Just Society: Respecting different interpretations promotes social harmony by fostering understanding, reducing conflict, and creating a more inclusive and equitable environment for all.

Challenges and Considerations:

While respecting different interpretations is essential for a healthy and productive society, it also presents challenges that require careful consideration.

Distinguishing Between Respectful Differences and Harmful Ideas: It is crucial to differentiate between respectful disagreements based on diverse perspectives and harmful ideas that promote violence, discrimination, or intolerance. While we should respect the right to hold differing opinions, we must also recognize that certain views are harmful and should be challenged and refuted.

The Role of Facts and Evidence: While interpretations may differ, it is important to ground discussions in facts and evidence. While subjective interpretations are unavoidable, decisions should be based on the best available evidence and data.

Balancing Respect with Accountability: Respecting different

interpretations should not be interpreted as condoning harmful behavior or silencing dissent. While individuals should be allowed to express their views, they should also be held accountable for the consequences of their actions and words. It fosters understanding, promotes dialogue, and enables individuals and groups to learn and grow from diverse perspectives. Embracing this principle requires acknowledging the subjective nature of interpretation, fostering empathy for others' viewpoints, and engaging in open and respectful dialogue. By promoting critical thinking, empathy, and open dialogue, we can build a more informed, inclusive, and just society where different interpretations are not only tolerated but celebrated as a source of strength and innovation.

Engaging in Open Dialogue

This exploration delves into the multifaceted nature of open dialogue, examining its principles, benefits, and challenges. We will explore strategies for effective engagement, recognizing the importance of active listening, thoughtful articulation, and a willingness to learn and adapt. Ultimately, this journey aims to empower individuals with the knowledge and skills to navigate complex conversations, fostering collaboration and progress in a world often marked by division.

The Power of Open Dialogue

Open dialogue is not simply about exchanging information; it is about fostering meaningful connections and building bridges across differences. It recognizes the inherent value in diverse perspectives and experiences, acknowledging that each individual holds unique insights and knowledge to contribute to collective understanding.

The power of open dialogue lies in its ability to:

Promote mutual understanding: By actively listening and engaging with diverse viewpoints, participants gain a deeper understanding of different perspectives, leading to greater empathy and appreciation for the complexities of human experience.

Generate creative solutions: Open dialogue fosters an environment of intellectual exploration, encouraging participants to share ideas, brainstorm solutions, and collaboratively address challenges with a sense of inclusivity and shared purpose.

Build trust and rapport: Open and respectful communication fosters trust and rapport among individuals, creating a foundation for meaningful relationships and collaborative endeavors.

Resolve conflicts constructively: Open dialogue provides a safe space for individuals to express their concerns and grievances, fostering constructive dialogue that seeks to understand and address underlying issues rather than escalate conflict.

Foster social change: By creating platforms for open and honest discussion on critical social issues, open dialogue empowers individuals to become active agents of change, promoting social justice, equality, and inclusivity.

Key Principles of Open Dialogue

Effective open dialogue hinges on a set of foundational principles, guiding participants towards respectful and productive engagement:

Respect for all participants: Open dialogue prioritizes the inherent dignity and value of each individual, regardless of their background, beliefs, or opinions. This means listening attentively, acknowledging different perspectives, and refraining from personal attacks or disrespectful language.

Openness to different viewpoints: Engaging in open dialogue requires a willingness to consider perspectives that may challenge one's own beliefs. It involves approaching discussions with curiosity and a genuine desire to understand others' points of view, even if they differ significantly from one's own.

Active listening and empathy: Active listening involves paying full attention to the speaker, understanding their message, and acknowledging their emotions. Empathy allows participants to connect with the speaker's perspective, fostering understanding and building bridges across differences.

Clarity of communication: Expressing thoughts and ideas clearly and concisely is crucial for effective dialogue. Participants should strive to articulate their views in a manner that is easily understood and avoids ambiguity.

Constructive feedback and critical thinking: Open dialogue encourages participants to offer constructive feedback, challenging ideas and assumptions while maintaining respect for the speaker. This promotes critical thinking and helps refine perspectives for greater clarity and understanding.

Flexibility and adaptability: Open dialogue is a dynamic process that requires flexibility and adaptability. Participants should be prepared to adjust their viewpoints, acknowledge new information, and adapt their communication style to facilitate productive engagement.

Strategies for Engaging in Open Dialogue

Engaging in open dialogue effectively requires a conscious effort to cultivate essential skills and adapt one's communication style. Here are some strategies to enhance your ability to participate in meaningful and productive conversations:

Active Listening: Pay full attention to the speaker, focusing on their words, tone, and non-verbal cues. Resist the urge to interrupt or formulate your response while they are speaking. Instead, try to paraphrase their message to ensure you've understood their perspective.

Empathy and Perspective-Taking: Try to see the world from the speaker's point of view. Consider their background, experiences, and values that may have shaped their beliefs and opinions. Even if you disagree, acknowledge their perspective and demonstrate understanding.

Clear and Concise Communication: Articulate your thoughts and ideas clearly and concisely, avoiding jargon or technical language that may be difficult to understand. Use "I" statements to express your own feelings and experiences, while acknowledging the other person's perspective.

Focus on Collaboration: Approach discussions with a collaborative mindset, seeking to build common ground and find solutions that benefit everyone. Avoid adversarial language or attempts to dominate the conversation.

Respectful Disagreement: It's perfectly acceptable to disagree with someone, but it's crucial to do so respectfully. State your disagreement clearly and calmly, avoiding personal attacks or inflammatory language. Focus on the issues at hand rather than attacking the person.

Seek Clarification: If you're unsure about something, ask for clarification. Don't be afraid to ask for definitions, examples, or explanations.

Seek Common Ground: Even when there are significant differences, look for areas of agreement. Highlight shared values or goals to foster a sense of common purpose.

Acknowledge Emotions: Be aware of your own emotions and the emotions of others. Acknowledge when emotions are running high, and try to create a space for everyone to express their feelings safely and respectfully.

Be Open to Learning: Engage in open dialogue with a genuine desire to learn and grow. Be willing to consider new information, revise your perspective, and expand your understanding of the world.

Challenges and Considerations in Open Dialogue

While open dialogue holds tremendous potential for fostering understanding and collaboration, it is not without its challenges:

Power Imbalances: Power imbalances can create barriers to genuine dialogue. Individuals with greater authority, resources, or social capital may have a greater influence on the conversation, silencing marginalized voices or discouraging dissent.

Emotional Triggers: Certain topics or viewpoints can trigger strong emotions, making it difficult to engage in calm and respectful dialogue. Participants may resort to defensive behavior, personal attacks, or emotional outbursts.

Cultural Differences: Communication styles and norms vary across cultures. Misunderstandings can arise due to differences in language, body language, or conversational etiquette.

Cognitive Biases: We are all susceptible to cognitive biases that can distort our perception of information and influence our interactions with others. Confirmation bias, for example, can lead us to seek out information that confirms our existing beliefs and dismiss evidence that contradicts them.

Time Constraints: Engaging in truly open dialogue requires time and effort. In fast-paced environments, individuals may not have the opportunity to listen deeply, reflect critically, or fully articulate their perspectives.

Lack of Trust: Open dialogue requires a foundation of trust among participants. In contexts where trust is lacking, individuals may be hesitant to share their views, engage in honest conversations, or acknowledge their own biases.

Strategies for Addressing Challenges

Addressing these challenges requires a conscious commitment to creating a safe and inclusive space for open dialogue. Here are some strategies:

Acknowledge Power Dynamics: Recognize and address power imbalances within the conversation. Individuals with greater authority should be mindful of their influence and create space for marginalized voices to be heard.

Cultivate Emotional Intelligence: Develop emotional intelligence by recognizing and managing your own emotions while understanding and respecting the emotions of others. This allows for more productive conversations, even when difficult topics are discussed.

Embrace Cultural Sensitivity: Be aware of cultural differences in communication styles and norms. Practice active listening to understand different perspectives and avoid making assumptions based on cultural stereotypes.

Challenge Cognitive Biases: Be aware of your own cognitive biases and take steps to challenge them. Seek out diverse sources of information, consider opposing viewpoints, and be open to revising your beliefs based on new evidence.

Prioritize Time for Reflection: Allocate sufficient time for participants to process information, reflect on their perspectives, and formulate their responses. Avoid rushing through conversations or expecting immediate agreement.

Build Trust Through Transparency: Foster trust by being transparent about your own biases and assumptions. Be willing to acknowledge your limitations and engage in conversations with humility.

Seek Facilitation and Mediation: Consider bringing in trained facilitators or mediators to guide conversations, manage conflicts, and ensure respectful and productive engagement.

Moving Forward: Cultivating Open Dialogue in Our World

Engaging in open dialogue is not a passive activity; it requires a conscious effort and a commitment to fostering understanding and collaboration. As we navigate an increasingly complex world, the ability to engage in meaningful conversations becomes essential for addressing shared challenges and building a more just and equitable society.

By embracing the principles and strategies outlined here, we can cultivate a culture of open dialogue, promoting empathy, respect, and constructive engagement. This journey begins with each of us, taking responsibility for our own communication styles and actively seeking opportunities to connect with others in meaningful ways. Let us commit to fostering a world where open dialogue thrives, bridging divides, sparking innovation, and paving the way for a brighter future.

Building Bridges of Understanding

This journey of building bridges begins with recognizing the very foundations upon which they must be built. It is crucial to acknowledge the existence of differences, not as barriers, but as opportunities for learning and growth. These differences can manifest in myriad ways – language, ethnicity, religion, political affiliation, socioeconomic status, and personal experiences all shape our worldviews and influence how we interact with the world. Embracing this inherent diversity is the first step towards fostering genuine understanding.

Moving beyond simple acceptance, we must cultivate curiosity and actively seek to understand perspectives that differ from our own. This journey of exploration requires a commitment to active listening, a willingness to engage with discomfort, and a genuine desire to learn. Engaging in open-minded dialogue, asking questions, and challenging our own assumptions can help us dismantle the walls of prejudice and build pathways to empathy.

The process of building bridges is inherently iterative and requires ongoing effort. We must continuously refine our understanding of others and engage in respectful dialogue even when opinions diverge. Patience, humility, and a commitment to finding common ground are essential tools in this process. It is within these spaces of shared understanding that we can begin to bridge the divides that separate us.

The Power of Communication: Building Bridges Through Dialogue

Communication is the lifeblood of any bridge, and it is through meaningful dialogue that we can truly connect with others and build bridges of understanding. Effective communication transcends mere words; it requires active listening, empathetic engagement, and a willingness to see the world through another's eyes.

One key element of effective communication lies in understanding the power of perspective. We must recognize that our own experiences shape our beliefs and values, and these personal lenses influence how we interpret the world. This realization encourages us to approach conversations with an open mind, actively seeking to understand the perspectives of others without judgment.

Active listening is another crucial component of building bridges through communication. It involves paying full attention to the speaker, both verbally and nonverbally, and acknowledging their thoughts and feelings without interrupting or dismissing their viewpoint. This attentive listening allows us to truly grasp the essence of another's perspective and fosters a sense of validation and respect.

Effective communication also requires the ability to express our own perspectives clearly and respectfully. This involves articulating our thoughts and feelings with clarity and sensitivity, while simultaneously considering the impact our words might have on others. By employing empathy and choosing our words carefully, we can foster a constructive and respectful dialogue that encourages understanding rather than conflict.

Building bridges through dialogue also necessitates a commitment to seeking common ground. Rather than focusing solely on differences, we should actively search for areas of shared interest and values. This approach allows us to build upon commonalities, fostering a sense of shared purpose and encouraging collaboration.

The Role of Education: Building Bridges Through Knowledge and Understanding

Education plays a vital role in building bridges of understanding by equipping individuals with the knowledge and skills necessary to navigate a diverse world. It serves as a foundation for critical thinking, empathy, and open-mindedness, fostering the ability to engage respectfully with diverse perspectives.

One crucial aspect of education in building bridges lies in fostering critical thinking skills. By developing the ability to analyze information, evaluate evidence, and challenge assumptions, individuals are better equipped to engage in informed dialogue and discern fact from fiction. This critical lens helps to dismantle harmful stereotypes and prejudices, promoting a more nuanced understanding of diverse experiences.

Empathy is another essential element of bridge-building. Education can cultivate this vital skill by exposing individuals to a wide range of perspectives, experiences, and cultures. Through literature, history, and the arts, individuals can learn to step into the shoes of others, developing a deeper understanding of their motivations, struggles, and aspirations. This empathetic understanding fosters a sense of connection and reduces the potential for misunderstanding and conflict.

Moreover, education can empower individuals to become active participants in building bridges of understanding. By providing knowledge about social issues, historical injustices, and current events, education equips individuals with the tools necessary to engage in constructive dialogue and contribute to positive change. This understanding allows individuals to become agents of understanding, actively promoting empathy and tolerance in their communities.

Building Bridges Across Cultures: Embracing Diversity and Fostering Intercultural Understanding

In a world increasingly interconnected, understanding and appreciating diverse cultures is vital for building bridges of understanding. This journey requires embracing cultural differences, challenging stereotypes, and fostering intercultural competence.

One crucial step towards building bridges across cultures is to actively challenge stereotypes and prejudices. These harmful generalizations often stem from ignorance and lack of exposure to diverse perspectives. By engaging with diverse individuals and learning about their experiences, we can dismantle these preconceived notions and develop a more accurate and nuanced understanding of different cultures.

Moreover, it is crucial to cultivate a sense of cultural humility. This involves acknowledging our own cultural biases, recognizing that our perspective is just one of many, and approaching other cultures with open-mindedness and respect. By embracing cultural differences rather than seeing them as deficits, we can create a more inclusive and tolerant environment.

Building bridges across cultures also requires developing intercultural competence. This involves understanding the nuances of communication, nonverbal cues, and cultural norms that vary across different societies. By developing this awareness, we can navigate intercultural interactions with sensitivity and avoid potential misunderstandings.

Building Bridges Through Art and Creativity: Connecting Across Divides

Art and creativity serve as powerful tools for building bridges of understanding, transcending language barriers and fostering empathy and connection. Through diverse art forms, we can explore different perspectives, challenge societal norms, and create spaces for dialogue and reflection.

Music, with its universal language, has the power to bridge cultural divides and evoke shared emotions. From traditional folk music to contemporary global genres, music can connect individuals from different backgrounds, fostering a sense of community and shared experience.

Visual art, in its myriad forms, allows for a powerful exploration of diverse cultures and perspectives. Through paintings, sculptures, photography, and film, artists can depict the nuances of human experience, challenge societal norms, and spark meaningful conversations about identity, diversity, and social justice.

Literature, with its ability to transport us into different worlds and minds, offers a profound means of building bridges of understanding. Through the exploration of diverse characters, narratives, and perspectives, literature can foster empathy, challenge prejudices, and broaden our understanding of human experiences.

The power of art and creativity lies in its ability to create spaces for dialogue, reflection, and shared experiences. By engaging with diverse art forms, we can gain a deeper understanding of different cultures and perspectives, fostering empathy, connection, and a shared appreciation for the richness of human expression.

Building Bridges in a Digital World: Navigating the Online Landscape

In our increasingly digital world, the need to build bridges of understanding extends to the online landscape. Social media, while offering opportunities for connection and shared experiences, can also fuel division and misinformation. Navigating this complex digital terrain requires a commitment to responsible communication, critical thinking, and digital literacy.

Building bridges online requires engaging in respectful and constructive dialogue. This involves being mindful of our words and tone, avoiding personal attacks, and striving to create a safe and inclusive environment for all participants. We must also be vigilant in identifying and challenging misinformation, promoting accurate and reliable information.

Developing digital literacy skills is essential for navigating the online landscape effectively. This involves being aware of the potential biases and limitations of online platforms, understanding the mechanics of information flow, and developing critical thinking skills to evaluate the validity of online information.

Building bridges online also requires a commitment to building genuine connections. Rather than focusing solely on surface-level interactions, we should strive to engage in meaningful dialogue, share diverse perspectives, and foster a sense of community. By embracing the potential of the digital world to connect and learn, we can build bridges that transcend physical boundaries and foster a more inclusive and informed online environment.

Building Bridges for a More Just and Equitable World

Building bridges of understanding is not just a matter of individual effort; it requires a collective commitment to creating a more just and equitable world. This involves challenging systems of oppression, promoting social justice, and advocating for the rights and dignity of all individuals.

One crucial aspect of building bridges for a more just world involves addressing systemic inequalities. This requires dismantling structures and systems that perpetuate discrimination and marginalization based on race, gender, socioeconomic status, sexual orientation, or other factors. This involves challenging discriminatory policies, promoting equitable access to resources, and working towards a society that values diversity and inclusivity.

Moreover, we must actively engage in promoting social justice. This involves advocating for the rights of marginalized groups, speaking out against injustice, and working towards a society where everyone has the opportunity to thrive. This commitment requires us to challenge our own biases, embrace diverse perspectives, and work collaboratively to create a more equitable world for all.

Building bridges of understanding is an ongoing journey, one that requires constant effort, reflection, and a commitment to creating a more just and equitable world. It is a journey that begins with recognizing our own biases, embracing diversity, and actively seeking to understand perspectives different from our own. Through open-minded dialogue, empathy, and a commitment to finding common ground, we can build bridges that connect us, heal divides, and create a world where understanding and respect prevail.

Chapter 7: Embracing the Messianic Jewish Community

Finding a Community that Fits

Understanding the Why: The Need for Belonging

The need for belonging is not simply a social nicety; it is a fundamental human need as essential as food, water, and shelter. From an evolutionary perspective, belonging to a group provided safety, resources, and increased chances of survival. This instinctual drive to connect persists in the modern world, albeit in different forms.

Psychologists and sociologists have extensively studied the benefits of belonging. Studies show that people who feel a strong sense of community report higher levels of happiness, well-being, and overall life satisfaction. They experience reduced stress, improved mental health, and a stronger sense of purpose. Conversely, isolation and lack of belonging can lead to increased feelings of loneliness, depression, and even physical health problems.

Defining Your Community: Knowing What You Seek

The journey of finding a community that fits starts with self-reflection. Before embarking on the search, it is crucial to understand what you seek in a community. This involves exploring your values, interests, and what truly matters to you. What kind of environment do you thrive in. What kind of people do you enjoy connecting with. What activities bring you joy and purpose.

Consider the following questions to guide your reflection:

Values and Beliefs: What are your core values and beliefs. Do you seek a community that shares your perspective on social justice, environmental sustainability, or spirituality.
Interests and Hobbies: What are your passions and hobbies. Are you interested in sports, arts, music, or community service.
Lifestyle and Values: What kind of lifestyle do you envision for yourself. Are you drawn to a rural, urban, or suburban environment. Do you prioritize family-oriented activities, intellectual pursuits, or social activism.
Shared Goals and Aspirations: Do you seek a community that is working towards a common goal, whether it's promoting social change, fostering artistic expression, or supporting local businesses.

Exploring the Landscape: Finding Your Tribe

Once you have a clear understanding of your values and desires, the search for community can begin. The possibilities are vast and diverse, so it's important to be open to exploring various avenues:

Online Communities: The digital age has revolutionized how we connect. Online platforms like social media groups, forums, and virtual meetups offer a vast network of individuals sharing common interests.
Local Organizations and Groups: Consider joining organizations related to your hobbies, interests, or passions. This could include sports clubs, book clubs, community gardens, religious groups, or political organizations.
Neighborhood Events and Activities: Attend local events like farmers markets, community festivals, or neighborhood potlucks to meet people with shared interests.
Volunteer Opportunities: Volunteering for a cause you believe in is a fantastic way to meet like-minded individuals and build a sense of

community.
Workplace Connections: While work may not always be the ideal place to find deep friendships, it can offer opportunities to connect with colleagues who share your professional interests.
Faith Communities: For those seeking spiritual connection, faith-based communities can provide a strong sense of belonging and purpose.

Building Connections: Cultivating Trust and Belonging

Finding a community is just the first step; the true magic happens when you build genuine connections within it. This requires effort, patience, and a willingness to be vulnerable. Here are some strategies to cultivate meaningful connections:

Be Authentic and Open: Be your true self and share your genuine interests, thoughts, and experiences. Vulnerability fosters trust and deeper connections.
Active Listening: Pay attention to what others have to say, show empathy, and engage in meaningful conversations.
Offer Support and Kindness: Be there for your community members, offering a helping hand when needed.
Contribute Your Unique Skills and Talents: Share your knowledge, passions, and expertise to enrich the community.
Be Patient and Persistent: Building lasting relationships takes time and effort. Don't get discouraged if you don't find immediate connection.

Navigating the Challenges: Managing Expectations and Conflicts

Finding a community that perfectly aligns with your every desire is unrealistic. Just as individuals are complex and diverse, so too are communities. There will be disagreements, differences of opinion, and occasional conflicts. The key is to navigate these challenges with grace, empathy, and a willingness to compromise.

Acknowledge Differences and Embrace Diversity: Respect the diverse perspectives within your community, even if you don't agree with them. Celebrate the richness that comes from different backgrounds, ideas, and experiences.

Communicate Openly and Respectfully: When disagreements arise, approach them with open communication, active listening, and a willingness to find common ground.

Focus on Shared Values and Goals: Remind yourself of the shared values and aspirations that brought you together in the first place.

Seek Resolution and Reconciliation: When conflicts arise, strive for resolution and reconciliation rather than allowing them to fester.

The Ongoing Journey: Growth and Transformation

Finding a community that fits is not a destination but an ongoing journey. As you grow and evolve, your needs and desires may change, and you may find yourself seeking new connections or deepening existing ones. Embrace this continuous process of self-discovery and connection.

By actively engaging in your community, contributing your unique talents, and fostering meaningful relationships, you can create a sense of belonging, purpose, and fulfillment. The journey of finding a community that fits is a journey of self-discovery, personal growth, and the profound joy of being part of something larger than yourself.

Exploring Various Messianic Jewish Synagogues

A Historical Tapestry: Tracing the Roots of Messianic Judaism

The emergence of Messianic Judaism is intricately woven into the tapestry of Jewish history. While traces of early Jewish believers in Jesus can be found in the first century CE, the modern movement gained momentum in the 20th century, fueled by various factors, including the rise of Zionism, the Holocaust, and a renewed interest in Jewish identity among Christian believers.

One significant catalyst for the movement's growth was the establishment of the Hebrew Christian Alliance in the 1930s. This organization, led by figures like the influential theologian and rabbi, Jacob Immanuel Schochet, aimed to bridge the gap between Jewish tradition and Christian faith. The Hebrew Christian Alliance provided a platform for Jewish believers in Jesus to explore their faith within a Jewish context, fostering a sense of belonging and identity.

The post-World War II era witnessed a surge in Messianic Jewish communities, particularly in the United States. The rise of Zionism and the establishment of the State of Israel in 1948 inspired many Jewish believers in Jesus to see their faith as deeply intertwined with Jewish identity and national aspirations. The desire to reconnect with their Jewish heritage, alongside a growing awareness of their unique position within both the Jewish and Christian worlds, fueled the emergence of distinct Messianic Jewish communities across the globe.

Theological Diversity: A Spectrum of Beliefs

Messianic Jewish synagogues are united by their belief in Yeshua (Jesus) as the Messiah, but their theological perspectives exhibit a wide spectrum of views. This diversity stems from different interpretations of Scripture, varying degrees of emphasis on Jewish tradition, and a range of understandings of the relationship between Judaism and Christianity.

Torah Observance: A significant point of differentiation lies in the level of Torah observance practiced within Messianic Jewish communities. Some communities embrace a traditional Jewish lifestyle, adhering to the dietary laws (kashrut), Sabbath observance, and other rituals, while others adopt a more relaxed approach, focusing on the core principles of their faith while integrating elements of their cultural background.

Messianic Identity: Another key area of theological diversity revolves around the concept of Messianic identity. Some communities emphasize the distinctness of their Messianic identity, seeing themselves as a separate branch of Judaism, while others view themselves as an integral part of the Jewish people, embracing a more inclusive vision of Jewish unity.

Relationship with Christianity: The relationship between Messianic Judaism and Christianity also varies considerably. Some communities maintain strong connections with evangelical Christian denominations, drawing inspiration from Christian theology and practices, while others seek to emphasize their distinctiveness as a Jewish expression of faith, maintaining a more autonomous approach to their theological development.

Worship Styles: A Blend of Tradition and Innovation

The worship practices within Messianic Jewish synagogues offer a fascinating blend of traditional Jewish elements and Christian influences. While the core elements of prayer, Torah study, and communal fellowship remain central to their worship experiences, they often incorporate Christian hymns, liturgical elements, and themes related to the life and teachings of Yeshua.

Synagogue Services: Messianic Jewish synagogues typically hold Shabbat services, often featuring a combination of traditional Jewish prayers and liturgical readings, interspersed with musical selections, teachings, and testimonies. The services are often characterized by a warm and welcoming atmosphere, with a strong emphasis on participation and fellowship.

Music and Liturgy: The music played in Messianic Jewish synagogues ranges from traditional Hebrew melodies to contemporary Christian songs. The liturgical elements often incorporate traditional Jewish prayers, such as the Shema and the Amidah, while also drawing inspiration from Christian hymns and liturgical practices.

Sabbath Celebration: The Sabbath is a central element of worship in Messianic Jewish communities. The day is set aside for rest, reflection, and communal gatherings, often featuring a festive meal and engaging in spiritual study and discussion.

Community Building: Fostering a Sense of Belonging

Messianic Jewish synagogues are not just places of worship; they serve as vibrant centers for community building. The shared faith and cultural heritage create a strong sense of belonging, providing a supportive environment for individuals and families seeking a deeper connection to their Jewish roots.

Education and Outreach: Many Messianic Jewish synagogues actively engage in educational programs, offering classes on Jewish history, theology, and culture. They also participate in outreach initiatives, seeking to connect with the broader Jewish community and share their faith.

Challenges and Opportunities: Navigating the Future of Messianic Judaism

As Messianic Judaism continues to evolve, it faces a number of challenges and opportunities in the contemporary world. These include:

Maintaining Theological Integrity: Navigating the complex theological landscape while preserving the authenticity of their faith is a constant challenge for Messianic Jewish communities.
Bridging the Gap with Traditional Judaism: Building meaningful relationships with the broader Jewish community and overcoming historical divisions remains a significant priority.

Addressing Internal Differences: Maintaining unity and fostering dialogue within the diverse spectrum of theological perspectives is crucial for the continued growth of the movement.
Engaging with the Next Generation: Reaching out to younger generations and cultivating a sense of ownership over their faith and heritage is vital for the long-term sustainability of Messianic Jewish communities.

Despite these challenges, Messianic Jewish synagogues continue to thrive, offering a unique and enriching expression of Jewish faith for individuals and families who find themselves at the intersection of Jewish tradition and Christian belief. By embracing their rich heritage, fostering a spirit of unity, and engaging with the contemporary world, they continue to play a vital role in the evolving landscape of Judaism and Christianity.

The Future of Messianic Jewish Synagogues: Embracing Diversity and Building Bridges

As Messianic Judaism moves forward, its future is likely to be shaped by its ability to embrace diversity, bridge historical divisions, and adapt to the changing landscape of faith. By fostering dialogue and understanding, promoting educational opportunities, and engaging with the broader Jewish community, Messianic Jewish synagogues can continue to offer a compelling and welcoming spiritual home for those seeking to explore their faith within a Jewish context.

A Call to Dialogue and Understanding

This exploration of the diverse world of Messianic Jewish synagogues has aimed to shed light on the richness and complexity of this vibrant movement. It is important to recognize that there are diverse perspectives within Messianic Judaism, and that generalizations about the movement as a whole can be misleading. Ultimately, understanding and appreciation for the unique experiences and theological perspectives of Messianic Jewish communities requires respectful dialogue and a willingness to engage with the complexities of their faith.

Conclusion

Messianic Jewish synagogues stand as a testament to the evolving nature of faith, demonstrating the power of tradition, innovation, and the human longing for connection. They offer a unique and compelling spiritual journey, weaving together the threads of Jewish tradition and Christian belief. As they continue to navigate the complexities of their faith and engage with the contemporary world, Messianic Jewish synagogues remain a vital and dynamic force within the wider tapestry of religious and cultural life. Their continued growth and development hold the potential to contribute meaningfully to the ongoing dialogue and understanding between Judaism and Christianity, fostering greater appreciation for the rich diversity of human experience and the unifying power of faith.

Building Relationships and Growing Together

Building meaningful relationships is an art form, a delicate dance of vulnerability, trust, and shared experiences. It requires a conscious effort to cultivate understanding, to bridge the gap between individual perspectives, and to navigate the inevitable ebb and flow of life's currents. This journey is not without its challenges, for within the depths of our relationships lie the potential for both profound joy and profound pain.

However, it is precisely in the face of these challenges that we have the opportunity to grow, not just individually but also collectively. When we choose to engage with our relationships with intention and compassion, we unlock a transformative power. We learn to communicate more effectively, to empathize with different viewpoints, and to navigate conflict with grace and understanding. The very act of building relationships, of connecting with others on a deeper level, pushes us beyond our comfort zones and compels us to evolve.

The Foundation of Trust: A Cornerstone of Connection

At the heart of every meaningful relationship lies trust, a delicate web woven from shared experiences, consistent actions, and mutual respect. Without trust, our interactions remain superficial, governed by suspicion and guarded communication. True connection, however, thrives on the fertile ground of trust, allowing us to be vulnerable, to share our vulnerabilities, and to know that we are accepted and supported, flaws and all.

Building trust is a gradual process, a slow and steady accumulation of shared experiences that solidify the foundation of our connection. It requires consistent actions that align with our words, a commitment to transparency and honesty, and a willingness to forgive missteps and learn from them. It also involves active listening, truly hearing the unspoken emotions beneath the surface of words, and acknowledging the perspectives of others, even when they differ from our own.

Trust, once established, is a powerful force that empowers us to take risks, to be our authentic selves, and to rely on the unwavering support of those we cherish. It provides a safe haven within which we can explore our vulnerabilities, express our needs, and celebrate our triumphs.

The Power of Vulnerability: A Gateway to Deeper Connection

Vulnerability, often perceived as weakness, is in fact the cornerstone of authentic connection. When we choose to lower our defenses, to reveal our true selves, we create a space for genuine intimacy. We invite others to see beyond the carefully constructed facades we present to the world, to witness our raw emotions, our imperfections, and our struggles.

Vulnerability is not about weakness; it is about courage. It is about acknowledging our humanness, embracing our imperfections, and trusting that our authentic selves are worthy of love and acceptance. It is about letting go of the need to be perfect, to always be in control, and to allow ourselves to be truly seen.

When we embrace vulnerability, we create a space for deep connection, allowing others to experience our full spectrum of emotions. We open ourselves up to the possibility of greater intimacy, of shared experiences that strengthen our bonds and deepen our understanding of one another.

The Importance of Active Listening: Building Bridges of Understanding

Communication is a two-way street, a dance of give and take where both parties play an active role. While expressing our thoughts and feelings is essential, active listening is equally crucial to building meaningful relationships.

Active listening goes beyond simply hearing the words spoken. It involves truly paying attention, engaging with the speaker's emotions, and demonstrating genuine interest in their perspective. It involves asking clarifying questions, paraphrasing to ensure understanding, and offering empathy without judgment.

Active listening is not about simply waiting for our turn to speak; it is about creating a safe space for others to be heard. It is about respecting their viewpoints, even when they differ from our own, and seeking to understand the underlying emotions driving their words.

By actively listening, we build bridges of understanding, fostering a sense of connection and respect that lays the foundation for healthy, fulfilling relationships.

The Art of Conflict Resolution: Navigating Disagreements with Grace and Understanding

Disagreements are an inevitable part of any relationship, a testament to the unique perspectives and experiences that shape each individual. Conflict, when approached with intention and compassion, can be an opportunity for growth, a chance to strengthen our bonds and deepen our understanding of one another.

Navigating conflict effectively requires a shift in perspective. Instead of viewing disagreements as a threat to our relationships, we can embrace them as opportunities for learning and growth. This shift begins with acknowledging our own role in the conflict, taking responsibility for our contributions, and seeking to understand the perspective of the other person.

Active listening, empathy, and a willingness to compromise are essential tools for resolving conflict constructively. It requires the courage to express our needs and desires clearly and respectfully, while also acknowledging the needs and desires of our counterpart.

The goal is not to win an argument or to prove our point; it is to find a solution that works for both parties, to build a bridge of understanding and compromise.

Cultivating Forgiveness: Releasing the Weight of Past Hurts

Forgiveness is a profound act of self-compassion and compassion for others. It is the conscious decision to release the grip of past hurts, to let go of resentment and anger, and to choose to move forward with open hearts. Forgiveness does not mean forgetting or condoning past actions; it is about freeing ourselves from the shackles of pain and choosing to focus on healing and growth.

Forgiveness is not a sign of weakness; it is a sign of strength. It takes courage to confront the pain of the past, to acknowledge the hurt we have experienced, and to choose to let it go.

When we forgive others, we set ourselves free from the emotional burden of resentment, allowing us to move forward with greater peace and clarity. We also open the door to the possibility of repairing broken relationships and building bridges of reconciliation.

The Importance of Shared Experiences: Weaving a Tapestry of Connection

Shared experiences, both large and small, form the very fabric of our relationships. They provide common ground, create lasting memories, and deepen our understanding of one another. Whether it's a shared meal, a journey to a new destination, or a heartfelt conversation under the stars, these moments weave a tapestry of connection that strengthens our bonds over time.

Shared experiences also provide opportunities for growth and learning. They challenge us to step outside of our comfort zones, to embrace new perspectives, and to discover hidden strengths we never knew we possessed.

From the laughter shared during a family game night to the quiet moments of reflection after a challenging hike, these shared experiences enrich our lives and create a legacy of memories that we carry with us long after the moment has passed.

Growing Together: The Power of Mutual Support and Encouragement

Relationships are not static entities; they are dynamic systems that evolve and transform over time. As we navigate the challenges and triumphs of life, we learn, we grow, and we change. When we choose to grow together, to support and encourage one another on this shared journey, we unlock a profound source of strength and resilience.

Mutual support involves being there for one another through thick and thin, celebrating each other's triumphs, offering a shoulder to lean on during times of struggle, and providing the space for each other to grow and evolve.

Encouragement is the fuel that propels us forward, the gentle nudge that reminds us of our potential and motivates us to strive for our dreams. It is the power of believing in one another, even when we doubt ourselves, and celebrating the unique gifts that each of us brings to the world.

The Enduring Gift of Relationships: Building a Legacy of Love and Connection

Building relationships and growing together is a lifelong journey, a tapestry woven with threads of trust, vulnerability, active listening, conflict resolution, forgiveness, shared experiences, and mutual support. It is a journey that requires conscious effort, a willingness to learn and grow, and a commitment to nurturing the connections that enrich our lives.

The rewards of this journey are immeasurable. The love, support, and understanding we receive from our relationships provide us with a sense of belonging, purpose, and resilience. They empower us to navigate the challenges of life with courage and grace, and they remind us that we are not alone in this world.

As we build relationships and grow together, we create a legacy of love and connection, a ripple effect that extends beyond our immediate circle, inspiring others to embrace the transformative power of human connection. This legacy is a testament to the enduring beauty of our shared humanity, a reminder that even in a world often characterized by division and isolation, the power of connection can still weave a tapestry of hope and healing.

Creating a Sense of Belonging

The Foundations of Belonging: Understanding the Need

Understanding the significance of belonging begins with acknowledging its profound impact on human well-being. Research consistently demonstrates a strong correlation between a sense of belonging and positive psychological outcomes. Individuals who feel a sense of belonging are more likely to experience:

Increased self-esteem and confidence: Knowing we are accepted and valued by others strengthens our sense of self-worth and empowers us to navigate life's challenges with greater resilience.
Reduced stress and anxiety: Feeling connected to a group provides a safety net, offering support and a sense of security, which mitigates the isolating effects of stress and anxiety.
Improved mental and physical health: Belonging fosters a sense of purpose and meaning, contributing to overall well-being and reducing the risk of depression, loneliness, and other mental health issues.
Enhanced productivity and creativity: Feeling part of a team or community encourages collaboration, open communication, and a shared sense of purpose, leading to greater productivity and innovation.

Furthermore, belonging is not just about individual benefits; it has far-reaching societal implications. Strong communities characterized by a sense of belonging are more resilient, cooperative, and effective in addressing shared challenges. They are more likely to foster civic engagement, promote social justice, and create a safer and more equitable environment for all.

Building Bridges of Belonging: Strategies for Creating Inclusive Environments

Creating a sense of belonging is not a one-size-fits-all endeavor. It requires a nuanced approach that acknowledges the diverse needs and experiences of individuals and communities. However, several key principles and strategies can guide this journey:

1. Cultivating a Culture of Welcoming and Inclusion:

Embrace diversity: Recognizing and valuing the unique perspectives, experiences, and identities of all individuals is crucial. Create a culture that celebrates diversity, challenges biases, and promotes equal opportunities for all.
Promote open communication: Encourage open and honest dialogue, fostering a safe space for individuals to share their thoughts and perspectives. Active listening, empathy, and a willingness to understand different viewpoints are essential.
Challenge stereotypes and biases: Be mindful of unconscious biases and actively challenge assumptions that perpetuate exclusion. Promote awareness and education about diversity and inclusivity.
Foster a sense of shared purpose: Define a common goal or mission that unites individuals and creates a sense of collective responsibility, fostering collaboration and teamwork.

2. Fostering Connection and Relationship Building:

Create opportunities for interaction: Organize events, workshops, and activities that encourage interaction and connection between individuals from diverse backgrounds.
Promote mentorship and support networks: Establish formal and informal mentorship programs to provide guidance, support, and opportunities for growth.
Facilitate cross-cultural understanding: Promote cultural exchange programs, workshops, and resources to enhance understanding and appreciation of different cultures and perspectives.
Celebrate successes and acknowledge contributions: Recognize

and acknowledge the achievements of individuals and groups, fostering a sense of pride and belonging.

3. Addressing Barriers and Promoting Accessibility:

Identify and dismantle barriers: Be proactive in identifying and addressing barriers that hinder inclusion, such as discrimination, prejudice, or lack of accessibility.
Promote equitable access: Ensure equal access to resources, opportunities, and services for all individuals, regardless of their background or abilities.
Provide support for marginalized groups: Create targeted programs and initiatives to provide support and empowerment for individuals and communities facing systemic barriers.
Foster a culture of accountability: Establish clear expectations and consequences for discriminatory behavior, creating a culture of accountability and respect.

4. Cultivating a Sense of Belonging Within Oneself:

Embrace self-acceptance: Recognize and appreciate your unique strengths and qualities, fostering a sense of self-love and acceptance.
Cultivate self-awareness: Gain a deeper understanding of your values, beliefs, and motivations, enhancing your ability to connect authentically with others.
Develop your social skills: Build confidence and competence in communicating, building relationships, and navigating social situations.
Seek out communities that align with your values: Actively engage in communities and activities that resonate with your interests and values, fostering a sense of belonging and purpose.

The Power of Belonging: Transforming Lives and Communities

Creating a sense of belonging is not just about creating inclusive spaces and fostering connections; it's about nurturing a sense of shared humanity, empathy, and understanding. It's about recognizing the inherent worth and dignity of every individual, regardless of their background, beliefs, or experiences. By fostering a culture of inclusion and belonging, we create a more just, equitable, and compassionate society, empowering individuals to thrive and contribute their unique talents and perspectives to the collective good.

Beyond the Book: Applying the Principles of Belonging in Everyday Life

The principles of creating a sense of belonging are not limited to formal institutions or organizations. They are applicable to all aspects of our lives, from our personal relationships to our interactions within the broader community. Here are a few practical ways to integrate these principles into our everyday lives:

Be mindful of your language and actions: Pay attention to your words and behaviors, ensuring they are inclusive and respectful of others. Avoid language that is discriminatory or perpetuates negative stereotypes.
Practice active listening: Make a conscious effort to listen attentively to others, seeking to understand their perspectives and experiences. Validate their feelings and opinions, even if you don't agree with them.
Show kindness and compassion: Extend acts of kindness and support to those around you, demonstrating empathy and a willingness to help.
Be a bridge builder: Reach out to individuals from diverse backgrounds, fostering connections and bridging divides. Challenge your own biases and assumptions, seeking to understand perspectives different from your own.
Get involved in your community: Volunteer your time, participate in local events, and engage in initiatives that promote social justice and community building.

By embracing the principles of belonging in our personal lives and within our communities, we can create a world where everyone feels a sense of acceptance, connection, and purpose. It is a journey that requires ongoing effort, but the rewards are immeasurable, leading to a more compassionate, just, and harmonious society for all.

Chapter 8: The Power of Worship and Prayer

Messianic Jewish Worship Traditions

At the core of Messianic Jewish worship lies the recognition of Yeshua (Jesus) as the Messiah, the fulfillment of Jewish hopes and prophecies. This belief informs the ways in which Messianic Jews approach their faith, particularly their worship practices. Unlike many traditional Christian denominations, where worship often centers around a Sunday service, Messianic Jewish worship embraces a more holistic approach, integrating various aspects of Jewish life into their spiritual practices.

This holistic approach is most evident in the emphasis on the Sabbath. For Messianic Jews, the Sabbath is not merely a day of rest but a sacred time for gathering, reflection, and spiritual renewal. Sabbath services, often held in synagogues or other communal spaces, are filled with familiar Jewish elements like prayer, Torah reading, and the singing of Hebrew hymns. Yet, these familiar practices are infused with the spirit of Yeshua, highlighting his centrality in Jewish scripture and history.

The integration of Jewish liturgical practices within a Messianic framework also extends to other areas of worship. The use of Hebrew in prayer and liturgy, the observance of holidays like Passover and Rosh Hashanah, and the incorporation of traditional Jewish blessings and customs all serve as tangible expressions of Messianic Jewish faith. These practices are not seen as mere cultural artifacts but as living expressions of a spiritual heritage that has been passed down through generations.

To further understand the distinctiveness of Messianic Jewish worship, it is helpful to delve into the historical and theological context that informs these practices.

A Tapestry of Faith: Historical Roots and Theological Foundations

The emergence of Messianic Judaism can be traced back to the early centuries of the Christian era. While the early Church was primarily composed of Jewish believers, a gradual shift occurred, leading to the emergence of a distinctly Christian identity separate from Judaism. This separation, however, did not fully sever the historical and theological connection between Judaism and Christianity.

The roots of Messianic Judaism can be found in the persistence of Jewish Christians, who maintained their connection to Jewish tradition and practices even as they embraced Yeshua as the Messiah. This continuity, while not always smooth or unchallenged, served as a vital thread connecting the faith of the early Church to the contemporary expression of Messianic Judaism.

The theological underpinnings of Messianic Jewish worship are rooted in the understanding of Yeshua as the fulfillment of Jewish prophecy and the culmination of the Jewish covenant. Messianic Jews believe that Yeshua's mission was not to abolish Jewish tradition but to fulfill it, bringing it to its ultimate realization. This belief is reflected in their worship practices, which often incorporate traditional Jewish elements while interpreting them through the lens of the Messiah.

The Power of Symbols: Unveiling the Meaning Behind the Practices

Messianic Jewish worship is rich with symbolism, drawing from both Jewish tradition and Christian theology. These symbols serve as bridges connecting the tangible aspects of worship with the deeper spiritual realities they represent.

For instance, the use of the menorah, a seven-branched candelabrum, is a prominent symbol in Messianic Jewish worship. The menorah, a symbol of light and hope in Jewish tradition, takes on a new dimension in Messianic Jewish context. It is interpreted as a representation of the light of Yeshua, the Messiah who illuminates the path to salvation.

Similarly, the use of Hebrew in prayer and liturgy is not merely a cultural practice but carries deep theological significance. Hebrew, the language of the Jewish scriptures and tradition, is seen as the language of the covenant, carrying within it the history and promises of God's relationship with his chosen people.

Beyond individual symbols, the very act of gathering together for worship holds profound meaning in Messianic Jewish tradition. The gathering of the community reflects the gathering of Israel, the people called to be God's chosen ones. This shared act of worship, marked by prayer, music, and the reading of scripture, becomes a tangible expression of the covenant relationship between God and his people, a relationship that finds its ultimate fulfillment in the person and work of Yeshua.

A Journey of Understanding: Embracing the Nuances of Messianic Jewish Worship

Exploring the world of Messianic Jewish worship traditions requires an open mind and a willingness to embrace the nuances of this rich and multifaceted faith expression. It is a journey of discovery, one that involves understanding the historical context, theological underpinnings, and the symbolic language that shapes these worship practices.

Key Themes and Practices:

The Sabbath: As the cornerstone of Jewish observance, the Sabbath holds a prominent place in Messianic Jewish worship. Sabbath services are filled with traditional elements like Torah reading, prayer, and the singing of Hebrew hymns, all infused with the spirit of Yeshua.

The Festivals: The observance of Jewish holidays like Passover, Rosh Hashanah, and Yom Kippur is integral to Messianic Jewish faith. These celebrations serve as opportunities to connect with the ancient covenant and to celebrate God's faithfulness to his people.

Hebrew Language: The use of Hebrew in prayer and liturgy underscores the deep connection between Messianic Jewish faith and its Jewish heritage. Hebrew is seen as the language of the covenant and the scriptures, carrying within it the richness of Jewish history and tradition.

Symbolism: Messianic Jewish worship is rich with symbols that convey profound theological meanings. Symbols like the menorah, the Star of David, and the use of the Hebrew language all carry layered meanings that speak to the unique nature of this faith expression.

Challenges and Opportunities:

While Messianic Judaism offers a vibrant and enriching expression of faith, it also faces unique challenges. These challenges often stem from the delicate balance that Messianic Jewish communities strive to maintain between their Jewish heritage and their Christian beliefs.

One significant challenge involves navigating the complexities of Jewish identity. Some Messianic Jewish communities are more closely aligned with traditional Jewish practices, while others embrace a more distinctly Christian perspective. This spectrum of perspectives can lead to internal debates and tensions within Messianic Jewish communities, particularly as they grapple with questions of identity and belonging.

Another challenge involves engaging in meaningful dialogue with both traditional Jewish and Christian communities. While Messianic Jewish communities seek to bridge the gap between Judaism and Christianity, they often encounter resistance from both sides. Traditional Jewish communities may view Messianic Judaism as a form of proselytism, while some Christian groups may question the legitimacy of Messianic Jewish practices.

Despite these challenges, Messianic Judaism offers significant opportunities for dialogue and understanding. The very existence of this faith expression challenges traditional boundaries and encourages conversations about the shared roots of Jewish and Christian faith. Messianic Jewish communities can play a vital role in fostering dialogue and reconciliation between these two often-divided faith traditions. They are a testament to the enduring power of the Jewish covenant and the transformative love of Yeshua, the Messiah. As Messianic Jewish communities continue to grow and adapt, their worship practices will continue to evolve, reflecting the ongoing dialogue between faith, tradition, and culture.

Through their unique blend of Jewish tradition and Christian faith, Messianic Jewish worship offers a powerful and inspiring example of how faith can bridge cultural divides and create a space for meaningful dialogue and spiritual renewal. The ongoing journey of Messianic Jewish worship is a story of resilience, hope, and the enduring power of faith in the face of diverse and evolving cultural landscapes.

Exploring Different Forms of Prayer

This exploration delves into the rich tapestry of prayer, examining its various forms and uncovering the profound impact it has on individuals and communities. From the structured and liturgical prayers of organized religions to the spontaneous and personal expressions of individual faith, we will uncover the common threads that bind these diverse practices, highlighting the transformative power of prayer in our lives.

The Liturgical Landscape: A Foundation of Structure and Shared Meaning

Within organized religions, prayer often takes on a structured and liturgical form. This structured approach, rooted in tradition and scripture, provides a framework for communal worship and fosters a shared sense of belonging. Liturgical prayers, often recited in unison, offer a collective voice to express gratitude, supplication, and praise.

For example, in the Catholic tradition, the Rosary, a series of prayers centered on the life of Mary, offers a structured path for contemplation and meditation. Similarly, the Jewish tradition utilizes the Shema, a declaration of faith recited daily, to reinforce the core tenets of Judaism. The Islamic tradition, with its five daily prayers, provides a rhythm for daily life, fostering a connection with the Divine throughout the day.

This structured approach to prayer is not without its criticisms. Some argue that it can stifle individual expression and creativity, potentially leading to rote repetition rather than genuine connection. However, proponents of liturgical prayer emphasize its role in fostering a sense of community and preserving sacred traditions. They argue that the shared experience of reciting ancient prayers can create a profound sense of unity and spiritual connection.

The Personal Journey: A Tapestry of Individual Expression

Beyond the structured confines of liturgical forms, prayer takes on a more personal and intimate dimension. Here, the individual's voice becomes paramount, allowing for a direct and unfiltered dialogue with the Divine. Personal prayer can take many forms, from heartfelt whispers to passionate pleas, from introspective meditations to joyful expressions of gratitude.

One common form of personal prayer is the spoken prayer, where individuals articulate their thoughts, desires, and concerns to a higher power. This can range from simple petitions for guidance and strength to elaborate expressions of praise and adoration. Another form is written prayer, where individuals pour out their thoughts and feelings on paper, allowing for a more reflective and deliberate approach to prayer.

Meditation, a practice that emphasizes quiet contemplation and mindfulness, also serves as a form of prayer for many. By focusing on the present moment and clearing the mind of distractions, individuals can cultivate a deeper sense of inner peace and connection with the Divine.

The Transformative Power of Prayer: A Journey of Healing and Growth

The transformative power of prayer lies not just in its ability to connect us with a higher power, but also in its potential to bring about profound personal growth and healing. When we engage in prayer, we embark on a journey of self-discovery, exploring our deepest desires, fears, and aspirations. This process can lead to a greater understanding of ourselves and a deeper sense of purpose.

Prayer can also serve as a powerful tool for healing. By offering our burdens and anxieties to a higher power, we release ourselves from the weight of our troubles and open ourselves to the possibility of peace and healing. Prayer can provide a source of strength and resilience in the face of adversity, reminding us that we are not alone in our struggles.

Exploring Different Forms of Prayer: A Path to Deeper Connection

The journey of exploring different forms of prayer is a lifelong endeavor, filled with personal discovery and spiritual growth. It is a path that invites us to step beyond our preconceived notions and embrace the diverse ways in which humanity has sought to connect with the sacred.

As we delve deeper into the richness of prayer, we discover not only its varied forms but also its profound impact on our lives. We realize that prayer is not a singular practice confined to a specific religious tradition, but rather a universal language that speaks to the depths of our being, reminding us of our inherent connection to something greater than ourselves.

Beyond the Words: The Essence of Prayer

Ultimately, the essence of prayer transcends any specific form or practice. It is a state of being, a profound sense of connection and reverence, a recognition of the divine presence within and around us. Whether we express our faith through structured liturgies or heartfelt whispers, the true essence of prayer lies in the sincerity of our hearts, the depth of our intentions, and the transformative power of our connection with the Divine.

This exploration is just the beginning of a journey. It is a journey that invites us to embrace the rich diversity of prayer, to discover its transformative power in our lives, and to find our own unique path to a deeper connection with the sacred. May this exploration inspire you to deepen your own practice of prayer, to discover the transformative power of this ancient and universal practice, and to experience the profound connection that awaits you on this journey of faith.

The Importance of Community Prayer

Community prayer, in particular, offers a unique avenue for individuals to transcend their personal boundaries and engage in a collective act of seeking solace, guidance, and support. It transcends mere words, evolving into a shared ritual that binds individuals together, fostering a sense of unity and shared purpose. This shared experience, whether in the quiet intimacy of a small group or the soaring grandeur of a public gathering, has the potential to create a powerful sense of community, fostering understanding, compassion, and a shared commitment to the greater good.

The Power of Collective Intention: Uniting Hearts and Minds

One of the most profound aspects of community prayer lies in the power of collective intention. When individuals gather together, their individual hopes, anxieties, and aspirations coalesce into a unified force, creating a powerful energy that transcends the limitations of individual experience. This collective intention, fueled by the shared vulnerability of the group, can serve as a catalyst for positive change, both within the individual and within the wider community.

Imagine a group of individuals, each burdened by their own personal struggles, coming together in a shared act of prayer. In that moment, the individual anxieties and burdens begin to dissolve, replaced by a sense of collective hope and shared purpose. The shared experience of vulnerability creates a sense of belonging, a recognition that we are not alone in our struggles, and that together, we have the strength to overcome adversity. This shared experience of vulnerability can be particularly powerful in times of crisis, offering solace and support to those who may be feeling overwhelmed by the weight of their individual burdens.

Furthermore, the act of collective intention can serve as a powerful catalyst for social change. By uniting individuals in a common purpose, community prayer can serve as a focal point for collective action, inspiring individuals to channel their energy towards achieving shared goals. This shared commitment can be seen in the numerous examples of communities coming together through prayer to address issues such as poverty, injustice, and environmental degradation.

Strengthening the Bonds of Empathy and Understanding

Community prayer fosters empathy and understanding by creating a space for individuals to connect on a deeper level. As individuals share their prayers, they open themselves up to the experiences of others, gaining a deeper understanding of their joys, their sorrows, and the challenges they face. This shared vulnerability breaks down barriers and creates a sense of connection that transcends superficial interactions.

In an increasingly polarized world, where differences are often emphasized at the expense of shared humanity, community prayer offers a powerful antidote. By creating a space for individuals from diverse backgrounds to come together in shared purpose, it encourages understanding and fosters a sense of unity that transcends differences in ethnicity, religion, or socio-economic status. This shared experience of prayer can serve as a bridge, connecting individuals across divides and fostering a sense of collective responsibility for the well-being of the community.

A Pathway for Spiritual Growth and Transformation

Beyond its immediate social impact, community prayer also serves as a powerful tool for individual spiritual growth and transformation. Engaging in the shared act of seeking guidance and connection with the divine, individuals can tap into a deeper sense of purpose and meaning, fostering a sense of inner peace and tranquility. This transformative journey can lead to a greater understanding of oneself, a deeper appreciation for the beauty of life, and a renewed commitment to living a life of service and compassion.

For many individuals, community prayer provides a vital connection to a spiritual realm, offering solace, inspiration, and a sense of belonging. This connection can serve as a source of strength during difficult times, offering comfort and guidance when faced with uncertainty and adversity. Furthermore, the act of engaging in shared prayer can serve as a catalyst for personal growth, encouraging individuals to reflect on their values, to develop a sense of gratitude, and to cultivate a more compassionate and understanding approach to life.

Building a Stronger Foundation for Collective Wellbeing

The importance of community prayer lies not just in its immediate impact but also in its potential to create a more just, compassionate, and equitable society. By fostering a sense of unity and purpose, by promoting empathy and understanding, and by providing a pathway for spiritual growth and transformation, community prayer serves as a powerful force for positive change, strengthening the bonds of community and contributing to the collective well-being of all.

In a world often characterized by division, isolation, and a relentless pursuit of individual gain, community prayer stands as a beacon of hope, offering a space for individuals to come together, to share their burdens, and to draw strength from one another. It is a powerful reminder that we are not alone in our journey, and that together, we have the potential to create a world filled with compassion, justice, and peace. It offers a unique opportunity to connect, to heal, and to transform, both on an individual and collective level. By embracing the power of shared intention, by nurturing empathy and understanding, and by seeking a deeper connection to the divine, we can harness the transformative potential of community prayer to build a more just, compassionate, and equitable world.

Let us, therefore, embrace this opportunity with open hearts and open minds. Let us gather together, not just in times of need, but also in times of celebration, to share our joys, our sorrows, and our hopes for a brighter future. Let us find strength in our collective voices, in our shared commitment to the well-being of our communities, and in our unwavering belief in the transformative power of prayer.

Personal Connection with God

While the specifics of this connection may vary greatly across different faiths and individual interpretations, certain core aspects remain common. These include:

1. The Role of Faith: Faith is the cornerstone of a personal connection with God. It is the act of believing in something unseen, a trust in the unseen power that governs the universe, and a commitment to its principles. This faith is not blind acceptance, but rather an informed decision, based on individual experiences, scriptures, teachings, and personal reflection. It is a leap of faith that allows individuals to transcend the limitations of their senses and embrace a reality beyond the tangible world.

2. The Importance of Prayer and Meditation: Prayer and meditation serve as fundamental tools for fostering and maintaining a personal connection with God. Prayer is a form of communication with the divine, an act of expressing gratitude, seeking guidance, confessing sins, or simply connecting with the source of ultimate power. Meditation, on the other hand, is a practice of focusing the mind, clearing distractions, and achieving a state of deep inner peace. It allows individuals to quiet their thoughts, connect with their inner selves, and open themselves to the presence of the divine.

3. The Significance of Personal Experiences: A personal connection with God is often shaped by individual experiences that resonate with the divine. These experiences can range from profound moments of spiritual awakening, to life-altering events, or even the subtle presence of grace in everyday life. Such experiences serve as tangible evidence of the divine presence and inspire individuals on their journey of faith. They provide glimpses into the unseen, offering glimpses of God's love, guidance, or intervention in their lives.

4. The Value of Reflection and Interpretation: Developing a personal connection with God requires active engagement with one's faith. This includes reflecting on personal experiences, interpreting scriptures and teachings, and engaging in meaningful conversations with spiritual leaders and fellow believers. Through these reflections, individuals can deepen their understanding of their faith, gain valuable insights, and draw closer to the divine.

5. The Journey of Transformation: The journey of developing a personal connection with God is fundamentally a journey of transformation. It is a process of shedding old habits, embracing new values, and aligning one's actions with the principles of faith. This transformation is often accompanied by a sense of growth, forgiveness, and spiritual liberation. It empowers individuals to live more authentically, with compassion, purpose, and a profound connection to a greater power.

Understanding the Different Dimensions of Personal Connection:

While the journey of developing a personal connection with God is individual, certain common themes emerge across different perspectives:

a. Cognitive Understanding: This dimension involves the intellectual exploration of religious teachings, scriptures, and philosophical concepts. It seeks to understand the nature of the divine, the principles of faith, and the implications of belief for one's life. This intellectual pursuit plays a significant role in shaping a person's faith foundation.

b. Emotional Connection: This dimension centers around the emotional experiences that accompany faith. It encompasses feelings of love, awe, gratitude, peace, and a sense of belonging. This emotional connection adds depth and richness to the individual's relationship with the divine, fostering a sense of intimacy and closeness.

c. Spiritual Experience: This dimension refers to the personal experiences that individuals perceive as divine interventions or manifestations of the divine presence. These can range from profound spiritual awakenings to subtle nudges and confirmations in daily life. Such experiences provide tangible evidence of the unseen and strengthen the individual's belief in the divine.

d. Behavioral Transformation: This dimension focuses on the impact of faith on one's actions and choices. It involves aligning one's behavior with the principles of faith, seeking to embody the values of compassion, forgiveness, service, and love. This transformation reflects the individual's commitment to living a life that honors their faith and reflects their connection with the divine.

The Importance of a Personal Connection with God:

A personal connection with God offers individuals numerous benefits, both personal and societal:

1. Personal Growth and Fulfillment: Connecting with a higher power provides individuals with a sense of purpose, meaning, and direction. It offers guidance and support during challenging times, fostering resilience, hope, and a sense of inner peace. This connection can also lead to greater self-awareness, compassion, and empathy.

2. Improved Mental and Emotional Well-being: Studies have shown that individuals with strong religious beliefs and practices often exhibit better mental and emotional well-being. They tend to experience less stress, anxiety, and depression, and show increased resilience in the face of adversity. This suggests that a connection with God can provide a source of comfort, strength, and hope, contributing to greater mental and emotional health.

3. Enhanced Moral Compass and Ethical Conduct: Faith often

provides individuals with a strong moral compass, guiding their choices and actions. It inspires them to live according to ethical principles, fostering compassion, forgiveness, and service to others. This can lead to greater social responsibility, a commitment to justice, and a desire to contribute to the betterment of society.

4. Building Stronger Communities: Religious communities often provide a sense of belonging, support, and shared values. This fosters a strong sense of community, providing individuals with a network of people who share their beliefs and support their journey of faith. This can be particularly important for individuals navigating life's challenges, offering a sense of belonging and a network of support.

The Challenges of Cultivating a Personal Connection:

While the benefits of a personal connection with God are significant, it is not without its challenges:

1. The Struggle with Doubt and Uncertainty: Faith is not a linear journey, and moments of doubt and uncertainty are common. These challenges can stem from personal experiences, conflicting information, or simply the complexities of life. Individuals may question their beliefs, struggle with reconciling faith with difficult realities, or grapple with the mystery of the divine.

2. The Role of Free Will and God's Will: Navigating the tension between free will and God's will can be a significant challenge. Individuals may struggle with reconciling their own desires with what they perceive as God's plan for their lives. This can lead to difficult choices, anxieties, and questions about divine intervention and the nature of faith.

3. The Impact of Life's Challenges: Life is filled with challenges, and faith can be tested during difficult times. Individuals may question their beliefs when confronted with pain, suffering, or injustice. They

may struggle to reconcile their faith with the realities of loss, grief, or the seemingly unfair nature of life's events.

4. The Importance of Finding the Right Path: The journey of developing a personal connection with God can be complex, and there may be multiple paths to explore. Individuals may need to navigate different religious traditions, explore different interpretations of faith, or find a spiritual path that resonates with their individual beliefs and experiences.

Overcoming the Challenges:

While the challenges of cultivating a personal connection with God are real, they can be overcome with patience, perseverance, and a willingness to learn and grow:

1. Embrace Doubt as Part of the Journey: Rather than viewing doubt as a sign of weakness, embrace it as an opportunity for growth. Allow yourself to ask difficult questions, explore different perspectives, and seek answers from trusted sources. This process of questioning and seeking can lead to deeper understanding and a more informed faith.

2. Engage in Active Dialogue and Reflection: Engage in meaningful conversations with fellow believers, spiritual leaders, and theologians. This dialogue can provide valuable insights, different perspectives, and a sense of community. Spend time in reflection, exploring your beliefs, experiences, and the implications of faith for your life.

3. Seek Guidance from Trusted Sources: Turn to scriptures, teachings, and the guidance of spiritual leaders for support and direction. This can provide a framework for understanding your faith, navigating challenging situations, and finding comfort and hope during difficult times.

4. Embrace the Power of Forgiveness: Recognize that forgiveness is a cornerstone of spiritual growth. Forgive yourself for your mistakes, and extend forgiveness to others. This act of grace can help release the burdens of the past and open your heart to a deeper connection with the divine.

5. Cultivate Gratitude and Appreciation: Focus on the good in your life and express gratitude for the blessings you have received. This practice can shift your perspective, increase your happiness, and cultivate a more positive and hopeful outlook on life. It is a process of faith, experience, and growth, characterized by both moments of joy and challenge. While this journey may be complex and demanding, it offers individuals profound rewards, including a sense of purpose, inner peace, moral grounding, and a deep sense of connection to something greater than themselves. By embracing faith, engaging in prayer and meditation, reflecting on personal experiences, and embracing the power of forgiveness, individuals can cultivate a meaningful and fulfilling relationship with the divine. This connection can provide them with guidance, support, and the strength to navigate the complexities of life, ultimately leading to a life of greater purpose, meaning, and fulfillment.

Chapter 9: Living Out Faith in Daily Life

Integrating Faith into Everyday Decisions

Integrating faith into everyday decisions is not a passive act of simply reciting prayers or adhering to rituals. Rather, it involves a conscious and deliberate process of reflection, discernment, and action. It is a journey of self-discovery, where we seek to align our choices with the values and principles that form the bedrock of our faith.

From the Abstract to the Concrete: A Framework for Decision-Making

The first step in this journey is to move beyond the abstract principles of our faith and bring them to life in the concrete realities of our daily lives. This involves asking ourselves: What does my faith truly teach me about the nature of good and evil, about justice and compassion, about love and responsibility.

For example, if our faith emphasizes the value of love and forgiveness, how does this principle translate into our interactions with others. Do we extend grace to those who have wronged us. Do we seek opportunities to build bridges rather than perpetuate divisions.

The answers to these questions may not always be easy or straightforward. Faith is not a set of rigid rules or a blueprint for every decision. Rather, it is a living, breathing force that invites us to grapple with moral dilemmas, to engage in ongoing dialogue with God or the divine, and to seek guidance through prayer, scripture, or other spiritual practices.

The Power of Discernment: Listening to the Inner Voice

Discernment is a crucial element of integrating faith into our decisions. It involves the practice of listening to our inner voice, paying attention to our intuitions and instincts, and seeking to discern the will of God or the divine within the complexities of our choices.

This process is not always a sudden revelation, but rather a gradual unfolding of understanding. It may involve engaging in quiet reflection, seeking advice from trusted mentors or spiritual guides, and observing the consequences of our past decisions.

Discernment can be a challenging endeavor, as it requires us to be honest with ourselves, to confront our own biases and desires, and to be open to the possibility that our initial instincts may not always align with the teachings of our faith.

The Role of Scripture and Tradition: Finding Guidance in the Past

Scripture and tradition can provide valuable guidance in our decision-making process. By reflecting on the stories and teachings of our faith, we can gain insights into the values and principles that have guided generations of believers before us.

However, it is important to approach scripture and tradition with a critical and discerning mind. We must avoid simply applying them as rigid rules or literal interpretations. Instead, we should strive to understand the underlying message, the universal principles that transcend time and culture, and apply them to the unique challenges we face in our own lives.

The Importance of Consultation: Seeking Wisdom from Others

While our own faith journey is deeply personal, it is also inherently relational. Engaging in dialogue with other believers, seeking advice from mentors and spiritual guides, and participating in faith communities can enrich our understanding of our faith and provide valuable perspectives on the challenges we face.

These conversations can help us to broaden our horizons, to challenge our assumptions, and to gain a more nuanced understanding of the complexities of our decisions.

The Impact of Decision-Making: Living Out Our Values

Ultimately, the true measure of our faith is not in our words or beliefs, but in our actions. It is in the choices we make, the way we treat others, and the impact we have on the world around us.

Integrating faith into everyday decisions is a lifelong journey, a process of continuous learning, reflection, and growth. It is a journey that requires courage, humility, and a willingness to embrace the uncertainty that often accompanies the path of faith.

Navigating the Gray Areas: When Choices Are Not Black and White

Life rarely presents us with clear-cut choices, neatly categorized as right or wrong. The reality is often far more complex, with shades of gray that defy easy categorization. In these instances, faith offers not a set of rigid rules, but a framework for discernment, a lens through which we can analyze the situation, weigh the consequences, and strive to align our actions with the values and principles that define our faith.

For example, consider the dilemma of a business owner facing the decision to close a factory, potentially affecting the livelihoods of many employees. While the decision may be motivated by financial necessity, the ethical implications are significant. If the business owner's faith emphasizes compassion and social responsibility, they may be compelled to explore alternative solutions, to seek ways to minimize the impact on their employees and to ensure their well-being.

The Importance of Context: Understanding the Nuances of Each Decision

Faith is not a static entity, applicable in the same way to every situation. It is a dynamic force, informed by context, culture, and personal experience. This means that our understanding of our faith, and how it guides our decision-making, will evolve over time.

For instance, a young person raised in a conservative environment may hold a different perspective on issues such as sexual orientation or gender identity than someone who has been exposed to more diverse perspectives. This does not necessarily mean that one perspective is more valid than the other, but rather that our faith journey is a continuous process of learning and growth, informed by our experiences and interactions with the world around us.

The Role of Grace: Accepting Our Imperfections and Seeking Forgiveness

Integrating faith into everyday decisions is not a guarantee of perfection. We will make mistakes, we will stumble, and we will fall short of the ideals we strive to achieve. This is the human condition, and it is an inherent part of the faith journey.

The beauty of faith lies in the promise of grace. It is the recognition that we are not perfect, that we need forgiveness and redemption. It is the assurance that even in our failures, we are loved and accepted, and that God or the divine offers us the opportunity to repent, to learn from our mistakes, and to grow closer to our faith.

Faith as a Source of Strength and Hope

In the face of difficult decisions, our faith can be a source of strength and hope. It can provide us with the courage to face our fears, the resilience to overcome obstacles, and the perseverance to continue striving for the good.

It reminds us that we are not alone in this journey, that we are supported by a power greater than ourselves, and that even in the midst of uncertainty, we can find peace and hope in the promise of God's love or the divine's presence. It is a journey of self-discovery, where we seek to align our choices with the values and principles that define our faith. This journey may be challenging, but it is also profoundly rewarding, offering us a deeper understanding of ourselves, our faith, and our place in the world.

As we move forward, let us embrace the ongoing dialogue with God or the divine, seek guidance through prayer and scripture, and strive to live out our faith in the concrete realities of our daily lives. Let us remember that our faith is not a destination, but a journey, a continuous process of growth and transformation that shapes every decision we make and defines the tapestry of our lives.

Applying Jewish Values to Modern Life

Tzedakah: Cultivating Justice and Compassion in a Globalized World

Tzedakah, often translated as "righteousness" or "charity," is more than just acts of giving; it's a fundamental principle ingrained in Jewish thought, emphasizing justice, compassion, and the responsibility to alleviate suffering. In a world increasingly defined by global interconnectedness and complex social issues, tzedakah transcends individual acts of charity and becomes a multifaceted lens through which we engage with societal challenges.

The modern world, with its interconnectedness, presents both opportunities and challenges for applying tzedakah. Globalization has facilitated the movement of goods, services, and people across borders, but it has also exacerbated economic inequalities and highlighted the vulnerability of marginalized communities. Applying tzedakah in this context necessitates a holistic approach that goes beyond individual acts of giving and embraces systemic change.

One practical application of tzedakah in the modern world involves advocating for fair trade practices, supporting sustainable development initiatives, and working towards a more equitable global economic system. This necessitates engaging with complex issues like corporate accountability, labor rights, and environmental justice. By challenging exploitative practices and advocating for policies that promote social and economic justice, we embody the spirit of tzedakah in a globalized world.

Furthermore, tzedakah extends beyond material giving and encompasses acts of kindness, empathy, and emotional support. In an increasingly isolated and digitalized world, connecting with our communities and offering emotional support becomes crucial. By extending a helping hand to those struggling with mental health issues, navigating personal crises, or facing social isolation, we embody the spirit of tzedakah in our daily interactions.

Tikkun Olam: Repairing the World in the Age of Technology

Tikkun olam, meaning "repairing the world," is a core Jewish value that emphasizes the responsibility of each individual to actively contribute to the betterment of society. In the face of unprecedented technological advancements, the concept of tikkun olam takes on a new dimension, challenging us to consider the ethical implications of technology and its impact on human life.

The rapid development and widespread adoption of artificial intelligence (AI), for example, raises profound ethical questions regarding data privacy, algorithmic bias, and the potential displacement of human labor. Applying the principles of tikkun olam requires engaging in critical dialogue about the ethical considerations surrounding AI and advocating for responsible development and implementation.

Similarly, the rise of social media platforms presents both opportunities and challenges for tikkun olam. While these platforms can be powerful tools for activism, social justice movements, and spreading awareness about important issues, they can also contribute to the spread of misinformation, hate speech, and online harassment. Applying tikkun olam in this context requires engaging in constructive online discourse, promoting digital literacy, and combating online hate speech.

Furthermore, the concept of tikkun olam extends to the environment, urging us to be responsible stewards of the planet. With climate change posing a growing threat to the future of humanity, applying tikkun olam in this context requires advocating for sustainable practices, reducing our carbon footprint, and actively working towards environmental justice.

Kavod: Dignity and Respect in a Diverse and Interconnected World

Kavod, meaning "honor" or "respect," is a fundamental Jewish value that emphasizes the inherent dignity and worth of every individual. In a world increasingly defined by diversity, globalization, and multiculturalism, kavod becomes a guiding principle for fostering understanding, empathy, and respectful dialogue across cultural, religious, and social divides.

Applying kavod in the modern world requires actively challenging prejudice and discrimination in all its forms. This involves acknowledging the historical and contemporary realities of racism, sexism, homophobia, and other forms of oppression and working towards creating a more just and equitable society.

Furthermore, kavod necessitates cultivating empathy and understanding for people with different perspectives and beliefs. Engaging in respectful dialogue, listening to others with an open mind, and seeking common ground even when we disagree are essential for building bridges and fostering a more harmonious world.

Shabbat: Reclaiming Time and Cultivating Meaning in a Fast-Paced World

Shabbat, the Jewish Sabbath, is a weekly observance that emphasizes rest, reflection, and connection. In a world characterized by relentless work, constant connectivity, and a relentless pursuit of productivity, Shabbat provides a powerful counter-narrative, reminding us of the importance of slowing down, disconnecting, and prioritizing our relationships.

Applying the principles of Shabbat in modern life involves intentionally carving out time for rest and rejuvenation. This may involve disconnecting from technology, spending time with loved ones, engaging in meaningful activities, and simply enjoying the present moment. By embracing Shabbat, we reclaim our time, cultivate mindfulness, and create space for meaningful reflection and connection. It is about embracing the wisdom and insights of Jewish thought and adapting them to the challenges and opportunities of the 21st century. Through the lenses of tzedakah, tikkun olam, kavod, and Shabbat, we can cultivate a more just, compassionate, and meaningful world for ourselves and generations to come.

By actively engaging with these values, we can contribute to building a more just and equitable society, fostering greater understanding and empathy, and reclaiming our time and our lives. In an increasingly complex and interconnected world, the enduring wisdom of Jewish tradition offers a powerful framework for navigating the present and creating a brighter future for all.

Finding Meaning and Purpose

Finding meaning and purpose is not a destination but a continuous process, a dynamic exploration of our values, beliefs, and aspirations. It is about connecting with something larger than ourselves, something that ignites a sense of passion and inspires us to live a life of purpose. This journey can be exhilarating, challenging, and ultimately, deeply rewarding.

The Nature of Meaning and Purpose

Before embarking on this exploration, it is essential to understand the nature of meaning and purpose. These concepts, though intertwined, are distinct.

Meaning refers to the significance we find in our experiences and actions. It is about discovering a sense of coherence and understanding in our lives, recognizing the value and relevance of our choices, and finding a connection to something larger than ourselves. Meaning can be derived from various sources, such as relationships, work, hobbies, art, faith, or nature.

Purpose, on the other hand, is about having a direction in life, a guiding force that propels us forward and gives our actions a sense of direction. Purpose is often associated with making a difference, contributing to something beyond ourselves, and leaving a positive impact on the world.

The Importance of Finding Meaning and Purpose

Finding meaning and purpose is not simply an intellectual exercise; it has profound implications for our overall well-being. A life lived with meaning and purpose is often characterized by:

Increased Happiness and Fulfillment: When we find meaning in our lives, we experience greater satisfaction and a sense of fulfillment. We feel connected to something larger than ourselves, giving us a sense of purpose and direction.
Improved Mental and Physical Health: Studies have shown a strong correlation between finding meaning in life and improved mental and physical health. Individuals with a sense of purpose often experience lower levels of stress, anxiety, and depression. They are also more likely to engage in healthy behaviors such as exercise and proper nutrition.
Enhanced Resilience: Meaning and purpose provide a framework for navigating life's inevitable challenges. When faced with adversity, individuals with a sense of purpose are more likely to persevere and find ways to overcome obstacles.
Greater Productivity and Motivation: A life filled with meaning and purpose is characterized by a strong drive to achieve goals and contribute to something meaningful. This intrinsic motivation leads to increased productivity and a higher sense of accomplishment.
Strengthened Relationships: Meaning and purpose can enhance our relationships with others. When we are living a life of purpose, we are more likely to inspire others, build meaningful connections, and contribute to a sense of community.

Exploring the Pathways to Meaning and Purpose

Finding meaning and purpose is a personal journey, and there is no one-size-fits-all approach. However, exploring various pathways can guide us toward a deeper understanding of ourselves and our place in the world.

1. Self-Reflection and Exploration:

Values Clarification: Begin by identifying your core values, the principles that guide your life and shape your choices. These values can be about honesty, compassion, creativity, knowledge, or any other principles that resonate with you.

Passion and Interests: Explore your passions and interests. What activities bring you joy, ignite your curiosity, and make you feel alive. Are there any skills or talents you have been neglecting.

Strengths and Weaknesses: Identify your strengths and weaknesses. What are you good at. What areas do you need to develop. Knowing your strengths can help you identify areas where you can contribute and make a difference.

Past Experiences: Reflect on past experiences, both positive and negative. What have you learned from them. What have they taught you about yourself and your values.

Life Purpose Statements: Consider crafting a life purpose statement, a concise declaration that reflects your values, passions, and aspirations. This can serve as a guiding compass in your life's journey.

2. Connection and Contribution:

Meaningful Relationships: Nurture your relationships with loved ones. Spending time with people who care about you and with whom you share meaningful connections can bring a sense of belonging and purpose.

Community Involvement: Engage in your community. Volunteering, participating in local initiatives, or simply connecting with your neighbors can create a sense of purpose and contribute to a shared sense of well-being.

Career Choice: Choose a career that aligns with your values and interests. A fulfilling career can provide a sense of purpose and contribute to your overall sense of meaning.

Artistic Expression: Explore creative outlets, such as writing, painting, music, or dance. These activities can help you express yourself, explore your creativity, and find meaning in your artistic expression.

Spiritual Practices: Engage in spiritual practices that resonate with you. Whether it's prayer, meditation, or connecting with nature, these practices can provide a sense of peace, purpose, and connection to something larger than ourselves.

3. Growth and Development:

Continuous Learning: Embrace a lifelong learning mindset. Expand your knowledge, skills, and perspectives through reading, taking classes, or engaging in meaningful conversations.
Personal Growth: Set goals for personal growth and development. Explore new interests, challenge yourself, and strive to become the best version of yourself.
Embracing Challenges: View challenges as opportunities for growth and learning. Embrace adversity as a chance to learn, adapt, and become more resilient.
Finding Meaning in Suffering: Even in times of suffering, we can find meaning. Reflect on the lessons learned, the strength gained, and the potential for growth and transformation.

4. Acceptance and Gratitude:

Acceptance of Imperfection: Embrace the fact that you are not perfect and that life will always have its ups and downs. Accept your flaws and imperfections and strive to learn and grow from them.
Practice Gratitude: Cultivate an attitude of gratitude. Focus on the good in your life, appreciate the little things, and express gratitude to those who have touched your life.
Living in the Present: Practice mindfulness and focus on living in the present moment. Appreciate the beauty of the everyday, savor experiences, and connect with the world around you.

Finding Meaning and Purpose in Adversity

While finding meaning and purpose is often associated with positive experiences, adversity can also be a powerful catalyst for self-discovery and growth. When faced with challenges, we can use these opportunities to:

Identify Our Core Values: Adversity can often reveal our true priorities and values. During difficult times, we are forced to confront our fears, vulnerabilities, and the things that truly matter.
Develop Resilience: Overcoming challenges can build resilience and equip us with the skills and strength to navigate future obstacles.
Gain Perspective: Adversity can help us gain a broader perspective on life and appreciate the value of the things we often take for granted.
Discover Hidden Strengths: When faced with difficult situations, we often discover hidden strengths and capabilities that we never knew we possessed.
Connect with a Greater Purpose: Suffering can also lead to a deeper understanding of our purpose. It can inspire us to help others, make a difference in the world, and find meaning in our shared human experience.

The Continual Journey of Meaning and Purpose

Finding meaning and purpose is an ongoing journey, a continuous process of self-discovery, reflection, and growth. It is not a static state but a dynamic and evolving aspect of our lives. As we grow, change, and encounter new experiences, our understanding of meaning and purpose will also evolve.

The search for meaning and purpose is a deeply personal quest. While there are common themes and pathways, the journey is unique to each individual. It is a process of exploration, introspection, and connection, a quest to discover our own unique path and contribute to something greater than ourselves. It is a journey that can lead us to a more fulfilling, joyful, and meaningful life.

Spreading the Message of Hope

This journey of spreading hope begins with a deep understanding of its multifaceted nature. Hope is not simply a passive sentiment; it is an active force, a potent catalyst for action. It fuels our resilience, propels us towards our goals, and empowers us to navigate life's inevitable challenges. Hope, in essence, is an act of defiance against despair, a testament to the human spirit's enduring capacity to dream, to believe, and to build a better tomorrow.

The act of spreading hope requires a nuanced approach, recognizing the diverse needs and challenges faced by individuals and communities. It demands a commitment to empathy, a willingness to listen and truly understand the struggles and aspirations of others. This understanding serves as the foundation for building bridges, fostering connections, and offering genuine support.

Spreading hope often translates into tangible actions, a tapestry woven with threads of compassion, kindness, and generosity. It can manifest in acts of service, lending a helping hand to those in need, offering a listening ear to those burdened by grief or loneliness, or simply sharing a smile and a word of encouragement. These small gestures, woven together, create a collective wave of hope, rippling outward and touching countless lives.

The power of storytelling, the human ability to share experiences and connect on an emotional level, plays a vital role in spreading hope. Sharing stories of resilience, of individuals who have overcome adversity and emerged stronger, inspires others to believe in their own potential for growth and transformation. These narratives, woven with threads of courage, perseverance, and compassion, act as beacons of light, guiding others through their own dark nights.

Beyond individual actions, the message of hope can be amplified through collective efforts, through creating spaces for dialogue and shared purpose. This can involve community initiatives that promote well-being, address social issues, or simply offer moments of shared joy and laughter. Building bridges across divides, fostering understanding and empathy, and promoting inclusive communities are vital steps in spreading a message of hope that resonates with a diverse audience.

Furthermore, it is crucial to acknowledge and address the systemic factors that contribute to despair and hopelessness. Tackling issues like poverty, inequality, and social injustice requires a collective effort, a commitment to creating a more just and equitable society for all. This effort not only spreads hope but also empowers individuals and communities to build a future free from the shackles of oppression and discrimination.

The media plays a significant role in shaping perceptions and disseminating messages of hope or despair. By prioritizing narratives that highlight resilience, compassion, and positive change, media outlets can contribute to a more hopeful and inspiring world. Journalism that focuses on solutions, celebrates human ingenuity, and champions the work of individuals and organizations working towards a better future can serve as a potent force for good. It is a shared responsibility, a collective commitment to fostering a world where resilience, compassion, and belief in a brighter tomorrow prevail. It is a journey that begins within ourselves, nurtured by self-belief, compassion, and a willingness to act. It is a journey that culminates in a ripple effect of hope, touching countless lives and creating a more just, compassionate, and inspiring world for generations to come.

The Message of Hope in Literature

Literature, with its boundless power to explore the human condition, offers a profound canvas for exploring the message of hope. Throughout history, authors have woven tales of resilience, courage, and the enduring human spirit, offering solace, inspiration, and a glimpse of the possibility of a better world. From the timeless tales of Homer's Odyssey, where Odysseus perseveres against countless trials and tribulations, to the poignant narratives of Victor Hugo's Les Misérables, which explores themes of redemption and social justice, literature stands as a testament to the enduring power of hope.

Hope in the Face of Adversity

Literature often delves into the complexities of human suffering and the trials that life throws our way. However, it is precisely within these narratives of hardship that the message of hope shines through with even greater brilliance. Characters grappling with loss, poverty, injustice, and personal struggles offer a powerful reflection of the human spirit's ability to endure and find strength even in the darkest of times.

The Power of Belief

Hope, in literature, often manifests as a belief in something greater than oneself, a belief in a better future, or a belief in the inherent goodness of humanity. It is this belief that propels characters forward, guiding them through their challenges and giving them the courage to fight for a better tomorrow.

The Importance of Community and Connection

Literature often highlights the power of community and connection in fostering hope. Characters finding solace and support in one another, forging bonds of friendship and love that help them weather life's storms, serve as a powerful testament to the enduring strength of human connection.

Hope as a Catalyst for Change

Literature frequently depicts hope as a catalyst for change, a driving force behind social movements, political reform, and personal transformation. Characters who dare to challenge societal norms, fight for justice, and advocate for a more equitable world embody the transformative power of hope, inspiring readers to embrace their own agency and strive for a better tomorrow.

Hope as a Source of Resilience

Hope, in literature, serves as a wellspring of resilience, enabling characters to navigate the complexities of life, endure hardship, and emerge stronger from their trials. It is this enduring spirit, this unwavering belief in the face of adversity, that resonates with readers and inspires them to find strength within themselves.

Hope for the Future

Literature, with its ability to transcend time and offer glimpses into different worlds, serves as a powerful reminder that hope is not merely a fleeting emotion but an enduring force that transcends generations. By exploring the enduring human spirit, the power of belief, and the transformative potential of collective action, literature offers a potent message of hope, inspiring readers to embrace a brighter future and contribute to a more just and compassionate world.

Spreading the Message of Hope Through Educational Initiatives

Education plays a critical role in nurturing hope and promoting a sense of agency within individuals and communities. By fostering critical thinking, empathy, and a deep understanding of the world's complexities, education empowers individuals to become active agents of change and contribute to a more hopeful future.

Literacy and Empowerment

Providing access to books, stories, and information is crucial for empowering individuals, fostering critical thinking, and broadening their horizons. Literacy programs, libraries, and community initiatives that promote reading and access to knowledge are essential for nurturing hope and empowering individuals to navigate challenges and make informed decisions.

Critical Thinking and Problem-Solving

Education should encourage critical thinking skills, enabling individuals to analyze complex issues, identify potential solutions, and engage in constructive dialogue. By equipping students with the tools to analyze information, challenge assumptions, and develop their own perspectives, education fosters a sense of agency and empowers them to contribute to positive change.

Empathy and Social Justice

Instilling a sense of empathy and understanding of social justice issues is crucial for fostering a more inclusive and compassionate society. Education that emphasizes diversity, equity, and inclusion, and explores the systemic factors contributing to inequalities, helps students develop a deeper understanding of the challenges faced by marginalized communities and empowers them to advocate for a more just world.

Community Engagement and Action

Integrating community engagement and service learning into educational programs empowers students to make a difference in their communities and connect with those facing challenges. By participating in service projects, volunteering their time, and collaborating with local organizations, students gain valuable experience, develop empathy, and build a sense of shared purpose.

Building a Culture of Hope

Education can play a vital role in building a culture of hope by promoting positive narratives, celebrating human ingenuity, and fostering a belief in the power of collective action. By highlighting stories of resilience, success, and community efforts that have made a positive impact, education can inspire students to believe in the possibility of a brighter future.

The Importance of Mentorship and Support

Providing mentorship and support to young people is crucial for nurturing hope and empowering them to overcome challenges. Teachers, mentors, and community leaders who offer guidance, encouragement, and a belief in their potential play a vital role in helping young people navigate difficult times and realize their aspirations. Through literacy, critical thinking, social justice education, community engagement, and mentorship, educational initiatives can empower individuals to become active agents of change, contribute to positive societal transformation, and pave the way for a future filled with hope and possibility.

The Role of Technology in Spreading the Message of Hope

In our increasingly interconnected world, technology plays a profound role in shaping perceptions, facilitating communication, and spreading messages of hope or despair. Harnessing the power of technology for good requires a conscious effort to prioritize ethical considerations, promote positive narratives, and empower individuals to become active agents of change.

Social Media and Positive Change

Social media platforms have become powerful tools for raising awareness, mobilizing communities, and amplifying messages of hope. By leveraging the reach and connectivity of these platforms, individuals and organizations can share stories of resilience, promote acts of kindness, and connect people across geographical boundaries to foster a sense of collective purpose.

Digital Storytelling and Empowerment

Digital storytelling platforms, with their capacity to reach a wide audience, offer a powerful medium for sharing narratives of hope, inspiration, and resilience. By utilizing these platforms to amplify the voices of marginalized communities, showcase innovative solutions to social problems, and celebrate the triumphs of ordinary people overcoming extraordinary challenges, we can create a more hopeful and empowering digital landscape.

Virtual Communities and Collaboration

Technology has fostered the rise of virtual communities, bringing together people from all walks of life to share experiences, support one another, and work towards common goals. Online platforms dedicated to fostering empathy, promoting social justice, and connecting people with shared values can serve as powerful tools for spreading hope and facilitating collective action.

Educational Technology and Access to Knowledge

Technology has revolutionized education, providing greater access to knowledge, fostering collaboration, and empowering individuals to learn at their own pace. By leveraging online learning platforms, digital resources, and interactive tools, we can create more inclusive and accessible educational opportunities, fostering hope and empowering individuals to pursue their dreams.

Ethical Considerations in Technology

It is crucial to approach the use of technology with a strong sense of ethical responsibility, recognizing the potential for misuse and the importance of promoting a positive and constructive online environment. Addressing issues of online harassment, misinformation, and the spread of negativity requires a collective effort to foster a more ethical and responsible digital landscape. By utilizing technology responsibly, prioritizing ethical considerations, promoting positive narratives, and empowering individuals to become agents of change, we can harness the power of technology to create a more hopeful, just, and connected world for generations to come.

Chapter 10: The Role of Social Justice

Jewish Values and Social Action

At the heart of Jewish values lies the concept of tikkun olam, a Hebrew phrase meaning "repairing the world. " This notion, deeply rooted in Jewish tradition, emphasizes the inherent obligation to actively participate in the betterment of society. Tikkun olam transcends individual aspirations, recognizing that each person has a responsibility to contribute to the collective well-being. This responsibility is not limited to Jewish communities; rather, it extends to the entire human family and the environment we share.

The pursuit of tikkun olam is informed by a myriad of Jewish values, each contributing to the tapestry of social action. Tzedakah, often translated as "charity" but encompassing a broader concept of justice and righteousness, underscores the importance of supporting the vulnerable and addressing systemic inequalities. Tzedakah is not simply an act of generosity but a moral imperative, a recognition of the inherent interconnectedness of all people and the obligation to alleviate suffering wherever it exists.

Chesed, meaning "loving kindness" or "acts of compassion," adds a layer of human connection to the pursuit of social justice. Chesed emphasizes the importance of acting with empathy and understanding, acknowledging the inherent dignity of every individual, regardless of background or circumstance. This value encourages active engagement with those in need, offering not just material support but also emotional and spiritual nourishment.

Mishpat, translated as "justice" or "judgment," underscores the importance of fairness and equality in all aspects of society. This value calls for the creation of a just legal system that safeguards individual rights and ensures that everyone has the opportunity to thrive. It also extends to the broader realm of social justice, demanding accountability for systemic injustices and advocating for equitable access to resources and opportunities.

Shalom, often translated as "peace," embodies a deep desire for harmony and well-being within and beyond the Jewish community. This value emphasizes the importance of non-violent conflict resolution, promoting dialogue and understanding between different groups. Shalom also speaks to the need for environmental stewardship, recognizing the interconnectedness of all living beings and the responsibility to preserve our planet for future generations.

The practical application of these values is evident throughout Jewish history, with countless examples of Jewish individuals and communities engaging in social action. From the prophets challenging injustice in ancient Israel to the social justice movements of the modern era, Jewish communities have consistently sought to embody tikkun olam in their daily lives.

Early Jewish Social Action:

The Jewish tradition has a long history of social action rooted in the teachings of the prophets. Figures like Amos, Hosea, and Isaiah spoke out against social injustices, condemning exploitation of the poor and advocating for fair treatment of the marginalized. They emphasized the importance of economic justice, the need for compassion, and the responsibility to care for the vulnerable.

The Torah itself outlines numerous laws and principles that guide social action. The laws of Shabbat, for example, emphasize the need for rest and rejuvenation, reminding us to prioritize well-being and create a more equitable society. The laws of kashrut, dietary laws that govern the consumption of food, reflect a concern for animal welfare and a commitment to ethical practices.

Medieval and Early Modern Social Action:

During the medieval period, Jewish communities established various institutions to support the poor and vulnerable. This included the development of "hevra kadisha," societies responsible for burying the dead, and "chevra shel chesed," organizations providing financial and other forms of assistance to those in need. These organizations served as precursors to modern-day social service agencies, demonstrating the longstanding commitment to social action within Jewish communities.

The development of Jewish mysticism during this period also influenced social action. The Kabbalah, a mystical tradition focused on understanding the divine through symbolism and contemplation, offered a spiritual dimension to the pursuit of tikkun olam. Kabbalistic thinkers emphasized the interconnectedness of all beings and the importance of individual actions in shaping the world.

Modern Jewish Social Action:

The 19th and 20th centuries saw a renewed emphasis on social action within Jewish communities. The emergence of Zionism, a movement advocating for the establishment of a Jewish state in Palestine, fueled a resurgence of activism focused on both political and social justice.

The horrors of the Holocaust, however, cast a long shadow, prompting Jewish communities to address not only their own needs but also the broader issues of human rights and social justice. This led to the creation of organizations like the Anti-Defamation League, dedicated to fighting antisemitism and promoting tolerance, and the

American Jewish Committee, advocating for human rights and social justice on a global scale.

Contemporary Jewish Social Action:

Today, Jewish communities continue to engage in a wide range of social action initiatives, reflecting the diverse values and priorities of the modern Jewish world. These initiatives encompass issues such as:

Fighting poverty and hunger: Organizations like MAZON: A Jewish Response to Hunger and the Jewish Federation's efforts in food security, food pantries, and community kitchens address the pressing need to alleviate hunger and provide food security for those in need.

Promoting environmental justice: Efforts to combat climate change and address environmental degradation, such as the work of the Jewish Environmental Action Network (JEAN) and the Eco-Judaism movement, emphasize the interconnectedness of humans and the natural world.

Advancing racial justice: The recent resurgence of the Black Lives Matter movement has spurred Jewish communities to actively engage in the fight against systemic racism. Jewish organizations and individuals have joined forces with other communities of color to advocate for social justice and address the long-standing issues of inequality and discrimination.

Promoting peace and reconciliation: Organizations like the Jewish Peace Fellowship and the American Jewish World Service actively promote peacebuilding initiatives, advocating for non-violent conflict resolution and supporting peace processes in conflict zones.

Supporting LGBTQ+ rights: Jewish communities have increasingly embraced the LGBTQ+ community, with organizations like Keshet advocating for full equality and inclusion for LGBTQ+ individuals within Jewish life. This includes fighting for marriage equality, promoting LGBTQ+ inclusion in synagogues and Jewish institutions,

and addressing issues of homophobia and transphobia.
Addressing systemic injustices: Jewish communities continue to challenge systemic injustices, including advocating for universal healthcare, economic fairness, and access to quality education for all.

The Future of Jewish Social Action:

The future of Jewish social action is marked by a renewed focus on intersectionality and solidarity. Jewish communities are increasingly recognizing the interconnectedness of different social justice issues and the need to work in coalition with other groups to achieve common goals. This includes building bridges between Jewish communities and communities of color, addressing the needs of marginalized groups within the Jewish community, and advocating for policies that promote social justice for all.

The Jewish tradition's emphasis on tikkun olam continues to inspire and guide contemporary social action. As Jewish communities continue to grapple with the complexities of the modern world, the values of tzedakah, chesed, mishpat, and shalom serve as a powerful compass, reminding us of our obligation to act justly, compassionately, and with a commitment to building a more just and equitable society. The commitment to tikkun olam, repairing the world, permeates Jewish thought and action, inspiring generations to strive for a better world. From the prophets of ancient Israel to contemporary social justice movements, Jewish communities have consistently sought to embody these values, demonstrating the enduring power of Jewish thought to shape the world around us.

This exploration has revealed the diverse and dynamic nature of Jewish social action, highlighting the ongoing evolution of Jewish engagement with the world's challenges. As Jewish communities continue to navigate the complexities of the 21st century, the values that have guided them for millennia will continue to inspire and empower them to create a more just and compassionate world for all.

Engaging in Advocacy and Outreach

Understanding the Power of Advocacy and Outreach

Advocacy and outreach are powerful tools for achieving social, economic, and environmental justice. They enable individuals and communities to have a voice and influence decision-making processes. By raising awareness, building coalitions, and engaging policymakers, advocates can push for change and ensure that the needs and perspectives of marginalized groups are heard and addressed.

Defining Key Terms

Before delving into the practical aspects of advocacy and outreach, it's essential to establish a clear understanding of key terminology:

Advocacy: Advocacy is the act of publicly supporting or recommending a cause or policy. It involves actively promoting a specific viewpoint or agenda to influence decision-making processes and public opinion.
Outreach: Outreach refers to the activities undertaken to connect with and engage individuals, communities, or target groups. It aims to build relationships, share information, and foster collaboration to achieve common goals.

The Importance of Strategic Planning

Effective advocacy and outreach require a well-defined strategy. This strategy should encompass the following elements:

Identifying the Target Audience: Understanding the target audience is crucial for tailoring messaging and communication strategies. Who are the key stakeholders who can influence the desired change. Who needs to be informed and engaged.

Defining the Issue: Clearly articulating the problem or issue at hand is essential for rallying support and building a strong case for action. This involves providing evidence, data, and compelling narratives to illustrate the problem's impact.

Developing Measurable Objectives: Setting specific, measurable, achievable, relevant, and time-bound (SMART) objectives helps track progress, evaluate effectiveness, and demonstrate impact.

Developing a Communication Plan: A well-articulated communication plan outlines the key messages, channels, and tactics to be employed to reach the target audience effectively.

Building Coalitions and Partnerships: Collaboration is essential for amplifying impact. Building coalitions with other organizations and individuals working towards similar goals strengthens advocacy efforts and expands reach.

Effective Communication Strategies

Successful advocacy and outreach rely on clear, concise, and compelling communication. Key strategies include:

Storytelling: Sharing personal stories and anecdotes can resonate deeply with audiences, humanizing the issue and fostering empathy.

Data and Evidence: Using credible data and research findings strengthens arguments and provides a factual basis for advocacy efforts.

Framing the Message: Framing the issue within a compelling narrative that resonates with the target audience's values and beliefs can influence perceptions and encourage action.

Tailoring Communication: Adapting communication style and language to the specific needs and characteristics of the target audience is crucial for effective engagement.

Navigating the Landscape of Advocacy and Outreach

The landscape of advocacy and outreach is constantly evolving, driven by technological advancements, shifting social dynamics, and changing political landscapes. Here are some key considerations:

Leveraging Technology: Social media platforms, online petition sites, and digital communication tools offer powerful avenues for outreach and mobilizing support.
Navigating Online Spaces: Engaging in respectful and constructive dialogue online is crucial for building trust and fostering positive interactions.
Addressing Misinformation and Disinformation: In an age of digital overload, it's essential to counter misinformation and disinformation by providing accurate information and fostering critical thinking skills.
Building Relationships with Policymakers: Engaging with policymakers through meetings, lobbying, and advocacy campaigns is essential for influencing policy decisions.
Understanding the Role of Media: Utilizing media outlets, including traditional news media and online platforms, to amplify the message and reach wider audiences is key for raising awareness.

Ethical Considerations in Advocacy and Outreach

Engaging in advocacy and outreach requires upholding ethical principles to ensure transparency, accountability, and integrity. Key considerations include:

Transparency and Disclosure: Being transparent about funding sources, affiliations, and potential conflicts of interest builds trust and credibility.
Respect for Diversity: Recognizing and respecting the diverse perspectives, values, and experiences of the target audience is crucial for building inclusive and equitable advocacy efforts.
Integrity and Accountability: Upholding ethical standards in all

communication and actions ensures that advocacy efforts are rooted in honesty and integrity.

Evaluating Advocacy and Outreach Efforts

Regularly evaluating advocacy and outreach efforts is essential for identifying areas of improvement, measuring impact, and demonstrating accountability. Key metrics for evaluation include:

Reach and Engagement: Tracking the number of individuals and organizations reached through advocacy and outreach activities.
Policy Changes: Measuring the influence of advocacy efforts on policy decisions and legislative outcomes.
Behavioral Change: Assessing the impact of advocacy efforts on individual behaviors and community practices.
Public Awareness: Gauging the effectiveness of campaigns in raising public awareness and understanding of the issue.

Examples of Effective Advocacy and Outreach

Numerous examples showcase the power of advocacy and outreach in achieving positive change:

The Disability Rights Movement: Through advocacy and activism, individuals with disabilities have successfully pushed for legislation guaranteeing equal rights, accessibility, and inclusion.
The Environmental Justice Movement: Environmental justice advocates have been instrumental in raising awareness about the disproportionate impact of environmental degradation on marginalized communities and securing policies to protect public health and the environment.
The LGBTQ+ Rights Movement: Advocacy and outreach efforts have played a pivotal role in advancing LGBTQ+ rights, including marriage equality, anti-discrimination laws, and increased visibility.

Conclusion

Engaging in advocacy and outreach is a dynamic and multifaceted process that demands strategic planning, skillful communication, and unwavering commitment. By understanding the principles, strategies, and ethical considerations outlined in this guide, individuals and organizations can effectively leverage their voices to advocate for positive change and create a more just and equitable world.

Further Reading

Advocacy and Outreach: A Guide for Nonprofits by The National Council of Nonprofits
The Advocacy Handbook: A Guide to Effective Advocacy for Nonprofit Organizations by the Center for Social Development
Advocacy & Outreach: A Guide to Getting Your Message Out by the Alliance for Justice

Key Takeaways

Advocacy and outreach are powerful tools for achieving social, economic, and environmental justice.
Strategic planning, effective communication, and ethical considerations are crucial for successful advocacy and outreach efforts.
Building relationships, leveraging technology, and navigating online spaces are key aspects of contemporary advocacy and outreach.
Evaluating advocacy and outreach activities regularly helps ensure accountability, measure impact, and identify areas for improvement.

By applying the principles and strategies outlined in this guide, individuals and organizations can effectively engage in advocacy and outreach to amplify their impact and create meaningful change in the world.

Fighting for Justice and Equality

The fight for justice and equality is multifaceted, encompassing a broad spectrum of issues. It encompasses the dismantling of discriminatory practices based on race, gender, sexual orientation, caste, and other social constructs. It calls for the fair distribution of resources, opportunities, and power, ensuring that all members of society have a chance to thrive. It demands accountability for past injustices and the implementation of policies that prevent future inequalities.

The Historical Landscape: A tapestry of triumphs and tribulations

The fight for justice and equality is not a modern phenomenon; it has deep roots in history. Throughout the ages, individuals and groups have challenged established power structures and fought for recognition of their rights.

In ancient Greece, the philosopher Socrates challenged the Athenian democracy, advocating for a more just and equitable system. In Roman times, the Stoic philosophers emphasized the inherent equality of all human beings, regardless of their social standing. These early movements laid the foundation for future struggles for justice and equality.

During the Middle Ages, the rise of Christianity brought with it a renewed focus on human dignity and the equal value of all individuals in the eyes of God. The Church, at times, championed the cause of the poor and marginalized, although it also played a role in perpetuating societal hierarchies.

The Renaissance saw a surge of intellectual and artistic exploration, which coincided with a growing awareness of human potential. This period witnessed the emergence of social reformers who challenged the established order and advocated for more just and equitable societies.

The Enlightenment, with its emphasis on reason and individual liberty, profoundly shaped the fight for justice and equality. Thinkers like John Locke and Jean-Jacques Rousseau argued for the inherent rights of all individuals, including the right to life, liberty, and property. These ideas served as the foundation for the American and French Revolutions, which challenged monarchical rule and advocated for democratic governance based on the principles of equality and liberty.

The Rise of Modern Movements: From Abolition to Civil Rights

The 19th century witnessed a wave of social movements that sought to dismantle systems of oppression and advance the cause of justice and equality. The abolitionist movement, which fought to end the transatlantic slave trade and abolish slavery, was a pivotal moment in the struggle for human rights. The movement garnered support from a wide range of individuals and groups, from religious leaders to politicians to ordinary citizens.

The fight for women's suffrage emerged as another crucial battle in the fight for equality. Women throughout the world fought for the right to vote, challenging the patriarchal norms that had denied them this fundamental right. The suffragist movement, marked by its unwavering determination and tireless advocacy, eventually achieved its goals, paving the way for greater political participation by women.

The 20th century saw the rise of civil rights movements across the globe. In the United States, the Civil Rights Movement, led by iconic figures like Martin Luther King Jr. and Malcolm X, fought for the equality of Black Americans, challenging segregation and discriminatory practices. The movement's success, marked by landmark legislation like the Civil Rights Act of 1964 and the Voting Rights Act of 1965, served as a beacon of hope for other marginalized groups.

Simultaneously, movements for indigenous rights, LGBTQ+ rights, and disability rights emerged, demanding recognition and respect for the diverse experiences and identities within society. These movements, fueled by a shared vision of justice and equality, challenged the status quo, pushing for systemic change and the creation of a more inclusive society.

Challenges and Triumphs: The ongoing struggle for a just world

The fight for justice and equality is an ongoing process, marked by both progress and setbacks. While significant strides have been made in dismantling oppressive systems and advancing the cause of human rights, there are still numerous challenges that require our collective attention.

Discrimination and Inequality: Persistent barriers to justice

Despite the progress made, discrimination and inequality persist in various forms, hindering the full realization of justice and equality for all. Systemic racism, sexism, homophobia, transphobia, and other forms of prejudice continue to permeate society, leading to disparities in access to resources, opportunities, and representation.

The persistence of these inequalities underscores the need for ongoing efforts to dismantle the structures that perpetuate them. This requires a multifaceted approach that tackles both individual biases and systemic injustices.

Economic Inequality: A widening gap

Economic inequality has become a defining feature of our times, with a growing gap between the wealthy and the rest of society. This disparity not only fuels social unrest but also undermines the very principles of justice and equality.

The fight for economic justice necessitates policies that promote fair wages, affordable housing, access to quality healthcare, and educational opportunities for all. It also requires addressing the systemic factors that contribute to wealth disparities, such as discriminatory lending practices, tax loopholes, and corporate influence on policy.

Climate Justice: A matter of survival

Climate change poses a significant threat to the future of humanity, disproportionately impacting marginalized communities who are often the most vulnerable to its effects. The fight for climate justice requires a global effort to reduce greenhouse gas emissions, promote sustainable development, and protect the environment.

The Role of Education and Awareness

Education plays a crucial role in promoting justice and equality by fostering critical thinking, empathy, and understanding of diverse perspectives. By providing individuals with knowledge about the historical and contemporary struggles for justice, we can empower them to become informed advocates for change.

The Power of Activism and Collective Action

The fight for justice and equality requires collective action. Grassroots movements, community organizations, and advocacy groups play a vital role in mobilizing people, raising awareness, and demanding accountability from those in power.

The Importance of Intersectionality

The fight for justice and equality must acknowledge the interconnectedness of various social identities. Intersectionality recognizes that people experience oppression in multiple ways based on their race, gender, sexual orientation, class, and other factors. By understanding the intersectional nature of inequality, we can develop more effective strategies for dismantling oppressive systems.

Building a Just and Equitable Future

The fight for justice and equality is not a sprint, but a marathon. It requires sustained effort, unwavering commitment, and a deep belief in the inherent worth of all individuals. By fostering dialogue, promoting understanding, and working together to dismantle oppressive systems, we can create a more just and equitable world for generations to come. It is a journey that requires us to challenge assumptions, embrace diversity, and work tirelessly to create a world where all individuals are treated with dignity, respect, and fairness. The path ahead may be fraught with obstacles, but by drawing upon the strength of our shared humanity and the lessons of history, we can continue to build a more just and equitable future for all.

Making a Difference in the World

Understanding Impact: Defining the Scope and Significance

Before we embark on our quest to make a difference, it's crucial to understand what impact truly means. It's not simply about doing good deeds or having grand ambitions. Impact is about creating tangible and lasting positive change. This change can occur at various levels – individual, community, national, or global – and its significance can be measured through different metrics.

For instance, impact can be measured by the number of lives affected, the reduction in suffering, the improvement in living standards, the advancement of knowledge, or the conservation of the environment. It's important to note that impact is not solely defined by grand, headline-grabbing actions. Often, the most profound changes are brought about by seemingly small, consistent efforts that ripple outwards, creating a cumulative effect of positive change.

Finding Your Purpose: Embracing Passion and Identifying Needs

The first step towards making a difference is identifying your purpose. What are you passionate about. What issues ignite your soul. What problems do you see in the world that you feel compelled to address. Answering these questions will guide you towards a path where your actions are fuelled by genuine conviction and a deep sense of meaning.

It's also crucial to consider the needs of the world around you. What are the pressing challenges facing your community, your country, or the global community. Researching these issues, understanding their complexities, and identifying potential solutions will provide you with a clear roadmap for your actions.

Developing Skills and Strategies: Equipping Yourself for Change

Once you've identified your purpose and the needs you wish to address, you need to develop the skills and strategies to make a tangible impact. This may involve acquiring formal education, gaining practical experience, or developing specific skills relevant to your chosen area of focus.

For example, if you're passionate about environmental conservation, you might pursue a degree in environmental science or work as a volunteer for an environmental organization. If you're passionate about social justice, you might learn about advocacy techniques, organize community events, or contribute to social media campaigns promoting awareness and change.

The Importance of Collaboration: Building Networks and Sharing

Resources

Making a difference is rarely a solitary endeavor. It often requires collaboration, the pooling of resources, and the synergy of diverse perspectives. Therefore, it's essential to build networks with like-minded individuals, connect with established organizations, and explore opportunities for collaborative projects.

Joining organizations, attending conferences, participating in online forums, and engaging in community events can all contribute to building valuable connections and expanding your sphere of influence. By sharing resources, knowledge, and expertise, you can amplify your impact and create a collective force for positive change.

Embracing Resilience and Adaptability: Navigating the Challenges

The journey of making a difference is rarely smooth sailing. You will encounter obstacles, setbacks, and moments of doubt. You may face opposition, experience failures, and encounter situations that test your resolve. However, it's through these challenges that we learn, grow, and refine our strategies.

Embracing resilience, adaptability, and a growth mindset are crucial for navigating these obstacles. Learning from our mistakes, adapting our approaches, and persevering in the face of adversity are essential for achieving lasting impact.

Celebrating Progress: Acknowledging Achievements and Inspiring Others

The journey of making a difference is not simply about achieving a final destination; it's about the journey itself, the continuous learning, and the impact we create along the way. Therefore, it's important to celebrate our progress, acknowledge our achievements, and inspire others to join the movement.

Sharing our stories, highlighting the positive changes we've witnessed, and demonstrating the power of collective action can motivate others to participate, contribute, and create a ripple effect of positive change.

Beyond Individual Impact: The Power of Collective Action

While individual efforts are essential, it's crucial to recognize the power of collective action. By working together, pooling resources, and coordinating efforts, we can amplify our impact and achieve goals that would be impossible to achieve alone.

This collective action can take various forms – from supporting grassroots movements to advocating for policy changes, from participating in global campaigns to empowering marginalized communities. The key is to recognize that we are all interconnected and that our individual actions, when combined with the efforts of others, can create a powerful force for positive change.

The Ongoing Journey: Continual Learning and Evolution

Making a difference is not a one-time event but an ongoing journey of continual learning, growth, and adaptation. As the world evolves, our understanding of issues changes, and new challenges emerge, we need to stay informed, adapt our strategies, and refine our approaches.

Embracing a lifelong learning mentality, engaging in critical reflection, and staying open to new perspectives will help us navigate the ever-changing landscape of social and global issues, ensuring that our efforts remain relevant and impactful.

The Power of Hope and Inspiration

In the face of complex global challenges, it's easy to feel

overwhelmed and discouraged. However, it's essential to remember the power of hope and inspiration. Witnessing the countless acts of kindness, the tireless efforts of individuals and organizations, and the positive changes taking place around the world can serve as a source of inspiration and motivation.

By focusing on the positive, celebrating the victories, and believing in the possibility of change, we can create a more just, equitable, and sustainable future for all.

Making a Difference: A Call to Action

The world needs individuals who are passionate, dedicated, and committed to making a difference. Whether you choose to address social injustice, promote environmental sustainability, advance scientific knowledge, or create artistic expressions of change, your actions matter.

Embrace your purpose, develop your skills, collaborate with others, and never give up on the belief that you can make a difference. Together, we can build a better world, one positive action at a time.

Chapter 11: Exploring the Arts and Culture

Jewish Music, Literature, and Art

A Symphony of Faith: The Power of Jewish Music

Music has been an intrinsic part of Jewish life for millennia, serving as a bridge between the sacred and the secular, a vehicle for communal expression, and a source of solace and inspiration. Jewish music is not a monolithic entity, but rather a vast and multifaceted landscape encompassing a diverse array of genres, styles, and traditions.

From Ancient Melodies to Modern Innovation:

The origins of Jewish music can be traced back to ancient biblical times, where music played a significant role in religious rituals and celebrations. The Hebrew Bible, filled with narratives of musical performance, attests to the deep-seated connection between music and faith. The development of synagogal music, a vital component of Jewish religious life, emerged during the period of the Second Temple. The "nusach," a liturgical musical tradition specific to each Jewish community, evolved over centuries, incorporating local influences and adapting to changing historical contexts.

The Influence of Diaspora and Renewal:

The diaspora, the dispersion of Jews from their homeland, profoundly shaped the evolution of Jewish music. Jewish communities scattered across the globe assimilated elements of local musical traditions, blending their unique melodies and rhythms with the broader musical landscape. The "piyyut," a form of liturgical poetry set to music, flourished during the Middle Ages, expressing the hopes, fears, and aspirations of Jews navigating life in exile.

The Rise of Modern Jewish Music:

The 19th and 20th centuries witnessed a remarkable resurgence in Jewish musical creativity. The Zionist movement, fueled by a desire for national revival, saw the emergence of "Yiddishkeit" music, drawing inspiration from folk traditions and celebrating Jewish identity. Composed in the Yiddish language, this music resonated with Jews around the world, becoming a powerful symbol of their cultural heritage. The Hebrew language, revitalized through the Zionist movement, also gave rise to a new wave of Jewish musical expression, including classical composers who explored the rich sonic potential of Hebrew.

Contemporary Sounds and Global Connections:

In the 21st century, Jewish music continues to evolve, reflecting the changing face of Jewish life and embracing a diverse range of influences. From the fusion of traditional Jewish melodies with contemporary musical genres to the rise of independent Jewish artists exploring new sonic territories, Jewish music remains a vital and dynamic force. The internet and global communication have facilitated a surge in cross-cultural collaboration, connecting Jewish musicians across geographical boundaries and forging new artistic partnerships.

Beyond the Notes: The Power of Music in Jewish Life

Jewish music transcends the realm of entertainment; it serves as a powerful tool for transmitting values, celebrating tradition, and fostering community. The melodies of prayer and the rhythms of Jewish celebrations create a sense of belonging and unity, weaving together generations past and present. Jewish music has also played a significant role in addressing social and political issues, raising awareness about Jewish persecution and advocating for justice.

The Written Word: A Journey Through Jewish Literature

Jewish literature, spanning millennia, constitutes a remarkable repository of human experience, exploring themes of faith, identity, survival, and the complexities of human relationships. The written word has served as a cornerstone of Jewish cultural life, allowing for the transmission of history, the expression of personal experiences, and the contemplation of profound questions about faith, morality, and existence.

From the Hebrew Bible to Modern Fiction:

The Hebrew Bible, considered the foundational text of Judaism, serves as a literary masterpiece, encompassing a diverse array of genres, including narratives, poetry, law, and prophecy. These texts, filled with vibrant characters, intricate plots, and philosophical insights, have deeply shaped the Jewish worldview and provided a framework for understanding the divine and human interaction.

The Power of Rabbinic Literature:

The development of the Talmud, a vast collection of rabbinic commentary on Jewish law and tradition, marked a pivotal moment in Jewish literary history. The Talmud, a product of centuries of scholarly debate and interpretation, exemplifies the intellectual dynamism of Jewish culture and the enduring significance of textual study.

The Flourishing of Medieval Jewish Literature:

The Middle Ages witnessed a prolific period in Jewish literary production. Hebrew poetry, known for its intricate rhyme schemes and profound philosophical themes, flourished during this time. Philosophers like Maimonides and Judah Halevi engaged in intellectual discourse, exploring the nature of faith, the role of reason, and the relationship between Judaism and other cultures. The "haggadah," the text used during the Passover Seder, serves as a testament to the power of storytelling and the importance of transmitting Jewish tradition through narrative.

Modern and Contemporary Voices:

The 19th and 20th centuries saw the emergence of a diverse range of Jewish literary voices, grappling with the challenges of modernity, the impact of the Holocaust, and the search for Jewish identity in a changing world. Writers like Isaac Bashevis Singer, Sholem Aleichem, and Chaim Potok explored themes of displacement, cultural assimilation, and the enduring power of Jewish tradition in the face of adversity. Contemporary Jewish literature continues to explore the complexities of Jewish life, addressing issues of gender, sexuality, religion, and the intersection of Jewish identity with global concerns.

The Visual Language: Jewish Art Through the Ages

Jewish art, an intricate tapestry woven with religious symbolism, cultural expression, and artistic innovation, offers a unique window into Jewish history and identity. From ancient synagogues adorned with intricate mosaics to contemporary Jewish artists pushing the boundaries of artistic expression, Jewish art reflects the multifaceted nature of Jewish life and the enduring power of creativity.

Ancient and Medieval Roots:

Jewish art, influenced by the cultural contexts in which it flourished, often incorporated artistic styles and techniques from surrounding societies. The art of ancient Israel, characterized by a blend of Egyptian and Mesopotamian influences, can be seen in the impressive architectural remains of synagogues and other structures. Medieval Jewish art, shaped by the cultural landscapes of Europe and the Middle East, incorporated motifs drawn from Jewish tradition and the broader artistic trends of the time.

From Illuminated Manuscripts to Synagogal Art:

The creation of illuminated manuscripts, adorned with intricate illustrations and decorative elements, played a crucial role in the preservation and transmission of Jewish texts. These manuscripts, often commissioned by wealthy patrons, showcased the artistic skills of Jewish scribes and illuminated the importance of visual art in Jewish religious and cultural life. Synagogue art, drawing inspiration from Jewish tradition and local artistic styles, often featured decorative patterns, symbolic motifs, and representations of biblical stories. The iconic "Lion of Judah," a symbol of strength and sovereignty, frequently adorned synagogues, serving as a visible reminder of Jewish identity.

The Impact of Modernity:

The rise of modern Jewish art, mirroring the broader shifts in artistic expression, saw a move towards abstraction, experimentation, and the exploration of new forms and techniques. The Holocaust, a defining event in Jewish history, left an indelible mark on Jewish art, prompting artists to grapple with the trauma of persecution and the enduring resilience of Jewish identity.

Contemporary Jewish Art: A Diverse Landscape:

Contemporary Jewish art is a vibrant and diverse landscape, encompassing a wide range of styles, mediums, and perspectives.

Jewish artists today explore themes of faith, identity, social justice, and the complexities of the contemporary world, using their creative voices to engage in dialogue, challenge conventions, and inspire reflection. From abstract expressionism to installation art, from photography to performance art, contemporary Jewish art continues to push the boundaries of artistic expression and engage with the multifaceted dimensions of Jewish experience. These artistic expressions, born out of resilience, faith, and creativity, have not only reflected the Jewish experience but have also shaped its trajectory, providing a platform for dialogue, reflection, and innovation. As we continue to explore the rich tapestry of Jewish culture, we recognize the enduring power of these artistic expressions to connect us to our past, inspire us in the present, and guide us towards a future filled with artistic exploration and cultural vibrancy.

Engaging with Contemporary Expressions

The Language of Change: Reflecting and Shaping the Modern World

Contemporary expressions are not mere fads; they are vibrant expressions of our collective experience. They reflect the ever-changing dynamics of our society, mirroring the concerns, aspirations, and innovations that define our present. From the emergence of social media and its influence on online discourse to the growing awareness of social justice issues, contemporary language reflects the ebb and flow of our collective consciousness. Consider the rise of terms like "cancel culture" or "woke. " These phrases, while often debated, encapsulate the anxieties and aspirations of a generation grappling with societal norms and power structures. They act as signposts, indicating the evolving nature of our values and priorities.

This reflection goes beyond simply mirroring current events. Contemporary expressions possess the power to shape our understanding of the world around us. By providing new ways to frame experiences, they can alter our perception of social dynamics, cultural trends, and even personal identities. The ubiquitous use of emojis, for instance, has reshaped the landscape of digital communication. These tiny icons, imbued with emotional nuance, offer a visual language that transcends linguistic barriers and fosters new avenues for expression. Their adoption highlights the growing need for brevity and visual storytelling in a fast-paced digital world.

However, the influence of contemporary expressions extends beyond mere communication. They can also spark social movements and redefine cultural landscapes. The rise of "hashtag activism" demonstrates the power of language to galvanize collective action. Hashtags, born from the digital realm, have become potent symbols of social change, uniting people around shared causes and amplifying marginalized voices. They have transformed online spaces into platforms for social activism, blurring the lines between virtual and physical realms.

Navigating the Labyrinth of Contemporary Language: A Journey of Understanding

Engaging with contemporary expressions is not simply a matter of adopting the latest slang or mastering the art of online communication. It requires a deeper understanding of the forces at play, the contexts that birth these expressions, and their potential impact on our lives. This understanding is crucial for navigating the ever-shifting landscape of language and its profound implications for social interaction, identity formation, and cultural understanding.

One vital aspect of engaging with contemporary expressions is recognizing their diversity. They are not monolithic; they reflect the myriad voices, perspectives, and experiences that make up our society. This diversity is reflected in the evolving nature of language itself, with dialects, regionalisms, and cultural specificities contributing to a vibrant tapestry of expression. Engaging with this diversity requires a willingness to be open-minded, accepting of difference, and respectful of the unique language practices of various communities.

Furthermore, engaging with contemporary expressions necessitates a critical lens. While these expressions can offer valuable insights into our world, they are not inherently objective. They are shaped by power dynamics, social biases, and cultural assumptions. To truly understand their meaning and impact, it is essential to analyze the contexts in which they are used, the ideologies they reflect, and the potential consequences of their adoption.

Bridging the Generational Gap: The Power of Dialogue and Empathy

Engaging with contemporary expressions also involves acknowledging the potential for generational divides. Older generations might struggle to understand the nuances of language used by younger generations, and vice versa. This disconnect can lead to misunderstandings, communication breakdowns, and even social friction. Bridging this gap requires empathy, a willingness to learn from each other, and a commitment to open dialogue.

Engaging in dialogue is essential to bridge this gap. It allows individuals from different generations to share their perspectives, explain their interpretations, and learn from each other's experiences. This dialogue can help to dismantle stereotypes, foster understanding, and create a more inclusive and harmonious society. It requires active listening, a willingness to ask questions, and a genuine desire to understand the perspectives of others.

Empathy plays a crucial role in navigating the complexities of contemporary expressions. By putting ourselves in the shoes of those using a particular language, we can gain a deeper appreciation for its significance and its connection to their experiences. Empathy allows us to see the world through different lenses, to recognize the underlying emotions and motivations behind expressions, and to foster a sense of connection and understanding.

Looking Ahead: The Future of Language and the Importance of Engagement

Engaging with contemporary expressions is not a passive activity; it is an ongoing process of learning, adaptation, and reflection. As our world continues to evolve, so too will the language we use to understand and communicate within it. The challenge lies in embracing this dynamism, recognizing the power of language, and using it to foster understanding, empathy, and social progress.

By embracing a spirit of open-mindedness, critical thinking, and empathetic dialogue, we can navigate the evolving landscape of language and utilize its power for positive change. This engagement is not merely about keeping up with the latest trends; it is about fostering a deeper understanding of ourselves, our society, and the world around us.

The Power of Language in the Digital Age: A New Frontier for Communication and Expression

In the digital age, the importance of engaging with contemporary expressions takes on an even more profound significance. Online spaces, from social media platforms to online forums and digital communities, have become central to communication, information sharing, and cultural interaction. The language used within these spaces, often shaped by the constraints and possibilities of digital platforms, plays a vital role in shaping our perceptions of the world and our interactions with others.

Understanding the nuances of digital language is essential for navigating these spaces effectively. This involves recognizing the unique characteristics of online communication, such as the use of emoticons, abbreviations, and online slang. It also requires an understanding of how online platforms influence the way we communicate, from the brevity encouraged by Twitter's character limits to the visual storytelling fostered by platforms like Instagram.

Engaging with contemporary expressions in the digital age also requires critical thinking about the role of online algorithms and the impact of social media on public discourse. These algorithms, designed to curate our online experiences, can inadvertently reinforce existing biases, create echo chambers, and contribute to the spread of misinformation. Recognizing these dynamics is crucial for navigating the digital landscape with discernment and engaging in responsible online interactions.

Cultivating Language Awareness: The Foundation for Effective Communication and Understanding

Engaging with contemporary expressions goes beyond simply understanding the latest slang or mastering the intricacies of digital platforms. It is about cultivating a broader awareness of language itself, recognizing its power and influence in shaping our thoughts, beliefs, and actions. This awareness forms the foundation for effective communication, fostering understanding, and contributing to a more inclusive and equitable society.

Here are some key elements of cultivating language awareness:

Understanding the evolution of language: Recognizing that language is a living entity, constantly evolving to reflect the changing realities of our world, is crucial. This involves appreciating the historical context of language, exploring the origins of words and expressions, and understanding how language has adapted to new technologies and social shifts.

Recognizing the power of language: Language is not merely a tool for conveying information; it is a potent force that shapes our perceptions, influences our behaviors, and constructs our realities. By recognizing this power, we can become more conscious of the language we use and the impact it has on ourselves and others.

Developing a critical lens: Cultivating a critical lens allows us to examine language objectively, recognizing its potential biases, exploring the power dynamics that underlie its use, and identifying the assumptions embedded within its structures. This critical lens empowers us to challenge harmful stereotypes, question dominant narratives, and advocate for more equitable and just forms of communication.

Promoting inclusive language: Striving to use language that is inclusive, respectful, and representative of diverse experiences is crucial for building bridges and fostering understanding. This involves being mindful of the language we use, challenging harmful stereotypes, and advocating for language that values diversity and inclusivity.

Engaging with Contemporary Expressions: A Collective Responsibility

Engaging with contemporary expressions is not a solitary pursuit; it is a collective responsibility. It requires a willingness to learn from each other, to challenge our own biases, and to work together to create a more inclusive and understanding society. It involves actively listening to diverse voices, engaging in thoughtful dialogue, and embracing the dynamic nature of language as a force for positive change.

In a world constantly in flux, embracing the evolving language around us is not just about keeping up with the latest trends, but about fostering deeper understanding and empathy. By engaging with contemporary expressions, we can navigate the complexities of communication, challenge assumptions, and contribute to a more just and equitable world for all.

Finding Inspiration and Understanding

The Genesis of Inspiration:

Inspiration often emerges from the most unexpected corners of our lives. It can be sparked by a chance encounter, a fleeting glimpse of beauty, a stirring melody, or the profound words of a wise teacher. The world is a tapestry woven with countless threads of inspiration, waiting to be unraveled. To access these hidden treasures, we must cultivate an open mind and a receptive heart.

Cultivating a Receptive Mind:

The first step on this journey of discovery is to embrace a spirit of openness. We must learn to shed preconceived notions and biases, allowing ourselves to be swept away by the currents of new ideas and experiences. Curiosity, that insatiable thirst for knowledge, becomes our compass. We must ask questions, challenge assumptions, and delve into the unknown with an unquenchable thirst for understanding.

The Role of Exploration:

Exploration is the fuel that ignites inspiration. It is the act of venturing beyond the familiar, of stepping into the unknown and embracing the uncertainties that lie ahead. Whether it's exploring a new city, delving into a foreign culture, or immersing ourselves in a new field of study, exploration expands our horizons and exposes us to fresh perspectives.

Finding Inspiration in the Everyday:

Inspiration isn't confined to grand gestures or monumental events. It can be found in the mundane, the ordinary, the everyday. The gentle rustle of leaves, the vibrant colors of a sunset, the laughter of children, the quiet moments of introspection – all these seemingly insignificant experiences hold the potential to ignite the spark of inspiration.

The Power of Observation:

Sharp observation is a key to unlocking inspiration. It involves paying close attention to the details of our surroundings, noticing the subtle nuances of human behavior, and appreciating the beauty in the ordinary. By honing our observational skills, we can cultivate a deeper understanding of the world and tap into the wellspring of inspiration that lies within it.

The Importance of Immersion:

Immersion is the act of diving headfirst into a particular subject, allowing ourselves to be fully absorbed in its intricacies. Whether it's a new hobby, a favorite book, or a passion project, immersion allows us to explore a subject in depth, uncovering its hidden depths and gaining a deeper understanding of its nuances.

The Art of Reflection:

Reflection is a crucial component of the inspiration-understanding journey. It allows us to process our experiences, contemplate their meaning, and connect the dots that weave together the tapestry of our understanding. Through introspection, we can cultivate a deeper sense of self-awareness and glean valuable insights that can guide our future endeavors.

The Role of Mentors and Guides:

Throughout our journey of discovery, we encounter individuals who serve as mentors and guides. They are the beacons of light who illuminate our path, offering wisdom, encouragement, and a fresh perspective. These individuals can be teachers, colleagues, friends, or family members – anyone who inspires us to grow and evolve.

The Impact of Collaboration:

Collaboration is a powerful catalyst for both inspiration and understanding. By working together with others, we can tap into a collective wisdom and gain access to perspectives that we might not have considered on our own. Collaboration fosters creativity, stimulates innovation, and accelerates the process of discovery.

The Role of Failure:

Failure, often viewed as a setback, is an integral part of the learning process. It is through our mistakes that we gain valuable insights, refine our strategies, and develop resilience. By embracing failure as an opportunity for growth, we can turn setbacks into stepping stones on our path to success.

The Importance of Perseverance:

The journey to inspiration and understanding is not always straightforward. There will be challenges, obstacles, and moments of doubt. Perseverance is the key to navigating these choppy waters. It is the unwavering commitment to our goals, the ability to bounce back from setbacks, and the determination to keep moving forward despite the odds.

The Power of Imagination:

Imagination is the crucible in which inspiration is forged. It allows us to transcend the limitations of reality, to envision new possibilities, and to explore the uncharted territories of the mind. Through imagination, we can break free from the constraints of convention and create something truly extraordinary.

The Quest for Understanding:

Understanding is the product of diligent inquiry, persistent exploration, and a willingness to challenge our assumptions. It is the accumulation of knowledge, the weaving together of facts and insights, and the development of a comprehensive framework for interpreting the world around us.

The Value of Knowledge:

Knowledge is the cornerstone of understanding. It provides the foundation upon which we build our intellectual edifice, equipping us with the tools and insights needed to navigate the complexities of life. The pursuit of knowledge is an ongoing journey, a constant quest to expand our horizons and deepen our understanding of the world.

The Role of Critical Thinking:

Critical thinking is the engine that drives understanding. It is the ability to analyze information, evaluate evidence, and form well-reasoned conclusions. Critical thinking empowers us to sift through the clutter of information, discern truth from fiction, and formulate informed opinions.

The Importance of Curiosity:

Curiosity is the spark that ignites the flame of understanding. It is the insatiable thirst for knowledge, the drive to explore the unknown, and the desire to make sense of the world around us. By cultivating a spirit of curiosity, we can unlock the door to countless insights and discoveries.

The Pursuit of Wisdom:

Wisdom is the ultimate goal of the journey of understanding. It is the culmination of knowledge, experience, and insight, a tapestry woven together with threads of intellectual growth and personal reflection. Wisdom guides our decisions, informs our actions, and shapes our understanding of the world.

The Interplay of Inspiration and Understanding:

Inspiration and understanding are inextricably intertwined. Inspiration ignites the spark of creativity, while understanding provides the framework for giving it shape and purpose. Together, they propel us forward on a journey of discovery, enriching our lives with new insights, innovative ideas, and a deeper appreciation for the world around us.

The Impact of Inspiration and Understanding:

Inspiration and understanding have the power to transform individuals and shape the course of history. They fuel innovation, drive progress, and inspire us to strive for a better world. By nurturing these essential forces, we unlock our potential and contribute to the betterment of society.

The Journey Continues:

This journey of exploration, discovery, and understanding is a lifelong endeavor. It is a path paved with challenges and rewards, a tapestry woven with threads of inspiration and insight. As we continue to traverse this path, we must remember to embrace curiosity, foster critical thinking, and cultivate a spirit of lifelong learning. For it is through this ongoing pursuit of inspiration and understanding that we truly unlock our potential and make a meaningful impact on the world.

Celebrating the Richness of Jewish Culture

The foundation of Jewish culture rests firmly on the Torah, the foundational text of Judaism, which encompasses not only religious law but also a rich tapestry of stories, poetry, and ethical teachings.

This foundation has shaped the Jewish worldview, fostering a deep connection to history, a commitment to ethical living, and a belief in the importance of education and intellectual exploration. Through the lens of the Torah, Jews have navigated the complexities of life, grappling with questions of morality, justice, and the meaning of existence. The ongoing exploration and interpretation of these texts, through centuries of commentary and debate, has contributed to the vibrancy and dynamism of Jewish thought.

Beyond the religious sphere, Jewish culture blossoms in the realm of social customs and traditions. From the warmth of Shabbat meals, where families gather to share stories and connect, to the joyous celebration of holidays like Passover and Hanukkah, these rituals weave a thread of continuity through time, uniting generations and fostering a sense of shared identity. The importance of community is deeply ingrained in Jewish culture, manifested in the strong bonds between individuals, families, and synagogues. These social structures serve as anchors of support, offering a sense of belonging and fostering a shared sense of purpose.

Jewish culture has also made profound contributions to the world of art and literature. From the evocative poetry of Yehuda HaLevi to the philosophical writings of Maimonides, Jewish thinkers and artists have enriched the global intellectual landscape. The tradition of storytelling, deeply embedded in the Jewish narrative, has found expression in folk tales, fables, and literary works that have captured the imagination of generations. Music, another vital element of Jewish culture, echoes the joys and sorrows of life, resonating with the human experience across cultures. The melodies of klezmer music, the spiritual depths of liturgical music, and the innovative compositions of contemporary Jewish artists all showcase the dynamism and diversity of Jewish musical expression.

One of the most striking aspects of Jewish culture is its remarkable capacity for adaptation and resilience. Through centuries of displacement and persecution, Jewish communities have adapted and thrived in diverse geographical locations, each leaving its unique mark on the global cultural landscape. From the vibrant, cosmopolitan culture of pre-war Eastern Europe to the pioneering spirit of early American Jewish communities, each diaspora has contributed to the richness and complexity of Jewish culture. This ability to adapt and reinvent itself, while maintaining core values and traditions, is a testament to the enduring strength of Jewish identity.

Celebrating the richness of Jewish culture is not merely an exercise in nostalgia; it is an act of engagement and empowerment. It involves understanding the historical context of Jewish traditions, recognizing the challenges and triumphs that shaped its evolution, and appreciating the diverse expressions of Jewish life across the globe. It also means engaging with the ongoing dialogue within Jewish communities, embracing the dynamism and evolution of Jewish thought and practice.

In today's world, marked by increasing globalization and cultural exchange, celebrating the richness of Jewish culture is more important than ever. It serves as a bridge between different communities, fostering understanding and appreciation for the diversity of human experience. It also provides a valuable perspective on the complexities of identity and belonging, reminding us that our cultural heritage is not static but constantly evolving.

To celebrate the richness of Jewish culture is to embrace its complexities, to appreciate its diversity, and to recognize its enduring power. It is to acknowledge the contributions of Jewish thinkers, artists, and communities throughout history, and to recognize the vital role that Jewish culture plays in shaping the world we live in. It is a celebration of resilience, creativity, and a shared legacy of faith, tradition, and a profound connection to the human experience.

Exploring the Tapestry: A Closer Look at Diverse Expressions of Jewish Culture

1. The World of Jewish Literature: From Ancient Texts to Modern Narratives

Jewish literature, a treasure trove of stories, poems, essays, and philosophical treatises, offers a unique window into the Jewish experience. Its scope encompasses centuries of writing, spanning diverse genres and styles, from the ancient Hebrew Bible to contemporary novels and plays.

a. The Hebrew Bible: A Foundation of Stories and Teachings

At the heart of Jewish literature lies the Hebrew Bible, a collection of sacred texts that holds profound significance for Jews and Christians alike. Its stories, from the creation narrative to the exodus from Egypt, provide a framework for understanding Jewish history, beliefs, and values. The Bible is not merely a collection of stories but also a source of ethical teachings, legal codes, and poetic expressions.

b. The Talmud: A Monument to Legal and Ethical Discourse

Building on the foundation of the Bible, the Talmud emerged as a monumental work of Jewish legal and ethical discourse. This collection of rabbinic discussions and interpretations of Jewish law offers insights into the intricacies of Jewish life, ethical dilemmas, and the ongoing evolution of Jewish tradition. Its complex structure and rich language reflect the intellectual vigor and adaptability of Jewish thought.

c. Medieval Jewish Philosophy: Exploring the Intersection of Faith and Reason

Medieval Jewish thinkers, like Maimonides, Judah Halevi, and Moses ben Nachman, engaged in profound philosophical explorations, grappling with the complexities of faith, reason, and the nature of

God. Their writings, filled with intellectual rigor and spiritual depth, reflect the ongoing dialogue between Jewish tradition and the broader intellectual currents of the time.

d. Modern Jewish Literature: Exploring Identity, Trauma, and the Human Condition

Modern Jewish literature, born out of the tumultuous events of the 20th century, explores themes of identity, trauma, and the human condition. Writers like Isaac Bashevis Singer, Elie Wiesel, and Chaim Potok offer powerful and moving narratives that reflect the struggles and triumphs of Jewish individuals and communities in the face of persecution, displacement, and the search for meaning in a changing world.

2. The Music of Jewish Culture: From Sacred Melodies to Modern Expressions

Jewish music, diverse and vibrant, encompasses a wide spectrum of styles, from traditional liturgical melodies to contemporary compositions. These melodies reflect the joys and sorrows, the triumphs and challenges, of the Jewish experience.

a. Liturgical Music: The Heart of Jewish Prayer and Ritual

Liturgical music, the heart of Jewish prayer and ritual, spans centuries of tradition, from ancient synagogue melodies to the hymns and chants of the Hasidic movement. The use of Hebrew, the language of prayer, imbues these melodies with a sense of spirituality and tradition.

b. Klezmer Music: The Soul of Jewish Folk Culture

Klezmer music, a lively and energetic folk tradition, originated in Eastern Europe and has become a vital part of Jewish culture worldwide. Its lively melodies, often played on instruments like the clarinet, violin, and accordion, express the joy, exuberance, and sometimes melancholy of Jewish life.

c. Modern Jewish Music: Exploring New Sounds and Themes

Contemporary Jewish composers and performers continue to innovate, pushing the boundaries of traditional styles and exploring new themes. From the folk-infused melodies of the Klezmatics to the experimental compositions of contemporary classical composers, modern Jewish music reflects the ever-evolving landscape of Jewish creativity.

3. The Visual Arts of Jewish Culture: From Ancient Mosaics to Modern Masterpieces

The visual arts have been an integral part of Jewish culture for millennia, with Jewish artists contributing to the global landscape of artistic expression.

a. Ancient Jewish Art: Echoes of Faith and Tradition

Ancient Jewish art, dating back to the Roman period, often features motifs drawn from the Hebrew Bible and Jewish tradition. From the intricate mosaics of synagogues in Galilee to the sculptures and paintings of the ancient world, these artworks provide insights into the religious beliefs and cultural practices of early Jewish communities.

b. Medieval Jewish Art: A Blend of Religious and Secular Themes

Medieval Jewish art, influenced by the surrounding cultures, combined religious themes with secular motifs, reflecting the integration of Jewish communities into wider society. From illuminated manuscripts to synagogue decorations, these artworks showcase the unique artistic sensibilities of Jewish artists during this period.

c. Modern Jewish Art: Exploring Identity, History, and the Human Condition

Modern Jewish artists, grappling with the complexities of identity and history, have produced a wide range of works that reflect the impact of 20th-century events on the Jewish experience. From the Expressionistic works of Chaim Soutine to the social realism of Mark Rothko, these artists explored themes of displacement, trauma, and the search for meaning in a changing world.

4. The Culinary Delights of Jewish Culture: A Tapestry of Flavors and Traditions

Jewish cuisine, a vibrant tapestry of flavors and traditions, reflects the diverse geographical locations and cultural influences that have shaped Jewish communities throughout history.

a. Traditional Jewish Dishes: A Legacy of Taste and Tradition

From the hearty stews and savory pastries of Eastern Europe to the fragrant spices and flavorful dishes of the Middle East, traditional Jewish dishes have been passed down through generations, embodying the warmth and comfort of home.

b. Jewish Food Around the World: A Fusion of Flavors and Influences

Jewish cuisine is not static but constantly evolving, as Jewish communities have adapted to new environments and embraced local culinary influences. From the bagels and lox of New York City to the falafel and hummus of Israel, Jewish food around the world is a testament to the adaptability and creativity of Jewish culture.

c. The Meaning of Food in Jewish Culture: Sharing, Celebration, and Community

In Jewish culture, food is more than sustenance; it is a means of sharing, celebration, and building community. The Shabbat meal, a weekly ritual of gathering and feasting, symbolizes the importance of family and community. The festive meals of holidays like Passover and Hanukkah reinforce the sense of togetherness and tradition that is central to Jewish life.

5. The Importance of Learning and Education in Jewish Culture

Learning and education have always held a central place in Jewish culture, with a strong emphasis on intellectual exploration and the pursuit of knowledge.

a. The Value of Textual Study and Debate

From the earliest days of rabbinic Judaism, textual study and debate have been cherished traditions, fostering a critical approach to learning and a commitment to the pursuit of knowledge.

b. The Role of Yeshivas and Schools in Jewish Education

Yeshivas, religious schools where students delve into Jewish texts and traditions, have played a vital role in Jewish education for centuries. Jewish schools, both religious and secular, continue to provide a strong foundation for Jewish identity and values.

c. The Pursuit of Knowledge and its Relevance to Modern Life

The emphasis on learning in Jewish culture is not limited to religious texts. Jewish communities have produced scholars and intellectuals who have made significant contributions to fields like science, philosophy, literature, and the arts. The pursuit of knowledge, a core value of Jewish culture, remains relevant in today's world, inspiring a commitment to lifelong learning and intellectual exploration.

6. The Resilience of Jewish Culture: A Legacy of Adaptation and

Survival

Jewish culture has endured through centuries of displacement, persecution, and change, a testament to its remarkable resilience and adaptability.

a. The Diaspora: A Journey of Adaptability and Continuity

The Jewish diaspora, the scattering of Jewish communities across the globe, has been a defining factor in the evolution of Jewish culture. While facing challenges, Jewish communities have adapted to new environments, blending with local cultures while preserving their own traditions.

b. The Holocaust: A Trauma and a Challenge

The Holocaust, the systematic genocide of European Jewry during World War II, was a defining moment in Jewish history, a tragedy that profoundly impacted Jewish culture and identity. Despite the immense loss and trauma, Jewish communities have shown remarkable resilience, rebuilding their lives and preserving their heritage.

c. The Future of Jewish Culture: A Legacy of Hope and Innovation

Jewish culture, enriched by its history, continues to adapt and evolve in the 21st century. New expressions of Jewish identity, art, and thought emerge, reflecting the ongoing dialogue between tradition and modernity. The future of Jewish culture holds the promise of continued creativity, resilience, and the celebration of its enduring legacy.

Celebrating the Richness of Jewish Culture: A Call to Action

Celebrating the richness of Jewish culture is not just a passive act of appreciation; it is a call to action, a commitment to understanding, preserving, and fostering this vibrant legacy.

a. Engaging with Jewish Culture Through Exploration and Education

Understanding Jewish culture begins with exploration, a willingness to engage with its history, traditions, and diverse expressions. Supporting Jewish education, museums, and cultural institutions is a vital step in ensuring that future generations can access and learn from this rich legacy.

b. Fostering Interfaith Dialogue and Understanding

Celebrating Jewish culture also involves building bridges between Jewish communities and other faiths and cultures. Promoting interfaith dialogue and understanding, challenging stereotypes, and fostering a culture of respect and inclusivity are crucial steps in promoting a more just and equitable world.

c. Embracing Jewish Creativity and Innovation

Jewish culture thrives on creativity and innovation. Supporting Jewish artists, musicians, writers, and thinkers, and encouraging new expressions of Jewish identity and art, is essential to ensuring the continued vibrancy of Jewish culture.

Conclusion

Celebrating the richness of Jewish culture is an act of respect, appreciation, and commitment. It is a recognition of the enduring impact of Jewish thought, art, and tradition on the world, and a commitment to preserving and fostering this vital legacy for future generations. By embracing the diversity, resilience, and dynamism of Jewish culture, we can contribute to a world that is more understanding, inclusive, and enriched by the vibrant tapestry of human experience.

Chapter 12: Facing Challenges and Questions

Addressing Common Doubts and Concerns

This exploration aims to address common doubts and concerns that arise in various aspects of life, providing a framework for navigating these uncertainties with clarity and resilience. We will delve into the psychological underpinnings of doubt and explore the different types of concerns that individuals encounter. This journey will equip you with the tools to acknowledge your doubts, analyze your concerns, and ultimately, find the answers that will guide you towards a more confident and fulfilling life.

The Nature of Doubt:

Doubt, in its purest form, is a healthy cognitive process. It represents a critical and inquisitive mind, questioning existing assumptions and seeking deeper understanding. It is the driving force behind scientific inquiry, artistic innovation, and personal growth. However, when left unchecked, doubt can morph into crippling self-doubt, hindering progress and perpetuating a cycle of uncertainty.

Understanding the nature of doubt requires examining its various facets:

1. Epistemological Doubt: This type of doubt concerns the validity of knowledge and the reliability of information. It explores the limits of human understanding and the inherent subjectivity of our perceptions. Questions like "How do we know what we know. " and

"Is there an objective reality. " fall under this category.

2. Existential Doubt: This existential questioning delves into the fundamental nature of existence and our place in the universe. It grapples with questions about life's purpose, the meaning of suffering, and the inevitability of death.

3. Moral Doubt: This type of doubt revolves around ethical dilemmas and the complexities of right and wrong. It challenges our values and moral compass, forcing us to confront difficult choices and grapple with conflicting perspectives.

4. Personal Doubt: This internal questioning focuses on our own abilities, worth, and potential. It manifests in self-doubt, insecurity, and feelings of inadequacy. It can stem from past experiences, societal expectations, or internalized beliefs.

5. Social Doubt: This type of doubt arises from questioning societal norms, established hierarchies, and the power dynamics within groups. It challenges conventional wisdom and encourages critical thinking about social structures and their impact on individuals.

While all these types of doubt can be valuable in prompting self-reflection and growth, it is crucial to differentiate between healthy skepticism and debilitating self-doubt.

The Shadow Side of Doubt:

When doubt lingers, intensifies, and takes root in our psyche, it can transform into a debilitating force, hindering our ability to make decisions, pursue goals, and experience joy. This negative manifestation of doubt often stems from:

1. Fear of Failure: This fear can paralyze us, preventing us from taking risks and pursuing opportunities. We may become overly cautious, avoiding situations where we might potentially experience

disappointment or judgment.

2. Perfectionism: The pursuit of flawless outcomes can lead to endless self-criticism and procrastination. It can trap us in a cycle of analyzing every detail, questioning our every move, and ultimately hindering our progress.

3. Lack of Confidence: Self-doubt can erode our confidence in our abilities, leading to feelings of inadequacy and helplessness. We may underestimate our strengths and overestimate our weaknesses, holding ourselves back from reaching our full potential.

4. Negative Self-Talk: Internalizing negative thoughts and beliefs about ourselves can create a self-fulfilling prophecy. This constant barrage of self-criticism and negativity can amplify feelings of doubt and make it difficult to see ourselves in a positive light.

5. Past Experiences: Negative experiences, whether personal or societal, can leave deep scars that fuel doubt and fear. Past failures, rejections, or betrayals can shape our perception of the world and ourselves, leading to a reluctance to trust and an unwillingness to take risks.

Addressing Doubt:

The journey to overcome debilitating doubt requires self-awareness, self-compassion, and a willingness to challenge our negative thought patterns. Here are some strategies to navigate doubt and reclaim your confidence:

1. Acknowledge and Accept Doubt: The first step to addressing doubt is acknowledging its presence. Don't try to suppress or deny it. Accept that doubt is a natural part of the human experience, and allow yourself to feel it without judgment.

2. Challenge Negative Thoughts: Become aware of your negative

self-talk and actively challenge those thoughts. Ask yourself: "Is this thought based on evidence, or is it just a fear. " "Would I say this to a friend. " Replace negative thoughts with more realistic and positive affirmations.

3. Focus on Your Strengths: Instead of dwelling on your weaknesses, focus on your strengths and accomplishments. Recognize your talents, skills, and past successes. Remind yourself of your resilience and ability to overcome challenges.

4. Practice Mindfulness: Mindfulness exercises can help you become more aware of your thoughts and emotions, allowing you to observe them without judgment. This practice can help you detach from negative thought patterns and create space for a more positive perspective.

5. Seek Support: Don't hesitate to reach out for support from friends, family, or professionals. Talking to trusted individuals about your doubts can help you gain a fresh perspective and feel less alone in your struggles.

6. Take Small Steps: Breaking down large goals into smaller, manageable steps can help reduce feelings of overwhelm and increase your confidence. Focus on making small progress every day, celebrating your successes along the way.

7. Cultivate Gratitude: Practice gratitude for the positive aspects of your life, even in the face of challenges. Focusing on what you are grateful for can shift your perspective, reducing negativity and fostering a sense of optimism.

Concerns: Navigating the Landscape of Worries

Concerns, unlike doubts, often stem from specific events or situations that evoke worry and anxiety. They can range from everyday anxieties about deadlines and finances to more profound concerns about health, relationships, or the future. Understanding the nature and origins of these concerns is crucial for effectively managing them.

Types of Concerns:

1. Practical Concerns: These concerns relate to tangible issues that require action and problem-solving. Examples include concerns about finances, deadlines, work projects, or household tasks.

2. Relational Concerns: These concerns relate to our relationships with others, including concerns about romantic partners, family members, friends, or colleagues. They can stem from conflicts, misunderstandings, or feelings of disconnection.

3. Health Concerns: Worries about physical or mental health are common. They can arise from personal experiences, family history, or media exposure to health issues.

4. Existential Concerns: These concerns delve into the big questions of life, death, and the meaning of existence. They can manifest as anxieties about the future, fears of the unknown, or a sense of existential angst.

5. Social Concerns: Worries about societal issues, such as climate change, political instability, or social injustice, can deeply impact individuals' well-being.

Addressing Concerns:

Navigating concerns requires a multifaceted approach that involves both emotional regulation and practical problem-solving. Here are some strategies to effectively address your concerns:

1. Identify and Define Your Concerns: The first step is to clearly define the source of your worry. What specific event, situation, or

thought is triggering your anxiety. The more specific you can be, the easier it will be to address the concern effectively.

2. Assess the Reality of Your Concerns: Once you have identified the source of your concern, assess its realistic likelihood and potential impact. Is this a genuine threat, or is it an exaggerated worry fueled by fear or uncertainty. Challenge your negative thought patterns and assess the evidence supporting your concern.

3. Develop a Plan of Action: If your concern stems from a practical issue, develop a plan of action to address it. Break down the problem into smaller steps, identify resources, and take action to resolve the situation.

4. Seek Support and Guidance: Don't hesitate to seek support from friends, family, or professionals. Sharing your concerns with trusted individuals can provide a sense of relief and perspective. Consider seeking professional help from a therapist or counselor if your worries are overwhelming or interfering with your daily life.

5. Practice Relaxation Techniques: Stress and anxiety can exacerbate concerns. Practice relaxation techniques such as deep breathing, meditation, or yoga to manage stress and calm your nervous system.

6. Focus on What You Can Control: It's important to acknowledge that you cannot control everything in life. Focus your energy on the things you can influence and let go of the things that are beyond your control.

7. Cultivate a Sense of Perspective: Remember that challenges are a part of life. Try to see your concerns within a broader context, remembering that you have faced difficult situations before and emerged stronger. By acknowledging our doubts, challenging negative thought patterns, and developing effective strategies for managing concerns, we can navigate uncertainty with greater clarity,

resilience, and confidence. Remember that doubt and concern are not weaknesses, but rather opportunities for growth and personal transformation. Embracing them with courage and curiosity can lead to a more fulfilling and meaningful life.

Navigating Difficult Life Experiences

This journey of navigating difficult life experiences is a multifaceted one, requiring a blend of emotional intelligence, cognitive skills, and a supportive network. We must first acknowledge that experiencing adversity is a natural part of human existence. No one is immune to the storms that life throws our way. Instead of fearing or avoiding these challenges, we need to understand them as opportunities for learning and growth. This shift in perspective is crucial for fostering resilience, a fundamental pillar in navigating difficult times.

Resilience is not about being impervious to pain or hardship. It is about the ability to adapt, bounce back, and learn from difficult experiences. It is the strength to rise again after falling, to pick up the pieces, and to move forward with renewed purpose. This resilience is cultivated through various strategies, both internal and external. Internally, we develop resilience by nurturing self-awareness, fostering emotional regulation, and cultivating positive coping mechanisms. This involves acknowledging and understanding our emotions, learning to manage them effectively, and finding healthy ways to deal with stress and distress.

External support is equally vital in navigating difficult life experiences. Building strong relationships, seeking professional guidance, and engaging in meaningful activities provide external resources that bolster our resilience. Our social support network acts as a buffer against adversity, offering encouragement, practical assistance, and a sense of belonging. Professional help, such as therapy or counseling, provides a safe space to process difficult emotions, develop coping strategies, and gain valuable insights.

Engaging in meaningful activities, whether it be volunteering, pursuing hobbies, or connecting with nature, provides a sense of purpose and belonging, fostering a positive outlook and promoting overall well-being.

The process of navigating difficult life experiences is not linear. There will be setbacks, moments of despair, and times when we feel overwhelmed. It is essential to acknowledge and accept these feelings without judgment. Self-compassion is a crucial component of navigating adversity. Treat yourself with the same kindness and understanding you would offer a friend going through a difficult time. Recognize that you are doing the best you can, given the circumstances. Allow yourself to feel the pain, process the emotions, and gradually work towards healing and growth.

Navigating difficult life experiences is not simply about overcoming adversity; it is about transforming ourselves in the process. These challenges, when faced with courage and resilience, have the power to unveil hidden strengths, redefine our values, and deepen our understanding of ourselves. We emerge from these experiences not only stronger but also wiser, more compassionate, and more equipped to face future challenges.

Beyond the Immediate: Building a Foundation for Lasting Growth

While addressing the immediate challenges is crucial, it is equally important to focus on building a foundation for lasting growth. This involves developing a mindset of continuous learning and growth, fostering self-care practices, and nurturing a sense of purpose and meaning in life.

1. Embracing a Growth Mindset:

A growth mindset, championed by psychologist Carol Dweck, is the belief that our abilities can be developed through dedication and effort. It contrasts with a fixed mindset, which sees abilities as innate and unchangeable. Embracing a growth mindset empowers us to view challenges as opportunities for learning and development. It encourages us to embrace mistakes as stepping stones on the path to growth, fostering a sense of agency and resilience.

2. Prioritizing Self-Care:

Self-care is not a luxury but a necessity, particularly when navigating difficult life experiences. It involves taking deliberate actions to protect and nurture our physical, mental, and emotional well-being. This includes getting enough sleep, eating nutritious food, engaging in regular physical activity, and practicing mindfulness or relaxation techniques. By prioritizing self-care, we replenish our resources, enhance our ability to cope, and foster a greater sense of balance and well-being.

3. Finding Meaning and Purpose:

One of the most powerful tools for navigating difficult life experiences is finding meaning and purpose in our lives. This can involve connecting with our values, exploring our passions, contributing to something larger than ourselves, or simply appreciating the beauty and wonder of the world around us. When we have a sense of purpose, we feel more connected, motivated, and resilient in the face of adversity.

4. Cultivating Gratitude:

Gratitude, the practice of appreciating the good things in our lives, has been shown to have a profound impact on our well-being. It shifts our focus from what is lacking to what is present, fostering a more positive outlook and promoting resilience. Cultivating gratitude can involve keeping a gratitude journal, expressing appreciation to others, or simply taking time to reflect on the blessings in our lives.

5. Building a Strong Support Network:

The importance of a strong social support network cannot be overstated, especially when navigating difficult life experiences. This network can provide emotional support, practical assistance, and a sense of belonging. It can involve family, friends, colleagues, mentors, or support groups. Building and nurturing these connections is crucial for maintaining our well-being and fostering resilience.

6. Seeking Professional Guidance:

When navigating particularly difficult life experiences, it can be beneficial to seek professional guidance. Therapists, counselors, or other mental health professionals can provide a safe and confidential space to process emotions, develop coping strategies, and gain valuable insights. Professional guidance can be particularly helpful for individuals experiencing trauma, grief, or chronic stress.

7. Engaging in Meaningful Activities:

Engaging in activities that bring us joy, purpose, and a sense of connection can be a powerful tool for navigating difficult life experiences. These activities might include hobbies, volunteering, creative pursuits, spending time in nature, or connecting with loved ones. By prioritizing these activities, we foster a sense of well-being, reduce stress, and strengthen our resilience.

Navigating difficult life experiences is a journey of resilience, growth, and transformation. It is not a smooth path, but one that unfolds through challenges, setbacks, and moments of deep reflection. By embracing a growth mindset, prioritizing self-care, finding meaning and purpose, and seeking support, we can navigate these difficult times, emerge stronger, and create a life filled with purpose, joy, and lasting fulfillment.

Finding Support and Guidance

The Power of Connection: A Foundation for Growth

Humans are inherently social creatures. Our innate need for connection is deeply rooted in our evolutionary history, where survival depended on collaboration and shared resources. This fundamental desire for belonging extends beyond basic survival; it fuels our emotional well-being and fosters a sense of purpose. Strong connections provide us with a sense of safety, belonging, and validation, creating a supportive network that helps us navigate life's challenges.

Within this network, we find a range of individuals who offer different forms of support. Mentors, with their vast experience and wisdom, guide us toward achieving our goals. Friends, with their unwavering support and understanding, provide a safe space for vulnerability and emotional expression. Family, with their unconditional love and unwavering loyalty, offer a constant source of comfort and encouragement. Each relationship serves a unique purpose, contributing to a tapestry of support that enriches our lives.

Seeking Guidance: Embracing Mentorship and Expertise

Throughout our lives, we encounter moments where we need guidance from those who have walked the path before us. This is where the concept of mentorship comes into play. Mentors act as guides, sharing their knowledge, experience, and insights to help us navigate specific challenges or achieve desired goals. They offer invaluable perspectives, challenge our assumptions, and provide constructive feedback that helps us grow both personally and professionally.

The benefits of mentorship extend beyond individual growth.

Mentorship fosters a culture of collaboration and knowledge sharing, creating a ripple effect that benefits entire organizations and communities. By investing in mentorship programs, businesses can cultivate a pipeline of talent, empower their employees, and foster a more inclusive and supportive workplace environment.

The Value of Diverse Perspectives: A Tapestry of Support

Finding support and guidance is not solely about seeking out one mentor or relying on a single source of wisdom. It's about cultivating a diverse network of individuals who offer different perspectives, skills, and experiences. This tapestry of support can provide us with a well-rounded understanding of the world, challenge our assumptions, and expose us to new ideas and approaches.

Building such a diverse network requires intentional effort. It involves actively seeking out individuals with different backgrounds, experiences, and perspectives. It means being open to learning from those who challenge our beliefs and push us beyond our comfort zones. By embracing diverse perspectives, we enrich our understanding of the world and cultivate a more inclusive and empathetic approach to life.

Navigating Challenges: Finding Support in Times of Need

Life is rarely a smooth journey. We inevitably encounter challenges and setbacks that test our resilience and push us to our limits. During these difficult times, having a supportive network becomes even more crucial. This network provides a safe space for vulnerability, a listening ear for our anxieties, and a source of encouragement to help us persevere.

The support we receive during challenging times can take various forms. It might be a friend offering a shoulder to cry on, a family member providing emotional support, or a therapist offering professional guidance. Whatever form it takes, this support plays a vital role in helping us navigate difficult emotions, regain our footing, and find meaning in our struggles.

Building Resilience: The Power of Self-Reflection and Growth

While external support plays a crucial role in our journey, it's equally important to cultivate inner resilience. This involves developing the ability to navigate challenges independently, to learn from our mistakes, and to find strength within ourselves. It requires self-reflection, introspection, and a willingness to embrace our vulnerabilities.

Building resilience requires a conscious effort to cultivate self-awareness, to understand our strengths and weaknesses, and to develop coping mechanisms for navigating stress and adversity. It involves practicing gratitude, fostering a positive mindset, and nurturing a sense of self-compassion. By developing inner strength, we become better equipped to face challenges, overcome obstacles, and thrive in the face of adversity.

Finding Support: A Continuous Journey of Growth and Development

Finding support and guidance is not a one-time event; it's an ongoing journey. As we evolve and grow, our needs and priorities change, requiring us to adapt and adjust our support networks accordingly. We may seek out new mentors, build new relationships, and refine our approaches to self-care and resilience.

The journey of finding support is a testament to our human capacity for connection, growth, and resilience. It's a journey that involves seeking wisdom from others, cultivating self-awareness, and embracing the power of vulnerability. By actively engaging in this journey, we empower ourselves to navigate life's complexities, achieve our goals, and live a more fulfilling and meaningful life.

Continuing the Conversation: Exploring the Landscape of Support

This exploration has merely scratched the surface of the vast and complex topic of finding support and guidance. There are countless dimensions to this journey, each worthy of . For instance, we could delve into:

The role of culture and social structures in shaping our access to support: How do societal norms and cultural values influence our experiences of seeking and receiving support. What are the systemic barriers that prevent individuals from accessing the support they need.
The impact of technology on our relationships and support networks: How has the digital age transformed the way we connect with others, seek guidance, and build community. What are the benefits and drawbacks of online support groups and virtual mentorship programs.
The evolving nature of mentorship and guidance in the workplace: How can organizations create a more supportive and inclusive environment that fosters mentorship and employee development. What are the best practices for implementing effective mentorship programs.

By engaging in these and other important conversations, we can deepen our understanding of the vital role of support and guidance in our lives. We can also identify ways to create a more supportive and equitable society where everyone has the opportunity to thrive.

Growing in Faith through Challenges

Our faith is not a static entity, impervious to the storms of life. Rather, it is a living, breathing force that thrives on the very challenges we face. As we navigate the complexities of life, our faith is put to the test, forcing us to confront our deepest fears, insecurities, and doubts. It is in these moments of vulnerability that we discover the true nature of our faith - not as a shield against pain but as a beacon of hope and a source of unwavering strength.

Challenges serve as catalysts for growth, forcing us to reevaluate our values, beliefs, and priorities. When confronted with suffering, we are compelled to delve deeper into our faith, seeking solace and meaning in the face of uncertainty. This introspection often leads to a reexamination of our relationship with the Divine, fostering a more profound understanding of God's presence, love, and purpose.

Take, for example, the story of Job in the Bible. He faced unimaginable suffering, losing his wealth, children, and even his health. Yet, through his trials, Job's faith was not diminished but deepened. He came to understand the immensity of God's power and the depths of His love, even in the midst of hardship. Job's story reminds us that our faith is not a guarantee of comfort or ease but a source of strength and resilience in the face of adversity.

Similarly, the apostle Paul, who experienced persecution, imprisonment, and hardship throughout his life, found strength and purpose in his unwavering faith. He wrote extensively about the transformative power of suffering, emphasizing that through trials, our character is refined, our faith strengthened, and our hope anchored in the enduring presence of God.

The process of growing in faith through challenges is not without its complexities. We may experience moments of doubt, frustration, and anger. We may question God's purpose and struggle to reconcile our pain with His love. These are natural responses to adversity, and they should not be dismissed or suppressed. Rather, they should be acknowledged, explored, and ultimately, surrendered to God.

It is through these moments of vulnerability that we learn to rely on God's grace and to embrace the power of His love. We discover that our faith is not a solitary endeavor but a shared journey with a compassionate and loving God who walks alongside us through every storm.

The Nature of Challenges and Their Impact on Faith

Challenges can manifest in various forms, ranging from personal struggles with health, relationships, or finances to societal injustices and global crises. These challenges can evoke a range of emotions, including fear, anxiety, anger, sadness, and even despair. The way we navigate these emotions and respond to adversity has a profound impact on our faith journey.

Navigating the Emotional Landscape of Challenges

When faced with adversity, it is essential to acknowledge and validate our emotions. Denying or suppressing our feelings only serves to create a barrier between ourselves and the transformative power of faith. Allow yourself to grieve, to feel anger, to experience the full spectrum of human emotion. This process of emotional release allows us to engage with our challenges more fully and authentically.

However, it is crucial to remember that our emotions should not be our sole guide. We must seek balance between acknowledging our feelings and allowing them to dictate our responses. Unchecked emotions can lead to unhealthy coping mechanisms, destructive behaviors, and a detachment from our faith.

The Role of Prayer and Spiritual Disciplines

Prayer becomes a lifeline in times of adversity. It provides a space for us to pour out our hearts to God, to express our pain, and to seek His guidance. Prayer is not simply a ritual but a profound conversation with the Divine. It allows us to tap into a source of strength, comfort, and wisdom that transcends our human limitations.

Alongside prayer, spiritual disciplines like Bible study, meditation, and acts of service can provide further support and deepen our faith. These practices cultivate a sense of connection to the Divine, offering us a framework for understanding God's will and purpose.

The Transformation of Suffering

While challenges can cause pain and suffering, they also hold the potential for profound transformation. Through adversity, we learn valuable lessons about ourselves, about God, and about the world around us. These experiences refine our character, build our resilience, and deepen our empathy for others who are struggling.

The Importance of Community and Support

Navigating challenges is not a solitary endeavor. We are called to live in community with others, and it is through this shared journey that we find strength, support, and encouragement. Sharing our burdens with others allows us to release our pain, to receive guidance, and to experience the power of collective faith.

Finding Purpose in the Midst of Challenges

While challenges may seem random and senseless, God often uses them to shape our lives and to reveal His purpose for us. By surrendering to God's will and seeking His guidance, we can discover hidden blessings and find new avenues for serving others.

The Enduring Hope of Faith

Ultimately, our faith is grounded in the unwavering hope of God's love and faithfulness. This hope is not a wishful thinking but a deep-seated belief in God's power, mercy, and redemptive plan. Even in the face of unimaginable suffering, our faith reminds us that we are not alone and that God is working all things for our good.

Embracing the Journey

Growing in faith through challenges is a lifelong journey. It is not about achieving a state of perfection or escaping all suffering but about embracing the process of transformation and drawing strength from God's grace. As we navigate the winding path of adversity, we learn to trust God's love, to rely on His strength, and to find purpose in the midst of our trials.

The Journey Continues

The journey of growing in faith through challenges is never truly finished. It is a continuous process of learning, adapting, and deepening our relationship with God. As we encounter new challenges, we can draw upon the lessons learned from our past experiences, trusting that God will continue to guide and strengthen us along the way.

The Legacy of Faith

Our journey of faith leaves a legacy that extends beyond ourselves. By sharing our stories of resilience and transformation, we inspire others to embrace their own challenges as opportunities for growth and to find solace in the enduring love of God. Through this collective tapestry of faith, we build a community of hope and resilience, reminding one another that even in the darkest of times, God's light shines brightly.

Conclusion

The challenges we face in life are not meant to crush us but to refine us. They are opportunities to discover the depths of our faith, to experience the transforming power of God's love, and to emerge from adversity with a deeper understanding of ourselves, God, and the world around us. Let us embrace the journey, drawing strength from God's grace and finding purpose in the midst of our trials, knowing that He walks with us every step of the way.

Personal Reflection

As you reflect on your own journey of faith, consider the following questions:

What are some of the challenges you have faced in your life.
How have these challenges impacted your faith.
What have you learned about yourself and about God through these experiences.
How can you use your experiences to encourage and support others who are facing challenges.

For of this topic, you may consider the following resources:

The Bible: Books such as Job, Psalms, and Romans offer profound insights into the nature of suffering and the transformative power of faith.
Books on spiritual growth and overcoming adversity: Consider exploring books by authors such as Henri Nouwen, Elisabeth Kübler-Ross, and John Ortberg.
Resources from your church or faith community: Many churches and faith communities offer support groups, Bible studies, and other resources to help individuals navigate life's challenges.

Remember: You are not alone in your journey. God is with you every step of the way, offering His love, grace, and unwavering support.

Chapter 13: The Importance of Family and Community

Building Strong Family Relationships

The Cornerstone of Connection: Communication

Effective communication forms the bedrock of any healthy relationship, and this holds especially true for families. It is through open dialogue that we bridge the gap between individual experiences, fostering empathy and understanding. However, communication within families can be complex, influenced by varying personalities, generational differences, and emotional baggage.

Active Listening: The Art of Hearing Beyond Words

Active listening is not simply about hearing the words spoken, but about truly comprehending the emotions and perspectives behind them. It involves paying full attention, engaging with non-verbal cues, and acknowledging the speaker's feelings without judgment. When we actively listen, we create a safe space for family members to express themselves freely, knowing they will be heard and validated.

Empathy: Stepping into Another's Shoes

Empathy is the ability to understand and share the feelings of another. When we practice empathy, we step outside of our own perspective and attempt to see the world through the eyes of our family members. This requires active listening, sensitivity to their needs, and a willingness to acknowledge their emotions, even if they differ from our own.

Effective Communication Strategies:

"I" Statements: "I" statements are a powerful tool for expressing our feelings and needs without blaming or attacking others. For example, instead of saying "You always make me feel ignored," try "I feel hurt when I don't get a chance to share my thoughts with you. "
Active Listening Techniques: Use verbal cues like "I see," "Go on," or "Tell me more" to demonstrate that you are paying attention. Reflect back what you hear to ensure understanding. For example, "So, what you're saying is that you feel overwhelmed with your workload. "
Setting Boundaries: Healthy boundaries are essential for maintaining personal space and emotional well-being. Clearly communicate what you need and expect from others. For example, "I need some quiet time after work to recharge. "
Conflict Resolution: Disagreements are inevitable in any family, but it is how we manage conflict that determines its impact on the relationship. Focus on finding solutions that meet the needs of all involved, rather than seeking to "win" an argument.

The Power of Shared Experiences:

Shared experiences play a crucial role in building strong family bonds. These experiences, whether large or small, create lasting memories and provide opportunities for connection, laughter, and mutual support.

Creating Meaningful Memories:

Family Traditions: Traditions, like holiday celebrations or weekly game nights, create a sense of continuity and belonging. They provide opportunities for consistent interaction and shared memories.

Family Vacations: Travel together, explore new places, and create unforgettable experiences that strengthen bonds and create lasting stories to share.
Everyday Moments: Don't underestimate the power of everyday moments. Sharing meals, playing games, or simply spending time together can create a sense of intimacy and connection.

Navigating the Challenges: The Dynamics of Family Life

Family life is not always a fairytale. Challenges are inevitable, and how we navigate them will significantly impact the strength and resilience of our relationships.

Generational Differences: Bridging the Gap

Generational differences can create communication barriers and misunderstandings. Older generations may have different values and perspectives than younger generations, leading to clashes in opinions and expectations.

Strategies for Bridging Generational Gaps:

Empathy and Understanding: Make an effort to understand the perspectives of different generations. Consider their life experiences and the values they hold dear.
Open Communication: Engage in open and honest conversations, encouraging all members to share their thoughts and feelings.
Respecting Differences: Acknowledge that everyone has a right to their own opinions and values, even if they differ from our own. Focus on finding common ground and appreciating the unique contributions of each generation.

Family Dynamics: The Impact of Roles and Relationships

The dynamic of a family is shaped by the complex interplay of individual personalities and the roles each member plays.

Understanding these dynamics can help us navigate potential conflicts and foster a more harmonious family unit.

Addressing Roles and Expectations:

Parental Roles: Parents play a crucial role in shaping the family dynamic. They set the tone for communication, establish boundaries, and model healthy relationships.
Sibling Relationships: Sibling relationships can be both supportive and challenging. Understanding the dynamics of sibling rivalry and the importance of sibling bonding is crucial.
Extended Family: Extended family members, like grandparents, aunts, and uncles, contribute to the richness of family life. Maintaining connections with extended family fosters a sense of belonging and shared history.

The Importance of Forgiveness and Reconciliation:

Forgiveness is essential for healing and moving forward from past hurts. It is a conscious decision to release resentment and bitterness, allowing for the possibility of reconciliation and restoring relationships.

Steps Towards Forgiveness:

Acknowledging the Hurt: Recognize the pain that has been caused and validate the emotions involved.
Choosing Forgiveness: Forgiveness is a choice. It is not condoning the hurtful behavior, but choosing to release the emotional burden it carries.
Reconciliation: Forgiveness can lead to reconciliation, where broken relationships are repaired and trust is rebuilt.

Building Resilience: Overcoming Adversity

Life throws unexpected challenges at all families. These challenges can test our relationships, but they can also strengthen them.

Strategies for Building Resilience:

Open Communication: Communicate openly and honestly about the challenges you are facing.
Shared Support: Lean on each other for support during difficult times. Sharing the burden can make it easier to bear.
Adaptability and Flexibility: Families that are adaptable and flexible are better equipped to navigate change and overcome adversity.

The Enduring Benefits of Strong Family Relationships:

Building strong family relationships is not just about creating a happy home, it is about creating a foundation for life. Strong family bonds provide a sense of belonging, love, and support that we can draw upon throughout our lives.

Benefits of Strong Family Relationships:

Emotional Well-being: Strong families provide a safe haven for emotional support, reducing stress and improving mental health.
Social Development: Families provide a foundation for learning social skills, fostering empathy, and developing healthy relationships.
Academic Success: Children from supportive families tend to perform better academically and have higher levels of motivation.
Physical Health: Strong family relationships are linked to improved physical health, including reduced risk of chronic diseases.
Life Satisfaction: Individuals with strong family bonds tend to report higher levels of life satisfaction and happiness. It is a journey worth undertaking, for the enduring legacy of a loving and supportive family is one of the greatest gifts we can pass down to future generations. By prioritizing connection, understanding, and forgiveness, we can cultivate a family environment where each

member feels valued, loved, and supported, creating a tapestry of love that stands the test of time.

Creating Meaningful Connections

At its core, the concept of "meaningful connection" speaks to the quality, not the quantity, of our interactions. It's about the depth of understanding, the resonance of shared values, the sense of mutual support and care that binds us to others. It's about feeling seen, heard, and valued, knowing that our presence makes a difference in the lives of those we cherish. This isn't solely a romantic pursuit, but a foundational element of a fulfilling life. It's about finding our tribe, our community of kindred spirits who enrich our world and inspire us to become better versions of ourselves.

Building Bridges: The Foundation of Meaningful Connections

The journey of building meaningful connections begins with a shift in perspective. Instead of viewing interactions as transactional, we must embrace a mindset of genuine interest and empathy. This means actively listening to understand, not just to respond, and extending kindness and compassion as a cornerstone of our interactions. We become mindful of our own communication style, striving to express ourselves clearly and respectfully, while simultaneously acknowledging and respecting the unique perspectives of others.

Empathy serves as the cornerstone of this process. It's about stepping outside of our own narratives and truly attempting to see the world through the eyes of another. This involves actively listening, asking questions, and seeking to understand their experiences, emotions, and motivations. By fostering empathy, we lay the foundation for authentic connection, creating a space where vulnerability can flourish and trust can blossom.

The Power of Shared Experiences: Weaving Threads of Connection

Shared experiences are the threads that weave together the intricate tapestry of meaningful connections. They serve as a common ground, a repository of memories and emotions that bind us to others. These experiences can be grand adventures or simple moments of shared laughter, but they all contribute to the rich fabric of our relationships. They allow us to see each other in a new light, to discover hidden strengths and shared vulnerabilities, and to forge deeper bonds of understanding and compassion.

Exploring new horizons together can be a powerful catalyst for connection. Whether it's embarking on a cross-country road trip, tackling a challenging hike, or simply trying a new restaurant, shared adventures create a sense of adventure and excitement that strengthens bonds. We learn to rely on each other, to navigate challenges together, and to celebrate victories as a united front. These shared experiences become touchstones, moments that we can revisit in our memories and rekindle the flames of connection.

Cultivating Intimacy: Sharing Our Stories and Vulnerability

Meaningful connections thrive on vulnerability. It's about letting go of the need to present a perfect facade and allowing others to see our true selves, flaws and all. Vulnerability is the act of opening ourselves to another, sharing our fears, our dreams, our insecurities, and our hopes. It's a testament to trust, a willingness to be seen and accepted for who we truly are.

By sharing our stories, we create space for connection and shared understanding. These stories might be about past experiences, personal struggles, or cherished memories. Through these narratives, we reveal our values, our vulnerabilities, and our dreams, allowing others to connect with us on a deeper, more meaningful level. This act of vulnerability creates a space for reciprocity, allowing us to witness the stories of others and to understand their journeys.

Nourishing the Connections: Practices for Growth and Nurturing

Once these connections are established, nurturing them requires intentionality and ongoing effort. Just as a garden needs constant tending, so too do our relationships require consistent attention and care. This involves committing to regular communication, showing appreciation, and making time for shared experiences. We can cultivate deeper connection through:

Active Listening: Giving others our undivided attention, asking clarifying questions, and reflecting back what we hear to ensure understanding.
Empathy and Compassion: Seeing the world through the eyes of others, acknowledging their emotions and experiences with empathy and kindness.
Open and Honest Communication: Expressing our thoughts and feelings clearly and respectfully, while simultaneously being open to hearing the perspectives of others.
Acts of Kindness: Making small gestures of care and appreciation, whether it's offering a helping hand, sending a thoughtful message, or simply being present for someone in need.
Making Time for Connection: Prioritizing spending quality time with loved ones, engaging in activities that foster shared experiences, and creating opportunities for meaningful conversations.

Navigating Challenges and Disagreements: Building Resilience and Empathy

Inevitably, challenges and disagreements will arise within our relationships. These moments are not signs of failure, but opportunities for growth and deeper understanding. We can navigate these complexities with empathy, active listening, and a willingness to compromise.

Disagreements are inevitable, but the key is to approach them with an attitude of collaboration, seeking common ground and respectful communication. Active listening becomes crucial, allowing each person to fully express their perspectives without judgment. Seeking to understand the root of the disagreement, rather than simply defending our own position, can pave the way for a resolution that honors the needs of all involved.

The Ever-Evolving Tapestry: Growth and Transformation

Meaningful connections are not static entities, but rather dynamic forces that evolve and transform with time. As we grow, learn, and face new challenges, our relationships will adapt and deepen, reflecting the journey of our shared experiences. This is the beauty of human connection: the potential for ongoing growth and transformation.

As we continue to nurture these vital threads in our lives, we create a vibrant tapestry of shared experiences, mutual support, and enduring love. This tapestry becomes a testament to the power of human connection, a reminder that even amidst the complexities of life, we are not alone. We are part of a vibrant network of support, a community of kindred spirits who inspire, challenge, and enrich our lives in ways we could never have imagined. It's about embracing vulnerability, fostering empathy, and nurturing the bonds that enrich our lives. It's about finding our tribe, building bridges of understanding, and weaving a tapestry of shared experiences that will last a lifetime. Let us embrace this journey with open hearts and open minds, ready to embrace the joy, the challenge, and the boundless possibilities that come with connecting with others on a meaningful level.

Finding Support and Encouragement

This exploration delves into the profound impact of support and encouragement on our individual and collective well-being. We will examine the various sources of support, from intimate relationships to broader communities, and explore the multifaceted ways in which encouragement fuels our growth and resilience. This journey will unpack the psychological mechanisms behind the effectiveness of support and encouragement, delving into the intricate interplay of emotions, motivation, and self-belief.

The Power of Connection: A Foundation for Support

At its core, support and encouragement stem from the fundamental human need for connection. We are social animals, wired for affiliation and belonging. Our social bonds provide a sense of security, purpose, and identity. These connections serve as a buffer against stress, loneliness, and isolation, fostering a sense of well-being and resilience.

In the realm of support, close relationships play a pivotal role. Family, friends, partners, and mentors can provide emotional, practical, and informational support, acting as a stable anchor in turbulent times. These relationships offer a safe space for vulnerability, where we can share our burdens, anxieties, and hopes without fear of judgment.

The Multiplicity of Support: A Tapestry of Resources

Support is not a monolithic concept, but rather a multifaceted phenomenon encompassing various forms and sources. While close relationships provide a crucial bedrock, support can also be found in broader communities, institutions, and even within ourselves.

Formal Support Networks:

Therapists and Counselors: These professionals offer a structured and confidential space for exploring our thoughts, feelings, and behaviors, helping us develop coping mechanisms and address specific challenges.

Support Groups: These gatherings bring together individuals facing similar struggles, creating a sense of community, shared understanding, and practical advice.

Social Services: Organizations dedicated to providing assistance in areas like housing, healthcare, education, and employment offer valuable resources and guidance for those in need.

Informal Support Networks:

Community Organizations: Local groups, clubs, and volunteer initiatives foster a sense of belonging and purpose, providing opportunities for social interaction, learning, and skill development.

Online Communities: Virtual platforms can provide a sense of connection and support, offering access to information, advice, and a feeling of belonging, particularly for individuals who may face social isolation.

Faith-Based Communities: Religious organizations often offer spiritual guidance, community support, and a sense of belonging, fostering a sense of hope and resilience.

Internal Support: Cultivating Self-Compassion and Resilience

While external support is invaluable, it is equally important to cultivate internal sources of support. Self-compassion, the ability to treat oneself with kindness, understanding, and acceptance, plays a critical role in navigating life's challenges. It allows us to recognize our vulnerabilities without succumbing to self-criticism, fostering resilience and personal growth.

Encouragement: Igniting Motivation and Confidence

Encouragement is the fuel that ignites our motivation and propels us forward in our pursuits. It can come from a variety of sources, including:

Positive Feedback: Acknowledgement of our efforts, strengths, and accomplishments from others, reinforcing our self-belief and confidence.

Words of Affirmation: Encouraging expressions of support, belief, and hope, providing a sense of validation and motivation.

Emotional Support: Empathy, understanding, and a willingness to listen, creating a safe space for vulnerability and emotional processing.

Practical Support: Concrete assistance with tasks, resources, or advice, helping us overcome obstacles and achieve our goals.

The Psychological Mechanisms of Support and Encouragement

The impact of support and encouragement is rooted in a complex interplay of psychological processes:

Stress Reduction: Social support acts as a buffer against stress, providing a sense of security and reducing the impact of negative experiences.

Increased Self-Efficacy: Encouragement fosters a belief in our capabilities, increasing our confidence and motivation to pursue our goals.

Improved Coping Strategies: Support helps us develop and utilize effective coping mechanisms for dealing with challenges and adversity.

Enhanced Emotional Regulation: Connection and encouragement provide a safe space for emotional processing, enabling us to manage our emotions effectively.

Increased Resilience: Support and encouragement foster a sense of hope and resilience, enabling us to bounce back from setbacks and navigate difficulties. It fosters a sense of belonging, validates our worth, and empowers us to overcome challenges and strive for personal growth. By cultivating and cherishing our support networks, both internal and external, we can navigate the complexities of life with greater resilience, confidence, and a sense of purpose.

The journey of finding support and encouragement is an ongoing process. It requires actively seeking out connections, nurturing existing relationships, and cultivating self-compassion. By embracing these principles, we can unlock the power of connection and create a foundation for personal and collective well-being.

Strengthening the Messianic Jewish Community

Theological Foundation: Building Bridges of Understanding

At the heart of the Messianic Jewish community lies a nuanced understanding of Jewish scripture and the person and work of Jesus. This necessitates a careful examination of the New Testament within the context of Jewish history and tradition. This theological framework, while rooted in the belief in Jesus as Messiah, emphasizes the continuity of Jewish identity and practice within the context of faith in Christ.

A key challenge for Messianic Jews lies in navigating the tension between their belief in Jesus as Messiah and the traditional Jewish understanding of the messianic expectation. This challenge requires theological clarity and sensitivity in communicating the uniqueness of Jesus within the framework of Jewish messianic thought. It necessitates a deep understanding of both Jewish and Christian perspectives, fostering a dialogue that honors both traditions while presenting a compelling case for the messianic claims of Jesus.

Cultural Identity: Embracing the Tapestry of Heritage

Strengthening the Messianic Jewish community also demands a firm grasp of its cultural identity. This necessitates the preservation and celebration of Jewish heritage and tradition, while acknowledging the unique aspects of Messianic Jewish practice. This means embracing the richness of Jewish tradition, including cultural practices, rituals, and celebrations, as integral components of Messianic Jewish life.

A crucial aspect of this cultural identity lies in fostering a sense of belonging within the broader Jewish community. This entails engaging in dialogue with other Jewish communities, promoting understanding and building bridges of connection. This requires a commitment to respectful and open communication, emphasizing shared values and common ground.

Outreach Strategies: Expanding the Circle of Faith

Outreach stands as a cornerstone of strengthening the Messianic Jewish community. This involves engaging with those who are seeking a deeper understanding of faith, particularly those who are drawn to both Jewish traditions and the message of Jesus. Effective outreach requires a multi-pronged approach, encompassing various channels of communication and engagement.

One crucial aspect of outreach is the establishment of welcoming and inclusive communities. This requires creating spaces where individuals can explore their faith, grapple with questions, and develop a sense of belonging. This necessitates a commitment to hospitality, understanding, and patience, recognizing that individual journeys of faith unfold at different paces.

Challenges and Opportunities

The Messianic Jewish community faces several challenges in its ongoing journey. One significant challenge lies in navigating the complex relationship with both the wider Jewish community and the broader Christian world. This necessitates sensitivity in communicating its unique identity, avoiding both assimilation and isolation.

Another challenge lies in the diverse theological perspectives within the Messianic Jewish community. This diversity, while enriching, can also create internal tensions and disagreements. It requires a commitment to respectful dialogue and a shared commitment to the fundamental tenets of faith.

Despite these challenges, the Messianic Jewish community also possesses significant opportunities for growth and impact. Its unique perspective allows it to contribute to the dialogue between Judaism and Christianity, fostering mutual understanding and respect. It also provides a compelling witness to the transformative power of faith, demonstrating the beauty and richness of a life grounded in both Jewish tradition and belief in Jesus as Messiah.

Moving Forward: Embracing the Journey

Strengthening the Messianic Jewish community requires a concerted effort from all its members. It calls for theological clarity, cultural awareness, effective outreach, and a deep commitment to building bridges of understanding within the Jewish community and the wider world. This journey requires courage, patience, and a shared vision of a vibrant and flourishing community that stands as a testament to the enduring power of faith and tradition.

The exploration of this topic can delve deeper into various aspects of the Messianic Jewish experience. Here are some potential avenues for further research and discussion:

Theological Perspectives: A detailed examination of various theological perspectives within the Messianic Jewish community, including their interpretations of scripture, messianic expectations, and the role of Jesus in Jewish history.
Cultural Identity: A deeper exploration of the intersection of Jewish tradition and Messianic Jewish practice, including the celebration of

holidays, observance of dietary laws, and the role of Hebrew language.

Outreach Strategies: A comprehensive analysis of various outreach approaches employed by Messianic Jewish communities, including online platforms, community events, and dialogue initiatives.

Challenges and Opportunities: A deeper discussion of the challenges and opportunities facing the Messianic Jewish community in the 21st century, including issues of acceptance, assimilation, and interfaith dialogue.

Historical Perspectives: An examination of the historical development of the Messianic Jewish movement, including its origins, key figures, and milestones.

By engaging in these explorations and fostering open dialogue, the Messianic Jewish community can continue to strengthen its identity, deepen its theological understanding, and expand its outreach, ultimately contributing to a richer and more interconnected world of faith.

Chapter 14: Sharing the Message of Messiah

Reaching Out to Others with the Gospel

This journey of sharing the Gospel begins with a heart overflowing with love. We must be driven by a genuine desire to see others experience the same transformative grace that we have received. This love is not a passive sentiment; it compels us to action. It leads us to build genuine relationships, to listen attentively, and to engage in meaningful conversations that transcend superficiality. We must remember that people are not just targets for our evangelistic efforts, but individuals with unique stories, experiences, and perspectives. To truly connect with them, we need to move beyond the "what" of our message to the "who" of our relationship.

This approach necessitates a deep understanding of the world we are navigating. The modern world, with its diverse cultures, ideologies, and spiritual landscapes, presents both challenges and opportunities for sharing the Gospel. We must be aware of the various perspectives and beliefs that shape people's lives, acknowledging that faith journeys are often complex and nuanced. It's not about imposing our beliefs or using fear as a motivator, but about engaging in thoughtful dialogue, respecting different viewpoints, and seeking common ground.

The very nature of the Gospel compels us to reach out with humility and compassion. The truth of the Gospel lies not in our own self-righteousness, but in the gracious love of God, who came to earth not to condemn, but to redeem. It's this spirit of humility that allows us to approach others with gentleness and understanding, recognizing that our own weaknesses and limitations are mirrored in the human experience.

Sharing the Gospel is not merely about sharing information but about sharing a life. It's about embodying the very love and forgiveness that we are proclaiming. Our words should be accompanied by actions that demonstrate the transformative power of Christ – actions of kindness, service, and generosity. We are called to be living embodiments of the Gospel, allowing our lives to speak louder than our words.

Building bridges of understanding is crucial. We must be willing to step outside our comfort zones and engage in meaningful conversations that transcend superficiality. This requires actively listening to others, seeking to understand their perspectives, and finding ways to connect with them on a human level. It's in these moments of genuine connection that the power of the Gospel can truly shine.

Our approach should be characterized by sensitivity and wisdom. We must be aware of the context in which we are sharing the Gospel, being mindful of cultural nuances and religious sensitivities. In a world often defined by division and conflict, our words and actions must be a force of reconciliation and peace.

Sharing the Gospel is not an act of imposing our will, but of offering a loving invitation. We present the truth of the Gospel, not as a burden, but as a liberating promise – a promise of hope, peace, and eternal life. This invitation must be accompanied by a spirit of respect, recognizing that ultimately, the choice to embrace the Gospel belongs to the individual.

The Gospel is not a static doctrine, but a dynamic force that continues to shape and transform lives. As we share the Gospel, we ourselves are transformed. We are challenged to grow in our own faith, to deepen our understanding of God's love, and to be more faithful witnesses in a world that desperately needs the light of Christ.

Sharing the Gospel in a Diverse World:

The world we live in is a tapestry of diverse cultures, backgrounds, and beliefs. As we embark on the journey of sharing the Gospel, we must acknowledge and embrace this diversity, recognizing that it enriches our understanding and enhances our ability to connect with others.

Understanding Cultural Nuances:

The Gospel message, while universal in its core principles, must be conveyed in a way that resonates with the specific cultural context. This requires sensitivity and understanding of the values, customs, and beliefs that shape people's lives. We must be mindful of language barriers, cultural sensitivities, and the ways in which the Gospel message might be received differently in various cultures.

Engaging in Interfaith Dialogue:

In a world where diverse faiths coexist, it's essential to engage in meaningful interfaith dialogue. This involves respectful listening, seeking common ground, and finding ways to bridge differences. Such dialogue allows us to learn from each other, foster understanding, and build relationships that transcend religious boundaries.

Embracing the Uniqueness of Each Individual:

We must remember that each person we encounter is unique, with their own individual stories, experiences, and perspectives. Sharing the Gospel effectively means recognizing and respecting these differences, tailoring our approach to meet the specific needs of each individual. It's about building genuine relationships, listening attentively, and seeking to understand where they are in their faith journey.

Sharing the Gospel in a Pluralistic Society:

In a society where multiple worldviews coexist, we must navigate the complexities of sharing the Gospel with sensitivity and respect. This requires acknowledging that people hold different beliefs and values, and that our own faith is not the only truth. We must be prepared to engage in respectful dialogue, presenting the Gospel as a source of hope and love, rather than a weapon of division.

Responding to Opposition and Criticism:

Sharing the Gospel may sometimes lead to opposition or criticism. We must be prepared to engage with such challenges with grace and humility, offering reasons for our beliefs in a way that is both compelling and respectful. Remember, the Gospel is not about forcing our views, but about offering a message of hope and love that can transform lives.

The Importance of Relationships:

At the heart of sharing the Gospel is the importance of building genuine relationships. These relationships provide the foundation for meaningful conversations, allowing us to connect with people on a personal level and share our faith in a way that is both authentic and impactful.

Investing in Long-Term Relationships:

Building meaningful relationships takes time and effort. We must be willing to invest in long-term relationships, showing consistent love, care, and support. This involves being present in the lives of others, celebrating their joys, and offering support during difficult times.

Sharing Life Experiences:

Sharing our own faith journey can be a powerful way to connect with others. By sharing personal experiences of how God has worked in our lives, we can demonstrate the transformative power of the Gospel in a tangible way.

Being a Living Example:

Our lives should be a reflection of the Gospel message. We are called to be living examples of Christ's love, grace, and forgiveness. This involves demonstrating compassion, generosity, and a commitment to serving others.

The Importance of Listening:

Active listening is essential for effective Gospel sharing. We must be willing to listen attentively to others, seeking to understand their perspectives and concerns. This creates a space for genuine dialogue and allows us to tailor our message to meet their specific needs.

Being Sensitive to the Spirit's Leading:

We must be sensitive to the leading of the Holy Spirit in our efforts to share the Gospel. This means being open to opportunities, trusting in God's timing, and allowing Him to guide our interactions with others.

The Power of Prayer:

Prayer is an essential part of reaching out to others with the Gospel. We must pray for guidance, wisdom, and boldness as we engage in these conversations. We should also pray for the people we are seeking to reach, asking God to open their hearts to His truth.

Sharing the Gospel with Confidence and Love:

Sharing the Gospel can be a challenging but rewarding journey. By embracing love, humility, and respect, we can effectively convey the transformative message of Christ to a world in need. Remember, the Gospel is a message of hope, peace, and reconciliation – a message that has the power to change lives.

Developing Evangelistic Strategies

Understanding the Essence of Evangelism

Before delving into specific strategies, it's crucial to define the essence of evangelism itself. It's not simply about converting people to a specific set of beliefs. Rather, it's about sharing a life-changing encounter with the person of Jesus Christ, inviting others to experience His love, forgiveness, and hope firsthand. It's a journey of relationship building, where genuine connection and understanding pave the way for sharing the transformative power of the Gospel.

Developing Effective Evangelistic Strategies

Developing effective evangelistic strategies requires a multifaceted approach that considers both the content of the message and the context in which it's shared. Here are some key principles to guide your approach:

1. Know Your Audience: The effectiveness of any communication hinges on understanding your audience. This applies even more so to evangelism. Who are you trying to reach. What are their concerns, needs, and aspirations. What language, metaphors, and examples will resonate with them. Understanding your audience allows you to tailor your message and approach to meet them where they are.

2. Build Relationships: Evangelism is not a one-time event but a process of relationship building. Genuine relationships require time, effort, and active listening. Seek to build genuine connections based on mutual respect, empathy, and shared values. This will foster trust and create an environment where the Gospel message can be shared naturally and authentically.

3. Embrace Authentic Sharing: The most powerful form of evangelism is sharing your own personal story of transformation. How did you encounter Jesus. What impact has His love and forgiveness had on your life. By sharing your own experiences, you make the Gospel message relatable and credible, demonstrating its transformative power in a tangible way.

4. Focus on the Person, Not the Problem: While it's important to address the challenges and concerns people face, the ultimate focus of evangelism should be on the person of Jesus Christ and the hope He offers. Present the Gospel as a solution to the human condition, a source of love, forgiveness, and eternal life.

5. Be Patient and Persistent: Sharing the Gospel is a long-term commitment, not a quick fix. Be patient with the process of nurturing relationships and allow the Holy Spirit to work in the hearts of others. Remember that the journey of faith is often gradual, with ups and downs along the way.

Specific Evangelistic Strategies:

Once you've established a foundation of understanding and relationship building, you can explore a variety of specific evangelistic strategies:

1. One-on-One Evangelism: This classic approach involves engaging in meaningful conversations with individuals, sharing your personal testimony and inviting them to explore their faith. Key aspects of one-on-one evangelism include:

Active Listening: Pay close attention to the other person's concerns, needs, and experiences. Seek to understand their perspective and build rapport before sharing your own.

Sharing Your Story: Share your personal encounter with Jesus Christ and the impact it has had on your life. Authenticity and vulnerability are key in building trust and connection.

Inviting Exploration: Invite the other person to explore their own faith and consider the claims of Christianity. Encourage them to ask questions, share their doubts, and explore the Gospel through Scripture and prayer.

2. Group Evangelism: Group evangelism involves sharing the Gospel with a small group of people in a more structured setting. This approach can be effective for building community and fostering a sense of belonging. Here are some common forms of group evangelism:

Small Group Studies: Gathering a group to discuss Scripture and explore the themes of faith together can create a safe space for sharing and learning.

Life Groups: Focus on building relationships and providing support through shared experiences, prayer, and spiritual growth.

Evangelistic Outreach Events: Organize events like dinners, conferences, or concerts that provide opportunities for people to hear the Gospel message in a relaxed and welcoming atmosphere.

3. Digital Evangelism: In today's digital age, utilizing online platforms offers a powerful way to reach a wider audience with the Gospel message. Here are some effective digital strategies:

Social Media: Engage in conversations on social media, share meaningful content related to faith, and utilize platform features like live video and stories to connect with followers.

Websites and Blogs: Create compelling content that addresses common questions and concerns about faith. Share personal testimonies, theological insights, and practical applications of the Gospel.

Online Communities: Participate in online communities and forums related to faith and spirituality. Share your experiences and insights, engage in discussions, and build relationships with individuals who are seeking answers.

4. Creative Evangelism: Embrace creativity and explore unique approaches to sharing the Gospel message. Consider these options:

Art and Music: Utilize visual arts, music, and storytelling to convey the Gospel message in an engaging and memorable way.

Community Service: Engage in service projects that demonstrate the love of Christ in action and create opportunities for conversations about faith.

Public Events: Organize events such as festivals, concerts, or public forums that attract a diverse audience and create a welcoming environment for sharing the Gospel.

Developing an Effective Evangelism Plan:

Creating an effective evangelism plan requires careful consideration and intentional planning. Here are some steps to guide your process:

1. Define Your Goals: What are you hoping to accomplish through your evangelistic efforts. Are you seeking to reach a specific demographic, build relationships, or share the Gospel message in a particular community. Defining your goals will provide a clear framework for your plan.

2. Identify Your Resources: What resources are available to you. Consider your time, skills, financial resources, and the support of your church or community.

3. Develop a Timeline: Establish a realistic timeline for implementing your evangelism plan. Consider the time required for relationship

building, event planning, and content creation.
4. Assign Roles and Responsibilities: If working with a team, clearly assign roles and responsibilities to ensure a coordinated effort.
5. Track and Evaluate: Regularly evaluate the effectiveness of your evangelism plan. Track your progress, identify areas for improvement, and adapt your approach based on feedback and results. Remember that the heart of evangelism lies in sharing the transformative power of Jesus Christ with authenticity, love, and compassion. By embracing the principles and strategies outlined in this guide, you can equip yourself with the tools you need to share the Gospel message effectively and see the love of God transform lives.

Creating Opportunities for Dialogue

This exploration delves into the intricate art of creating opportunities for dialogue, examining its multifaceted nature and highlighting its transformative potential. We will delve into the principles that guide effective dialogue, exploring the crucial elements of active listening, empathy, and respectful communication. We will also uncover the practical strategies that can be employed to foster such environments, emphasizing the importance of building trust, establishing common ground, and navigating conflict constructively.

The Essence of Dialogue: More Than Just Words

Dialogue, at its core, is a process of mutual exploration and understanding. It goes beyond mere conversation, where individuals exchange ideas and opinions in a linear fashion. Dialogue, instead, involves a shared journey of discovery, where participants actively listen, engage in genuine curiosity, and strive to understand perspectives that may differ from their own. This inherent pursuit of shared understanding sets dialogue apart, making it a powerful tool for bridging divides, building consensus, and fostering collaboration.

Creating the Foundation: Building Trust and Establishing Common Ground

The foundation of any successful dialogue lies in building trust and establishing common ground. Trust, in this context, refers to the belief that participants will engage in good faith, listen attentively, and respect each other's viewpoints, even when they disagree. Establishing common ground, on the other hand, involves identifying shared goals, values, and experiences that can serve as a starting point for meaningful interaction.

Active Listening: The Bedrock of Meaningful Dialogue

Active listening, a fundamental pillar of effective dialogue, goes beyond simply hearing words. It involves actively paying attention to both the verbal and nonverbal cues of the speaker, demonstrating genuine interest and seeking clarification when necessary. This practice fosters a sense of respect and encourages the speaker to feel heard and understood, paving the way for genuine exchange and deeper understanding.

Empathy: The Bridge to Understanding

Empathy, the ability to understand and share the feelings of another, is crucial in facilitating dialogue. By stepping into the shoes of the other participant, we gain a deeper appreciation for their perspective and motivations, even if we disagree with their views. This process of empathetic understanding helps to bridge divides and create a space for genuine connection and shared learning.

Respectful Communication: The Key to Productive Interaction

Respectful communication, characterized by honesty, kindness, and a willingness to listen, forms the bedrock of productive dialogue. It involves treating each participant with dignity, regardless of their viewpoints, and avoiding personal attacks or judgmental language.

Respectful communication fosters an environment where individuals feel safe to share their thoughts and ideas, knowing that they will be treated with respect and consideration.

Navigating Conflict: Transforming Challenges into Opportunities

Conflicts are inevitable in any dialogue, but they need not be seen as obstacles. Instead, they can be viewed as opportunities for deeper understanding and growth. By embracing conflict constructively, we can engage in respectful debate, explore differing perspectives, and strive to reach a mutually acceptable resolution. This process of constructive conflict resolution strengthens relationships, enhances problem-solving abilities, and ultimately leads to more resilient and collaborative outcomes.

The Power of Facilitators: Guiding the Dialogue Process

In many instances, the success of a dialogue depends on the presence of a skilled facilitator. Facilitators play a crucial role in setting the tone, establishing ground rules, and guiding the conversation in a productive direction. They ensure that all participants have a chance to share their perspectives, encourage active listening, and help to navigate potential conflicts constructively. Facilitators act as neutral guides, empowering participants to engage in meaningful dialogue and achieve shared goals.

Creating Dialogue Opportunities in Various Contexts

The art of creating opportunities for dialogue is applicable across a wide range of contexts, from personal relationships to professional settings, community initiatives, and even international relations. Here are just a few examples:

Personal Relationships: Engaging in open and honest conversations with loved ones, focusing on active listening, empathy, and respectful communication, can strengthen bonds and deepen understanding.

Workplace Settings: Establishing open communication channels, fostering a culture of inclusivity and respect, and encouraging diverse perspectives can lead to more innovative solutions and improved teamwork.

Community Initiatives: Organizing public forums, town hall meetings, and community dialogues on issues of shared concern can empower citizens to participate in decision-making processes and build stronger communities.

International Relations: Diplomatic dialogues, cross-cultural exchanges, and international conferences can promote understanding, foster cooperation, and contribute to the resolution of global challenges.

The Transformative Power of Dialogue

The transformative power of dialogue lies in its ability to bridge divides, build understanding, and foster collaboration. By engaging in meaningful dialogue, we move beyond superficial exchanges to delve into the complexities of human experience, discovering shared values, building bridges across differences, and forging lasting connections. By embracing the principles of active listening, empathy, and respectful communication, we can create spaces for genuine understanding, fostering collaboration, innovation, and lasting change. The art of creating opportunities for dialogue is a skill that can be cultivated, a practice that can be refined, and a commitment that can transform the world we live in. It is a journey worth embarking upon, one that promises to enrich our lives and empower us to build a more just, equitable, and harmonious future.

Sharing the Hope of Yeshua

This journey begins with a personal encounter with Yeshua. It's about recognizing the depth of God's love for us, even in our imperfections, and accepting His free gift of forgiveness and salvation through the sacrifice of His Son. This encounter is not a passive event; it's a dynamic exchange where the Holy Spirit opens our hearts to the truth of God's word and empowers us to walk in His light.

Once we experience this transformative grace, it becomes a natural overflow to share it with others. Sharing the hope of Yeshua is not about forcing our beliefs on anyone, but about offering the same compassion and understanding that we ourselves have received. It's about demonstrating the love of God in tangible ways, through acts of kindness, empathy, and service. It's about offering a listening ear, a comforting presence, and a genuine desire to help others find the same peace and hope we have found.

This sharing can take many forms. It could be a simple conversation with a friend, offering encouragement and support during a difficult time. It could be a prayer offered for someone in need, expressing the weight of our faith and the power of God's intercession. It could be a compassionate act of service, extending a helping hand to those around us.

In all these ways, we share the hope of Yeshua, not as a burden, but as a gift. We share it because we understand its true value, because we have tasted its sweetness, and because we know it can transform lives.

Sharing this hope also involves engaging in deep and meaningful conversations. It's about acknowledging the questions and doubts that often arise, and responding with patience, humility, and a spirit of truth-seeking. It's about understanding different perspectives, recognizing the complexities of faith, and engaging in respectful dialogue that allows for honest exploration and mutual understanding.

This kind of dialogue is not about winning an argument but about fostering genuine connection and building bridges of understanding. It's about recognizing that faith is not a static dogma, but a living, dynamic experience that continues to evolve and deepen throughout our lives.

Sharing the hope of Yeshua is a journey of lifelong learning and growth. It's about constantly deepening our own understanding of God's word, cultivating a heart of compassion, and allowing the Holy Spirit to guide us in all our interactions with others. It's about living a life that reflects the love of God, demonstrating His grace and mercy in tangible ways, and offering hope and encouragement to those who need it most.

The Importance of Context and Understanding

When sharing the hope of Yeshua, it's crucial to understand the context and background of the person we're engaging with. We must approach each encounter with sensitivity, recognizing that everyone comes with their own unique experiences, beliefs, and questions.

For example, when talking with someone from a different cultural or religious background, it's important to approach the conversation with humility and respect. We should be willing to listen to their perspective, acknowledge their beliefs, and engage in a genuine exchange of ideas. Sharing our faith should not be about imposing our own beliefs, but about fostering understanding and building bridges of connection.

It's also important to remember that faith is a deeply personal experience. We should avoid making assumptions or judgments about someone's faith journey. We should recognize that their understanding of God and their relationship with Him may be different from our own. Our goal should be to offer encouragement and support, not to impose our own beliefs or judge their path.

Sharing the Hope of Yeshua in a World of Uncertainty

In a world increasingly defined by uncertainty and fear, the hope of Yeshua shines even brighter. It offers a foundation of truth and stability in a world of flux, a source of strength and resilience in the face of adversity.

Sharing this hope is not simply about sharing a set of doctrines or beliefs, but about offering a path to a life transformed. It's about sharing a journey of love, forgiveness, and redemption, a journey that leads to a deeper understanding of ourselves, our purpose in the world, and our relationship with God.

This journey starts with a personal encounter with Yeshua, an experience that changes our hearts, renews our minds, and sets us on a path of transformation. It's about recognizing the depth of God's love, accepting His gift of salvation, and allowing the Holy Spirit to guide our steps.

Sharing the Hope of Yeshua Through Acts of Kindness

Sharing the hope of Yeshua is not limited to words; it's also expressed through acts of kindness, compassion, and service. These actions are tangible expressions of God's love, demonstrating the power of His grace and mercy in the world.

A simple act of kindness, such as offering a helping hand to someone in need, can be a powerful witness to God's love. It can break down barriers, build bridges of connection, and offer a glimmer of hope to those who are struggling.

Similarly, acts of compassion and service can be powerful expressions of faith. When we reach out to those in need, offering comfort, support, and encouragement, we are reflecting the heart of God and demonstrating His love for all people.

Sharing the Hope of Yeshua in a World of Division

In a world often marked by division and conflict, the message of Yeshua offers a powerful message of unity and reconciliation. It's a message that transcends cultural, racial, and religious boundaries, calling us to love our neighbors as ourselves.

Sharing this hope means engaging in dialogue with those who hold different beliefs, listening with compassion, and seeking common ground. It means fostering understanding, building bridges of connection, and working towards a world where differences are celebrated and unity is fostered.

Sharing the Hope of Yeshua Through Prayer

Prayer is a powerful tool for sharing the hope of Yeshua. It's a way of connecting with God, expressing our faith, and interceding on behalf of others. It's also a way of sharing our concerns, anxieties, and hopes, entrusting them to God's care and trusting in His wisdom and guidance.

When we pray for others, we are acknowledging their needs, expressing our love and concern, and placing them in the hands of God. This simple act of faith can offer a powerful source of comfort, strength, and encouragement.

Sharing the Hope of Yeshua Through Music

Music is a powerful tool for sharing the hope of Yeshua. It can transcend language barriers, expressing emotions and truths that words cannot convey. It can evoke feelings of joy, peace, and hope, inspiring us to connect with God and each other.

Music can also be a bridge for sharing our faith with others. Through songs of praise, worship, and testimony, we can express our love for God, share our stories of faith, and invite others to join in the journey of faith.

Sharing the Hope of Yeshua Through Stories

Sharing the stories of our faith can be a powerful way to connect with others and inspire them to explore the hope of Yeshua. These stories can offer glimpses into the lives of those who have been transformed by faith, demonstrating the power of God's love and the reality of His presence in our lives.

By sharing these stories, we are not only offering a glimpse into our own faith journey, but also inspiring others to consider the possibility of a deeper relationship with God. These stories can offer encouragement, hope, and a sense of possibility, inviting others to explore the transformative power of faith.

Sharing the Hope of Yeshua Through Acts of Service

Acts of service are a tangible expression of our love for God and our neighbors. They are a way of demonstrating the hope of Yeshua through practical actions, offering tangible help and support to those in need.

These acts of service can take many forms. We can volunteer at local organizations, donate to charities, offer assistance to those in our community, or simply offer a listening ear to someone who is struggling.

Through these acts of service, we are sharing the hope of Yeshua in a practical way, demonstrating the love of God in tangible ways, and offering encouragement to those who need it most.

Sharing the Hope of Yeshua Through Our Lives

Ultimately, sharing the hope of Yeshua is about living a life that reflects His love, His grace, and His mercy. It's about demonstrating the transformative power of faith through our daily actions, our words, and our relationships.

It's about being a beacon of hope in a world often marked by darkness, offering a listening ear, a compassionate heart, and a genuine desire to help others find the same peace and joy that we have found in Yeshua.

Sharing the hope of Yeshua is a lifelong journey, a journey that requires dedication, commitment, and a willingness to be transformed by the love of God. It's a journey that leads to a deeper understanding of ourselves, our purpose in the world, and the power of God's love to change lives.

It's a journey worth taking.

Chapter 15: Building a Legacy of Faith

Passing on Jewish Faith to Future Generations

The Jewish concept of "tikkun olam" - "repairing the world" - underscores the critical role of each generation in shaping the future. Passing on the faith, therefore, is not merely a passive act of inheritance, but an active commitment to contributing to the ongoing evolution of the Jewish people. This responsibility transcends the mere transmission of religious practices and beliefs; it encompasses the embodiment of Jewish values, the nurturing of a sense of belonging to a vibrant community, and the fostering of a deep connection to the rich tapestry of Jewish history and culture.

However, the landscape of intergenerational transmission has shifted significantly in recent decades. The rise of secularization, assimilation, and a growing awareness of diverse identities has presented new challenges to traditional models of Jewish education and communal engagement. Gone are the days when Jewish identity was primarily defined by geographic proximity and familial lineage. Today, young people navigate a world of myriad options, making choices based on personal values, social connections, and a desire for meaning and purpose in a complex and ever-changing world.

This shift necessitates a paradigm shift in how we approach the transmission of Jewish faith. Gone are the days of "one size fits all" approaches that rely solely on rigid adherence to tradition. Instead, we must embrace a pluralistic and inclusive vision that allows for individual expression and diverse pathways to Jewish engagement. This requires a nuanced understanding of the diverse motivations and needs of younger generations, fostering a dialogue that acknowledges their unique experiences and aspirations.

Building Bridges: Cultivating a Sense of Belonging

At the heart of successful intergenerational transmission lies the creation of a sense of belonging, a feeling of being part of something larger than oneself. This requires building bridges of understanding and connection between generations, fostering a sense of shared history, values, and aspirations. The following strategies offer a framework for creating a vibrant and inclusive Jewish community that resonates with younger generations:

Embracing the Power of Storytelling: Judaism is a faith steeped in narrative, and stories hold the power to connect us to our past, inspire our present, and guide us towards a meaningful future. Sharing stories, both personal and communal, can help younger generations connect to the rich tapestry of Jewish history, values, and traditions. This might involve exploring family histories, sharing anecdotes about Jewish life in different eras, or engaging with Jewish literature and folklore.

Creating Meaningful Rituals: Rituals provide a framework for shared experience, offering moments of connection and reflection. While traditional rituals hold significance, it is crucial to adapt them to contemporary realities and empower younger generations to create new rituals that resonate with their experiences. This might involve exploring alternative forms of Shabbat celebration, creating new rituals for life cycle events, or incorporating contemporary artistic expressions into traditional practices.

Fostering Intergenerational Dialogue: Open and honest dialogue between generations is essential for bridging the gap between different perspectives and fostering a sense of shared understanding. Creating spaces for intergenerational conversations, workshops, and mentorship programs can provide platforms for exploring common values, addressing concerns, and building bridges of understanding.

Embracing Inclusive Language and Practices: Judaism is a diverse faith, with a spectrum of beliefs and practices. It is vital to create an inclusive environment that embraces diverse voices and perspectives, ensuring that all individuals feel welcome and respected. This might involve using inclusive language, exploring alternative interpretations of tradition, and offering diverse pathways for Jewish engagement.

Beyond the Walls: Engaging with the Wider World

The transmission of faith extends beyond the confines of the synagogue or community center. It requires engaging with the wider world, actively promoting Jewish values and contributing to the broader tapestry of human experience. This can involve:

Social Action and Tikkun Olam: The Jewish tradition emphasizes the importance of social justice and repairing the world. Encouraging young people to engage in social action projects, advocating for human rights, and working towards a more just and equitable society can infuse their Jewish identity with a sense of purpose and meaning.

Interfaith Dialogue and Building Bridges: In a world increasingly defined by diversity, interfaith dialogue is essential for building understanding and fostering peaceful coexistence. Encouraging young people to engage in interfaith dialogue, learning about other faiths, and building bridges of understanding can promote a sense of global citizenship and foster a spirit of collaboration.

Creative Expression and Jewish Arts: Art, music, literature, and film offer powerful platforms for exploring Jewish themes, values, and experiences. Encouraging young people to engage with Jewish arts, whether as creators or consumers, can help them connect with their heritage in meaningful and engaging ways.

The Power of Choice and Agency

Ultimately, the success of intergenerational transmission hinges on fostering a sense of agency and empowering young people to make informed choices about their Jewish identity. This requires:

Respecting Individual Choice: Jewish identity is a personal journey, and individuals should be empowered to explore different paths and make choices that resonate with their own values and aspirations. Providing Meaningful Education: A strong foundation in Jewish education is essential for informed choices. This might involve engaging in formal religious studies, exploring Jewish history and culture, or participating in experiential learning programs. Cultivating a Sense of Curiosity: Encouraging a sense of curiosity and exploration allows young people to discover the depth and breadth of Jewish tradition, fostering a lifelong connection to their heritage.

The Future of Jewish Tradition

The future of Jewish tradition lies in the hands of the next generation. By fostering a sense of belonging, encouraging meaningful engagement, and respecting individual choice, we can ensure that the Jewish faith continues to thrive, adapting to the challenges and opportunities of the 21st century. It is a journey that requires patience, understanding, and a shared commitment to building a future where Jewish tradition remains a vibrant and enriching source of meaning and purpose for generations to come.

Raising Children with a Messianic Jewish Identity

Embracing the Jewish Heritage:

At the heart of raising children with a Messianic Jewish identity lies the paramount importance of nurturing a profound connection to their Jewish heritage. This involves exposing them to the rich tapestry of Jewish culture, history, and tradition, creating a foundation upon which their Messianic faith can flourish. It is crucial to introduce them to the foundational elements of Judaism, including the Hebrew language, the Torah, and the holidays.

Hebrew Language:

Learning Hebrew, the language of the Jewish people, opens a gateway to understanding Jewish literature, prayer, and cultural expressions. Incorporating Hebrew into their daily lives, through simple phrases, songs, or even storybooks, can help children develop a sense of familiarity and connection to their heritage.

Torah Study:

Engaging in Torah study, the foundational text of Judaism, fosters a deeper understanding of Jewish history, law, and ethics. This can be achieved through age-appropriate methods, such as storytelling, parables, and interactive discussions, making Torah study both engaging and enriching.

Jewish Holidays:

Celebrating Jewish holidays, from Passover to Hanukkah, provides a tangible connection to their heritage and offers opportunities for family bonding and cultural immersion. These celebrations should be infused with meaning, allowing children to understand the historical significance and the enduring values embodied within each tradition.

Messianic Faith Integration:

While deeply rooted in Jewish tradition, Messianic Judaism also embraces the teachings of Jesus as the Messiah, offering a unique perspective on Jewish scripture and a profound understanding of

God's plan for salvation. Integrating these beliefs into their upbringing is essential for nurturing a holistic Messianic Jewish identity.

Jesus, the Jewish Messiah:

Introducing Jesus as the Jewish Messiah, the promised King and Savior, should be approached with sensitivity and understanding. Explaining his life, teachings, and sacrifice through the lens of Jewish tradition and scripture can help children grasp the profound meaning of his role in their lives and in the Jewish narrative.

Messianic Jewish Theology:

Nurturing a comprehensive understanding of Messianic Jewish theology, including the unique perspectives on prophecy, the nature of God, and the role of the Holy Spirit, is crucial for building a solid foundation in their faith. Engaging in open discussions, theological exploration, and the study of Messianic Jewish writings can deepen their knowledge and foster a sense of connection to their spiritual heritage.

Community and Belonging:

A sense of community is paramount in shaping a child's identity, and the Messianic Jewish community provides a unique and supportive environment for spiritual growth and cultural immersion. Engaging in the life of the community through worship services, social events, and outreach programs allows children to connect with others who share their faith and heritage, fostering a sense of belonging and support.

Worship and Prayer:

Participating in worship services, where the integration of Jewish tradition and Christian faith is evident, allows children to experience the vibrant spiritual life of the Messianic Jewish community. Engaging in prayer, both personal and communal, fosters a deep connection to God and cultivates a sense of spiritual awareness.

Outreach and Sharing:

Engaging in outreach initiatives, where children can share their faith and culture with others, fosters a sense of purpose and responsibility. This could involve participating in community service projects, sharing their stories with others, or simply being kind and welcoming to those from different backgrounds.

Challenges and Navigating Differences:

Raising children with a Messianic Jewish identity often involves navigating challenges and differences. Understanding the complexities of Jewish and Christian traditions, as well as the sometimes conflicting views of various communities, requires open communication, sensitivity, and a willingness to learn and grow.

Interfaith Relationships:

Messianic Jewish families may encounter interfaith relationships, requiring open dialogues and a respectful understanding of the different faiths involved. This presents an opportunity for fostering unity and compassion, while also upholding the values and beliefs of their faith.

Anti-Semitism and Prejudice:

Unfortunately, the Messianic Jewish community, like other Jewish groups, faces anti-Semitism and prejudice. It is essential to equip children with the tools to understand and address these issues, fostering a sense of resilience and advocacy for their faith and heritage. By fostering a deep connection to Jewish heritage, integrating the teachings of Jesus as the Jewish Messiah, and nurturing a strong sense of community and belonging, parents can guide their children toward a fulfilling life rooted in both their Jewish identity and their Messianic faith.

Creating a Culture of Faith

This essay explores the creation and cultivation of a culture of faith, navigating the challenges of a rapidly changing world while embracing the enduring power of belief. We'll delve into the key elements that foster a strong culture of faith, examining how individuals and communities can nurture an environment where faith thrives, offering a sense of purpose, connection, and spiritual fulfillment.

Understanding the Foundation: The Nature of Faith

Before delving into the dynamics of a culture of faith, we must first understand the essence of faith itself. While often associated with religious beliefs, faith transcends specific doctrines. It embodies a fundamental trust in something beyond the tangible, a belief in the unseen, a conviction that guides our actions and shapes our outlook. This "something" can be a deity, a set of principles, or a profound sense of purpose and meaning. Faith, in its essence, acts as a compass, guiding us through life's complexities, offering solace in times of hardship, and inspiring us to strive for a better world.

Cultivating a Culture of Faith: Fostering Belonging and Growth

Creating a vibrant culture of faith requires more than just shared beliefs. It necessitates an environment that fosters connection, encourages spiritual growth, and promotes a sense of belonging. This can be achieved through various avenues, each contributing to a richer understanding and expression of faith:

1. Cultivating a Spirit of Openness and Dialogue:

A healthy culture of faith welcomes diverse perspectives and encourages open dialogue. This doesn't imply a compromise of core beliefs, but rather a willingness to engage with others, learn from their experiences, and find common ground. This spirit of openness fosters intellectual curiosity, promotes deeper understanding of different faith expressions, and nurtures empathy and respect for those holding different beliefs.

2. Embracing the Power of Ritual and Tradition:

Rituals, whether religious or secular, provide a framework for shared experience, reinforcing values and fostering a sense of connection. In a culture of faith, rituals can be seen as expressions of belief, offering a tangible way to connect with the spiritual realm and strengthen the bonds of community. These rituals can range from regular prayer gatherings and communal worship services to more informal practices like sharing meals, engaging in acts of service, or celebrating milestones together.

3. Fostering Spiritual Growth through Education and Exploration:

A vibrant culture of faith encourages continuous learning and exploration. This can involve studying sacred texts, engaging in spiritual practices like meditation or reflection, or exploring different faith traditions. By creating opportunities for ongoing learning, individuals can deepen their understanding of their faith, challenge their assumptions, and develop a more nuanced and informed perspective.

4. Embracing the Role of Faith in Action:

Faith is not meant to be a passive concept but a call to action. By connecting our beliefs with tangible actions, we bring our faith to life, translating our convictions into tangible expressions of compassion, justice, and love. This can involve volunteering in our communities, advocating for the marginalized, or simply living out our values in our daily interactions.

5. Nurturing a Sense of Belonging: Building a Supportive Community

A strong culture of faith fosters a sense of community, providing a space where individuals feel supported, accepted, and valued for who they are. This sense of belonging is crucial, offering a sense of safety and encouragement, allowing individuals to explore their faith journey with confidence and support. Creating opportunities for meaningful connections, fostering mentorship relationships, and promoting a spirit of inclusivity are key to building a vibrant and supportive community.

Navigating the Challenges of a Changing World:

The creation and sustenance of a culture of faith in the modern world presents unique challenges. The rise of secularism, technological advancements, and globalization all contribute to a landscape where faith is often questioned, marginalized, or even actively opposed. In such a context, fostering a vibrant culture of faith requires a renewed commitment to the following:

1. Embracing Interfaith Dialogue:

As the world becomes increasingly interconnected, understanding different faith traditions becomes crucial. Interfaith dialogue allows for mutual learning, promoting understanding and respect between diverse communities. It can help dismantle stereotypes, highlight shared values, and foster collaboration on common concerns like social justice and environmental protection.

2. Addressing Faith-Based Conflict:

While faith can be a source of unity and peace, it can also be exploited to justify conflict and violence. Addressing these issues requires open dialogue, critical analysis of religious texts and teachings, and fostering a culture of peace and reconciliation. This can involve engaging in respectful debate, promoting non-violent conflict resolution strategies, and emphasizing the shared human values that transcend religious boundaries.

3. Navigating the Impact of Technology:

Technology has profoundly impacted our lives, and faith is no exception. While technology can offer new platforms for faith-based communities to connect and share resources, it also poses challenges. The proliferation of misinformation, the potential for online harassment, and the constant pressure to be "connected" can erode the spiritual foundations of faith. A healthy culture of faith must address these challenges, offering guidance on navigating the digital landscape while maintaining a focus on spiritual growth and authentic connection.

The Enduring Power of Belief:

Despite the challenges of a changing world, the need for faith remains strong. Faith offers a sense of purpose, hope, and connection that transcends the limitations of the physical world. In a culture where individualism often dominates, faith provides a foundation for shared values, community, and a belief in something greater than ourselves. Creating a culture of faith is not about imposing beliefs or silencing dissent, but about nurturing an environment where faith thrives, offering solace, inspiration, and a deeper sense of meaning to individuals and communities alike. It demands openness, dialogue, and a commitment to fostering an environment where belief can flourish, transcending the boundaries of specific doctrines and creating a space for shared understanding and meaningful connection. As we navigate the complexities of a changing world, the enduring power of faith offers a beacon of hope, guiding us towards a future where belief, compassion, and a shared sense of purpose shape the world we create together.

Leaving a Lasting Impact

This exploration begins with understanding the multifaceted nature of impact. It's not solely about achieving grand feats or amassing wealth, but rather about fostering positive change that resonates far beyond our own existence. It's about leaving behind a legacy, not merely in terms of material possessions or accolades, but in the form of inspiration, knowledge, or a positive shift in the collective human experience.

We can approach this journey of leaving a lasting impact through various lenses, each offering unique insights and pathways:

1. The Impact of Ideas and Innovation:

The world is a canvas painted with the strokes of human ingenuity. Every new invention, every groundbreaking discovery, every original thought leaves an imprint on our collective consciousness. The impact of ideas is a testament to the power of human imagination and its ability to shape our reality.

Take, for instance, the revolutionary theories of Albert Einstein, whose work on relativity fundamentally altered our understanding of space, time, and gravity. His ideas, once relegated to the realm of theoretical physics, became the foundation for countless technological advancements, from GPS navigation to nuclear energy. This enduring influence underscores the enduring power of groundbreaking ideas to shape the course of human history.

Beyond scientific breakthroughs, the impact of ideas extends to the realm of art, literature, and philosophy. Shakespeare's plays, for example, continue to resonate with audiences centuries later, exploring universal themes of love, loss, and human nature. The enduring power of these literary works speaks to the lasting impact of artistic expression and its capacity to transcend time and connect us across generations.

2. The Impact of Actions and Deeds:

While ideas hold immense power, their true impact often manifests through our actions. Every act of kindness, every act of courage, every act of selfless service contributes to a ripple effect of positive change. It is through these concrete expressions of our values that we leave an indelible mark on the world.

The life of Nelson Mandela serves as a poignant example. His relentless pursuit of justice and equality, his unwavering commitment to peaceful resistance against apartheid, inspired millions around the world. His legacy lies not only in the dismantling of a brutal regime, but also in the enduring principles of forgiveness, reconciliation, and the pursuit of a more just and equitable world.

On a smaller scale, each act of volunteerism, each donation to charity, each effort to help those in need contributes to a collective tapestry of compassion and empathy. These acts may seem insignificant in the grand scheme of things, but their cumulative impact is profound. They build bridges of understanding, foster a sense of shared humanity, and contribute to a world where kindness and compassion prevail.

3. The Impact of Education and Mentorship:

Education is the cornerstone of societal progress, empowering individuals to understand the world around them, to contribute to its betterment, and to leave a lasting legacy of their own. The impact of education is not confined to the acquisition of knowledge; it extends to the cultivation of critical thinking, problem-solving skills, and the ability to navigate the complexities of life with wisdom and empathy.

The role of mentors in this process is invaluable. They provide guidance, encouragement, and a sense of direction, helping individuals to unlock their potential and pursue their passions. The impact of a mentor can be transformative, shaping the trajectory of a student's life and inspiring them to leave their own mark on the world.

The legacy of a teacher extends far beyond the classroom, echoing through the lives of their students, their students' students, and so on. This ripple effect of knowledge and inspiration creates a chain of positive change that continues to resonate for generations to come.

4. The Impact of Stewardship and Conservation:

We are stewards of our planet, entrusted with the responsibility of safeguarding its resources for future generations. The impact of our actions on the environment has far-reaching consequences, shaping the world we leave behind. Every effort to reduce our carbon footprint, to protect endangered species, to promote sustainable practices contributes to a more sustainable and resilient future.

The legacy of conservationists like Jane Goodall and Wangari Maathai stands as a testament to the power of individual action. Through their tireless efforts to protect endangered chimpanzees and plant millions of trees, respectively, they inspired countless others to join the movement for environmental stewardship. Their impact extends not only to the preservation of biodiversity, but also to the fostering of a deeper sense of interconnectedness between humanity and the natural world.

5. The Impact of Legacy and Inspiration:

Leaving a lasting impact isn't solely about what we accomplish in our lifetime, but also about the legacy we leave behind. This legacy encompasses the values we embody, the stories we share, and the inspiration we ignite in others. It's about creating a ripple effect that extends beyond our own existence, motivating future generations to strive for a better world.

The legacy of Martin Luther King Jr. is a powerful example. His unwavering commitment to racial equality and his belief in the power of nonviolent resistance continue to inspire activists and social justice advocates today. His message of hope, love, and unity resonates across generations, serving as a guiding light in the pursuit of a more just and equitable society.

Leaving a lasting impact is about recognizing that our lives are interconnected with the lives of others, that our actions ripple outward and touch countless lives. It's about embracing the power of human connection, of shared purpose, and of the collective pursuit of a brighter future.

The Path Toward Meaningful Contribution:

Navigating this path toward leaving a lasting impact requires a combination of conscious intention, purposeful action, and a deep sense of personal conviction. Here are some key principles to guide our journey:

Identify Your Passion: The first step is to discover what truly ignites your passion, what you feel compelled to contribute to the world. This passion will be your guiding star, providing the motivation and energy to persevere through challenges and obstacles.
Develop Your Skills and Knowledge: Once you've identified your passion, invest in developing the skills and knowledge necessary to make a meaningful contribution. This may involve formal education, hands-on experience, or mentorship from those who have already achieved success in your chosen field.
Embrace Purposeful Action: Passion and knowledge are powerful tools, but they need to be translated into tangible action. Seek out opportunities to apply your skills and knowledge to make a difference in the world, whether through volunteer work, advocacy, entrepreneurship, or simply by living your life in accordance with

your values.

Foster Collaboration and Community: Leaving a lasting impact rarely happens in isolation. Surround yourself with like-minded individuals, collaborate with others who share your vision, and build a supportive community that amplifies your efforts and accelerates progress toward a common goal.

Embrace Continuous Learning and Growth: The pursuit of a lasting impact is a lifelong journey, one that requires continuous learning, adaptation, and resilience. Embrace challenges as opportunities for growth, seek out new perspectives, and stay informed about the evolving needs of the world around you. It's about recognizing that our individual lives are woven into the fabric of humanity, and that we have the power to make a difference.

This journey is not without its challenges. We may face setbacks, encounter resistance, and question our own capabilities along the way. But it's through these challenges that we grow, learn, and ultimately discover the true meaning of our contribution to the world.

By embracing a spirit of purpose, compassion, and unwavering commitment, we can each leave a lasting impact that transcends the boundaries of our individual lives, shaping the world for generations to come. And in doing so, we create a legacy of hope, inspiration, and positive change that will continue to resonate far beyond our own time.

Chapter 16: The Future of Messianic Judaism

Exploring Potential Challenges and Opportunities

I. Recognizing the Importance of Strategic Foresight

The world today is characterized by unprecedented change, driven by forces such as technological innovation, globalization, climate change, and geopolitical shifts. These forces are interconnected and dynamic, creating a complex landscape that is difficult to predict with certainty. However, while predicting the future with absolute precision may be impossible, understanding the key trends and drivers of change can equip us with the tools to make informed decisions and navigate uncertainty.

Strategic foresight is not simply about predicting the future; it's about understanding the potential range of futures and their implications. It involves:

Identifying Key Trends: Recognizing emerging patterns and long-term trajectories that shape the future. These might include technological advancements, demographic shifts, environmental changes, or social movements.
Analyzing Drivers of Change: Understanding the forces that are shaping these trends, whether they be political, economic, social, technological, environmental, or legal factors (PESTEL).
Developing Scenarios: Creating plausible and impactful future scenarios based on the interplay of identified trends and drivers.

This allows us to explore potential futures and their implications.
Assessing Impacts: Evaluating the potential risks and opportunities associated with each scenario, considering their implications for individuals, organizations, and society as a whole.
Developing Strategies: Formulating proactive plans and actions to navigate the potential challenges and seize the opportunities arising from different future scenarios.

II. Identifying Potential Challenges

Challenges are inherent to any dynamic system, and the future is no exception. Recognizing potential challenges allows us to develop strategies to mitigate their negative impacts and build resilience. Some key areas to consider when identifying potential challenges include:

A. Technological Disruption:

The rapid pace of technological innovation can disrupt established industries, business models, and even social structures. Potential challenges in this domain include:

Job displacement: Automation and artificial intelligence may lead to the displacement of workers in certain sectors, requiring reskilling and upskilling initiatives.
Cybersecurity threats: Increasing reliance on technology also brings heightened cybersecurity risks, requiring robust defenses and proactive measures to protect data and infrastructure.
Digital divide: Unequal access to technology can exacerbate existing social and economic inequalities, requiring policies to bridge the digital divide.
Ethical considerations: Emerging technologies like artificial intelligence raise ethical concerns regarding bias, privacy, and the potential for unintended consequences.

B. Environmental Challenges:

Climate change and its consequences pose significant challenges to ecosystems, economies, and societies. Key concerns include:

Climate-related disasters: Increased frequency and severity of extreme weather events, such as hurricanes, droughts, and floods, necessitate adaptation measures and disaster preparedness.
Resource depletion: Rising demand for resources like water and energy, coupled with environmental degradation, requires sustainable resource management strategies.
Biodiversity loss: The decline of species and ecosystems disrupts natural processes and jeopardizes ecosystem services, requiring conservation efforts and habitat restoration.
Environmental pollution: Air, water, and soil pollution pose risks to human health and environmental sustainability, demanding regulations and sustainable practices.

C. Social and Economic Challenges:

Social and economic inequalities, demographic shifts, and political polarization are significant challenges with far-reaching consequences. Key considerations include:

Income inequality: Widening income gaps can lead to social unrest, economic instability, and reduced social mobility. Addressing this requires policies aimed at promoting equitable distribution of wealth and opportunities.
Aging populations: Declining birth rates and increasing life expectancy lead to an aging population, presenting challenges for social security systems, healthcare provision, and economic growth.
Migration and displacement: Factors like climate change, conflict, and poverty drive migration and displacement, creating challenges for host countries and necessitating humanitarian aid and integration policies.
Political polarization: Growing polarization and distrust in institutions can undermine societal cohesion and hinder effective

governance, requiring efforts to promote dialogue, consensus-building, and civic engagement.

III. Identifying Potential Opportunities

Alongside challenges, the future also presents a wealth of opportunities for individuals, organizations, and societies. Recognizing and capitalizing on these opportunities is crucial for achieving growth, innovation, and progress.

A. Technological Advancements:

Technological breakthroughs offer exciting possibilities for improving lives, solving global challenges, and driving economic growth. Key opportunities include:

Innovation in healthcare: Advancements in artificial intelligence, biotechnology, and telemedicine hold the potential to revolutionize healthcare delivery, improve treatment outcomes, and increase access to care.
Sustainable technologies: Developing and deploying clean energy technologies, renewable resources, and sustainable materials can mitigate climate change and create new industries.
Enhanced communication and collaboration: Advancements in communication technologies enable greater connectivity and collaboration, facilitating knowledge sharing, innovation, and international cooperation.
Increased efficiency and productivity: Automation and artificial intelligence can streamline processes, improve efficiency, and free up human resources for higher-value tasks.

B. Environmental Opportunities:

Addressing environmental challenges can create both opportunities for sustainability and economic growth. Key considerations include:

Green economy: Investing in renewable energy, sustainable agriculture, and circular economy models can create new jobs, stimulate innovation, and reduce environmental impact.
Ecotourism and conservation: Developing responsible tourism practices and protecting natural environments can generate economic benefits while safeguarding biodiversity.
Climate adaptation: Investing in climate-resilient infrastructure, disaster preparedness, and adaptation strategies can mitigate the negative impacts of climate change and build resilience.

C. Social and Economic Opportunities:

Addressing societal needs and promoting inclusivity can unlock new opportunities for growth and progress. Key areas to focus on include:

Social entrepreneurship: Creating businesses that address social and environmental challenges while generating economic returns.
Skill development and education: Investing in education and skills development can empower individuals, promote social mobility, and enhance economic productivity.
Promoting diversity and inclusion: Creating inclusive societies that value diversity can foster innovation, creativity, and economic growth.

IV. Developing a Strategic Foresight Framework

To effectively navigate the complex landscape of potential challenges and opportunities, a comprehensive strategic foresight framework is essential. This framework should include the following steps:

1. Define the Scope: Clearly identify the focus of the foresight exercise, whether it's a specific industry, organization, or a broader societal issue.
2. Identify Key Trends: Research and analyze emerging trends that

are likely to shape the future landscape within the defined scope.
3. Analyze Drivers of Change: Identify the forces that are driving these trends, considering political, economic, social, technological, environmental, and legal factors (PESTEL).
4. Develop Scenarios: Create plausible and impactful future scenarios based on the interplay of identified trends and drivers. Consider various combinations of trends and their potential outcomes.
5. Assess Impacts: Evaluate the potential risks and opportunities associated with each scenario. Consider how each scenario might impact individuals, organizations, and society as a whole.
6. Develop Strategies: Formulate proactive plans and actions to navigate the potential challenges and seize the opportunities arising from different future scenarios.
7. Monitor and Adapt: Continuously monitor the evolving landscape, update scenarios as needed, and adapt strategies based on new information and emerging trends.

V. The Benefits of Strategic Foresight

Investing in strategic foresight offers numerous benefits for individuals, organizations, and societies:

Enhanced Decision-Making: By understanding potential future scenarios, decision-makers can make more informed and strategic choices.
Increased Resilience: Identifying and preparing for potential challenges enhances resilience and the ability to navigate unexpected disruptions.
Competitive Advantage: Seizing opportunities early can provide a significant competitive advantage in a rapidly evolving landscape.
Sustainable Development: Strategic foresight can guide investments and policies toward a more sustainable and equitable future.
Social Cohesion: Understanding and addressing potential societal challenges can strengthen social cohesion and build a more resilient and inclusive society.

VI. Conclusion

Exploring potential challenges and opportunities is not about predicting the future with certainty; it's about developing a deeper understanding of the forces shaping our world and equipping ourselves with the tools to navigate uncertainty. By embracing a strategic foresight framework, we can move from reactive to proactive decision-making, building resilience, seizing opportunities, and creating a more informed and prosperous future for all.

Envisioning a Thriving Future

Envisioning a thriving future is not about predicting the future with absolute certainty. It's about exploring possibilities, envisioning alternative pathways, and igniting a collective commitment to creating a world that nurtures both humanity and the planet. This vision is not a utopian fantasy but a practical roadmap that guides our actions today, laying the foundation for a future where prosperity is shared, resources are managed responsibly, and generations to come can inherit a world teeming with life and opportunity.

A Shift in Perspective: Embracing Sustainability as the Cornerstone of Progress

The concept of sustainability, often reduced to environmental conservation, encompasses a much broader vision. It's a holistic approach that recognizes the interconnectedness of our social, economic, and environmental systems. A sustainable future is one where economic growth is coupled with social justice and environmental responsibility. It's a future where we consume resources wisely, mitigate climate change, and ensure equitable access to essential services like healthcare, education, and clean water.

This shift in perspective demands a move away from the traditional paradigm of limitless growth. Instead, we must embrace a model of sustainable development that prioritizes circular economies, renewable energy sources, and responsible consumption patterns. This means rethinking our current production and consumption systems, transitioning to a model where waste is minimized, resources are reused, and natural capital is preserved for future generations.

Building a Just and Equitable Future: Bridging the Gap of Inequality

A thriving future cannot be built on a foundation of inequality. Social justice is an integral part of sustainability, recognizing that everyone deserves a fair chance to live a fulfilling life. This means addressing the systemic issues that perpetuate poverty, discrimination, and marginalization. It means investing in education, healthcare, and social safety nets to empower individuals and communities, particularly those most vulnerable to the negative impacts of climate change and economic instability.

Achieving social justice requires a commitment to dismantling oppressive systems and fostering inclusivity. It involves ensuring equal access to resources, opportunities, and decision-making power. It also means recognizing and valuing the diverse contributions of all members of society, creating a sense of shared ownership and responsibility in shaping a more equitable future.

A Global Perspective: Recognizing Interdependence and Shared Responsibility

The challenges we face today, from climate change to pandemics, are not confined to national borders. They are global in scope, demanding international collaboration and a shared sense of responsibility. The interconnectedness of our world requires a shift from nationalistic perspectives to a more inclusive and collaborative approach.

Global cooperation is not just a moral imperative, it's a pragmatic necessity. It allows us to leverage collective expertise, resources, and innovation to address complex problems. It also fosters understanding and empathy, building bridges between cultures and fostering a sense of shared humanity.

The Role of Technology: Balancing Innovation with Ethical Considerations

Technology has the potential to be a powerful force for good, enabling us to overcome existing challenges and create a more sustainable and equitable future. Innovations in renewable energy, biotechnology, and artificial intelligence offer promising solutions for addressing climate change, improving healthcare, and enhancing our quality of life.

However, technology must be harnessed responsibly. We must carefully consider the ethical implications of new technologies, ensuring they are used in ways that benefit humanity and the planet. This requires robust frameworks for regulating technology, fostering transparency, and ensuring equitable access to its benefits.

The Power of Individual Action: Embracing a Collective Shift in Behavior

While systemic change is crucial, individual actions play a vital role in shaping a thriving future. Every individual has the power to make choices that contribute to a more sustainable and just world. We can reduce our carbon footprint, support local businesses, advocate for policies that promote social justice, and engage in community initiatives that foster a sense of shared responsibility.

Furthermore, embracing a shift in values and mindset is essential. We need to move beyond consumerism and materialism, prioritizing experiences and connections over possessions. We need to cultivate empathy and compassion for all living beings, recognizing our interconnectedness with the natural world and each other.

Moving Forward with Hope and Resilience: Embracing a Future of Possibilities

Envisioning a thriving future is a hopeful endeavor, a testament to our capacity for collective action and our innate desire for a better world. This vision is not a guarantee but a compass, guiding our actions towards a future where sustainability and well-being are interwoven into the fabric of our lives.

It is a future where we learn to live in harmony with the planet, where social justice is a reality, and where technology empowers us to create a world that is both prosperous and sustainable. This is a future that is within our grasp, if we choose to embrace the challenges and opportunities that lie ahead with courage, creativity, and a shared commitment to building a brighter future for all. It's a journey that requires us to embrace both the challenges and opportunities that lie ahead, recognizing that each individual has the power to contribute to a more sustainable and just world. It's a journey that demands hope, resilience, and a belief in our collective capacity to create a future that is truly thriving for all.

Building Unity and Strength

This exploration delves into the multifaceted realm of building unity and strength, examining the intricate web of factors that contribute to its creation and the enduring challenges that often impede its progress. We will navigate the diverse terrains of personal relationships, social structures, and global alliances, seeking to understand the fundamental principles and practical strategies that empower us to build unity and foster strength, both within ourselves and within our communities.

The Foundations of Unity: Shared Values and Common Ground

The bedrock of unity lies in the shared values and aspirations that bind individuals together. When we find common ground, whether it's a belief in justice, a passion for artistic expression, or a commitment to environmental stewardship, a sense of belonging emerges. This shared understanding fosters empathy, encourages collaboration, and provides a platform for collective action.

Consider the power of shared traditions and rituals. They weave a tapestry of shared experiences, connecting generations and fostering a sense of continuity. Whether it's a religious ceremony, a cultural celebration, or simply a shared meal around a table, these rituals serve as powerful reminders of our interconnectedness.

The strength of a community is further amplified when its members actively cultivate empathy and compassion. By understanding and valuing each other's perspectives, even when they differ, we create a space for respectful dialogue and compromise. This willingness to embrace diversity strengthens our collective resolve and fosters a sense of unity that transcends individual differences.

Building Bridges: The Art of Effective Communication

Effective communication is the lifeblood of unity. It allows us to bridge divides, clarify misunderstandings, and forge deeper connections. Active listening, open dialogue, and a genuine desire to understand different perspectives are crucial elements of this process.

The challenge lies in creating spaces where diverse voices can be heard, where ideas can be exchanged without fear of judgment, and where constructive criticism is valued as a catalyst for growth. Fostering open and inclusive communication requires cultivating a culture of respect, where differences are not perceived as threats but as opportunities for enrichment.

Technology, in its various forms, plays a pivotal role in bridging geographical and cultural gaps. Social media platforms, online forums, and virtual communication tools can connect individuals across borders, fostering understanding and collaboration on a global scale. However, it's crucial to acknowledge the potential pitfalls of these technologies, recognizing the need for responsible use and the importance of cultivating authentic connections that transcend virtual realms.

Cultivating Strength: Embracing Diversity and Shared Responsibility

The strength of a community lies not in homogeneity but in its diversity. By valuing individual strengths and perspectives, we create a tapestry of talent and experience, enriching our collective wisdom and resilience.

This requires embracing inclusivity, actively seeking out diverse voices, and ensuring that all members feel valued and empowered to contribute their unique gifts. True strength arises from the recognition that individual success is inextricably linked to the well-being of the collective.

Shared responsibility is another cornerstone of strength. When individuals and communities recognize their collective stake in the shared future, they are more likely to act in ways that benefit the whole. This sense of shared ownership fosters a commitment to social justice, environmental sustainability, and long-term well-being.

The Challenges of Unity: Overcoming Division and Fostering Trust

Building unity and strength is not a linear path. It is often fraught with challenges, requiring constant effort and a willingness to confront ingrained biases and societal divisions.

One of the most formidable challenges lies in overcoming entrenched inequality and systemic discrimination. Addressing issues of poverty, access to education, and healthcare disparities is essential for fostering a just and equitable society, laying the foundation for true unity and shared prosperity.

The erosion of trust, fueled by misinformation, political polarization, and a culture of distrust, further complicates the task of building unity. Addressing these issues requires a renewed focus on fostering critical thinking skills, promoting media literacy, and encouraging constructive dialogue across ideological divides.

Navigating the Future: Embracing Innovation and Collaboration

The challenges of the 21st century demand innovative approaches to building unity and strength. Climate change, economic instability, and global pandemics underscore the interconnected nature of our world, highlighting the need for international collaboration and shared responsibility.

This requires embracing new technologies, fostering cross-cultural understanding, and promoting global citizenship. Embracing a mindset of collaboration, where shared solutions are prioritized over individual gains, is crucial for navigating the complex challenges of our time.

The Power of Hope and Collective Action

The journey of building unity and strength is ultimately a testament to the power of hope and collective action. Despite the obstacles, human history is replete with examples of communities overcoming adversity, forging bonds of solidarity, and achieving remarkable feats of progress.

By embracing the values of empathy, understanding, and shared responsibility, by engaging in meaningful dialogue and prioritizing collective action, we can create a future where unity and strength serve as beacons of hope, guiding us towards a world where all individuals and communities thrive.

Concluding Thoughts: A Call to Action

This exploration of building unity and strength is not simply an academic exercise. It is a call to action. It is a call to engage in meaningful dialogue, to build bridges across divides, and to actively contribute to the creation of a more just, equitable, and resilient world.

The journey ahead may be fraught with challenges, but the rewards of a united and empowered humanity are immeasurable. Let us embrace the spirit of collaboration, the power of shared purpose, and the enduring hope that, together, we can create a future where unity and strength are the hallmarks of our shared human journey.

Leaving a Legacy of Faith

Building Foundations: A Legacy of Faith Begins Within

The journey of leaving a legacy of faith begins not with grand pronouncements or outward gestures, but with a profound internal transformation. It requires a deliberate and conscious commitment to living a life authentically aligned with our faith. This journey is not a sprint, but a lifelong marathon, demanding unwavering dedication and a constant striving for spiritual growth. It entails immersing ourselves in the teachings of our faith, engaging in regular prayer and reflection, and seeking to live out the tenets of our beliefs in every aspect of our lives.

This internal transformation is characterized by a profound sense of purpose and a deep-rooted desire to serve others. It is fueled by a love for God and a genuine concern for the well-being of our fellow human beings. This inner work is the cornerstone of a lasting legacy of faith, for it creates a foundation of character, values, and convictions that will influence generations to come.

Living Out Our Faith: Embracing the Tapestry of Life

Leaving a legacy of faith is not a passive act of simply observing religious practices. It is an active, dynamic engagement with the world around us, where faith becomes a guiding light, illuminating the path towards meaningful living. This engagement unfolds in the tapestry of our daily lives, woven with threads of relationships, work, community, and service.

In our relationships, faith fosters compassion, forgiveness, and understanding. It empowers us to build bridges, mend broken connections, and extend grace to those who may be different from ourselves. It teaches us to prioritize love over judgment, acceptance over exclusion, and reconciliation over bitterness.

In our work, faith inspires us to strive for excellence, to seek integrity in all our dealings, and to treat each person with dignity and respect. It challenges us to view our work not merely as a means to an end, but as an opportunity to contribute to the greater good, leaving a positive impact on the world around us.

In our communities, faith compels us to participate in the lives of others, offering support and assistance to those in need. It motivates us to work towards social justice, to advocate for the marginalized, and to fight against injustice and inequality.

In our service, faith encourages us to go beyond our comfort zones, to step into the unknown, and to offer ourselves in love and service to others. It empowers us to become agents of change, bringing hope and healing to a world in need.

Passing the Torch: Inspiring Future Generations

The legacy of faith is not solely about personal transformation; it is also about actively shaping the lives of future generations. This involves sharing our faith with those around us, not through coercion or indoctrination, but through the power of example and inspiration. It means living our lives with integrity, demonstrating the transformative power of faith, and creating a space where others feel safe and welcome to explore their own spiritual journeys.

This passing of the torch can take many forms. It can be found in the simple act of sharing a heartfelt prayer with a loved one, in offering words of encouragement to someone struggling, or in guiding a child towards a deeper understanding of their faith. It can also be found in the pursuit of creative endeavors, where art, music, writing, or other forms of expression become channels for conveying the beauty and truth of our faith.

Through our actions, our words, and our presence, we can inspire others to embrace a life of faith, to seek a deeper understanding of their own spiritual identity, and to discover the joy and purpose that come from living a life guided by God's love.

A Legacy that Endures: Leaving an Imprint on Eternity

Leaving a legacy of faith is not about seeking earthly accolades or recognition. It is about seeking a connection to something far greater than ourselves, something that transcends the boundaries of time and space. It is about leaving an imprint on eternity, a testament to the power of faith to transform lives and create lasting positive change in the world.

The legacy we leave behind will be judged not by the number of followers we gather or the wealth we accumulate, but by the impact we have on the lives of others. It will be measured in the acts of kindness we extend, the words of encouragement we share, and the love and compassion we radiate into the world.

Leaving a legacy of faith is a journey of ongoing transformation, a lifelong pursuit of love, service, and spiritual growth. It is a journey that begins within, blossoms outwards, and ultimately inspires generations to come. It is a journey that offers the promise of an enduring impact, a legacy that will continue to inspire and empower long after we have gone.

Chapter 17: Personal Reflections and Testimonies

Sharing Stories of Faith and Transformation

The act of sharing such stories is a testament to the inherent human need for connection. We are social beings, driven by a primal urge to belong and to share our experiences with others. When we share stories of faith and transformation, we open ourselves up to vulnerability, allowing others to glimpse into the depths of our souls and understand the profound impact faith has had on our lives. This act of vulnerability fosters connection, creating a sense of shared humanity and understanding.

Beyond connection, sharing stories of faith and transformation serves as a powerful tool for cultivating meaning. In a world often characterized by uncertainty and chaos, these stories provide a compass, guiding us towards a sense of purpose and direction. By hearing about the journeys of others, we gain insights into the challenges they have faced, the lessons they have learned, and the transformative power of faith in navigating life's complexities. These stories remind us that we are not alone in our struggles, offering comfort and inspiration as we navigate our own paths.

Furthermore, sharing stories of faith and transformation serves as a catalyst for personal growth. These narratives often highlight moments of adversity and the resilience required to overcome obstacles. By hearing about the journeys of others, we are inspired to confront our own challenges with renewed strength and courage. The stories also serve as a reminder of the transformative power of faith, offering hope and encouragement as we embark on our own journeys of spiritual exploration and growth.

However, the act of sharing stories of faith and transformation requires a delicate balance of sensitivity and authenticity. It is crucial to approach these narratives with respect for individual experiences and beliefs. Sharing stories should not be about proselytizing or imposing beliefs on others, but rather about fostering understanding and empathy. Authenticity is equally important, as genuine stories resonate deeply and inspire genuine connection.

The Power of Personal Narratives

The power of personal narratives in exploring faith and transformation lies in their ability to transcend the abstract and theoretical. They humanize the spiritual journey, bringing faith and its transformative power into the realm of lived experience. These stories offer a unique window into the complexities of human belief, revealing how faith shapes values, influences choices, and ultimately impacts the trajectory of life.

Consider the individual who, after experiencing a personal crisis, finds solace and strength in a newfound faith. Their story, shared with others, offers a testament to the power of faith in times of hardship, providing a source of hope and encouragement.

Or perhaps the story revolves around an individual whose life has been irrevocably transformed by a deeply held belief. They may recount moments of spiritual awakening, acts of service inspired by their faith, or the profound impact faith has had on their relationships. These stories offer glimpses into the transformative potential of faith, inspiring others to consider its role in their own lives.

Navigating the Landscape of Faith and Transformation

Sharing stories of faith and transformation is a complex and multifaceted endeavor, requiring careful consideration of the nuances involved. Here are some key considerations:

Respecting Diversity of Beliefs: Recognizing the vast spectrum of beliefs and spiritual practices across the globe is essential. Stories should be shared with respect for the diversity of faith traditions, avoiding any form of judgment or dismissal of differing beliefs.
Embracing Vulnerability: Sharing stories of faith and transformation often requires vulnerability. The individuals sharing these stories may be revealing personal struggles, moments of doubt, or profound spiritual experiences. It is important to create a safe and supportive environment where vulnerability can be embraced without fear of judgment or dismissal.
Promoting Open Dialogue: Sharing stories can serve as a springboard for open and respectful dialogue about faith and its impact on individuals and communities. Creating spaces for dialogue allows for a deeper exploration of different perspectives, fostering understanding and mutual respect.
Addressing the Challenges: Faith and transformation are not always smooth journeys. Sharing stories can also involve acknowledging the challenges, doubts, and moments of uncertainty that can accompany spiritual growth. These narratives offer a more balanced and honest portrayal of faith, recognizing the complexity of human experience.

The Impact of Sharing Stories

Sharing stories of faith and transformation has a profound impact on both the storyteller and the listener. For the storyteller, it serves as a cathartic experience, providing an outlet for reflection, processing, and integrating their own experiences. The act of sharing can also strengthen their faith, reminding them of the power and impact of their beliefs.

For the listener, these stories offer a sense of connection, understanding, and inspiration. They provide a glimpse into the diverse ways in which faith manifests in the world, fostering empathy and respect for different beliefs. These stories can also serve as a source of comfort and strength, particularly for those who are navigating their own journeys of faith and transformation.

Beyond Personal Narratives: Exploring the Impact of Storytelling in Faith-Based Communities

The impact of sharing stories extends far beyond individual narratives. Faith-based communities often use storytelling as a powerful tool for building community, fostering spiritual growth, and transmitting values and traditions across generations.

Consider the role of storytelling in religious ceremonies and rituals. Parables, myths, and legends shared during these ceremonies often convey profound spiritual teachings, inspiring awe and reverence. These narratives serve as a bridge between past and present, connecting individuals to a shared history and collective identity.

Storytelling is also an integral part of many faith-based educational programs. Sharing the stories of faith figures, historical events, and personal journeys can deepen understanding of religious teachings, cultivate a sense of belonging within the community, and inspire individuals to live out their faith in their daily lives.

Furthermore, storytelling plays a vital role in addressing social issues and promoting justice. Faith-based organizations often use storytelling to raise awareness about systemic injustices, share the stories of those who have been marginalized, and inspire action for positive change.

The Future of Sharing Stories of Faith and Transformation

In an increasingly interconnected world, the power of sharing stories of faith and transformation will continue to grow. As people from diverse backgrounds and beliefs come together, these stories will offer a bridge of understanding, fostering empathy and respect across cultural and religious divides.

Technological advancements also present new avenues for sharing stories. Online platforms, social media, and digital storytelling initiatives offer opportunities to connect with wider audiences and expand the reach of these transformative narratives.

Furthermore, the growing interest in personal development and spiritual growth suggests a continued desire for stories that offer guidance, inspiration, and a sense of meaning. Sharing stories of faith and transformation will remain a vital source of comfort, hope, and connection in a world that often feels fragmented and uncertain. These narratives transcend individual experiences, offering a tapestry of human experience that resonates across cultures, backgrounds, and beliefs. By embracing vulnerability, promoting open dialogue, and respecting diversity, we can create spaces where these stories can be shared with authenticity and impact, transforming lives and fostering a deeper understanding of the human spirit.

Inspiring Others Through Personal Experiences

Inspiring others through personal experiences is not about boasting or seeking validation. It is about fostering a sense of shared humanity, forging connections through relatable struggles and triumphs, and offering a beacon of hope that resonates deeply with the individual listener. It is about embracing the power of vulnerability, acknowledging our imperfections, and recognizing that even in our darkest moments, there is potential for growth and transformation.

This journey of inspiring others through personal experience begins with a deep understanding of the power of storytelling. Stories, at their core, are universal. They weave together threads of emotion, experience, and reflection, creating a tapestry that speaks to the human condition. Sharing our stories is an act of vulnerability, a willingness to open ourselves up to judgment and scrutiny. But it is also an act of courage, a testament to our resilience and our willingness to connect with others on a profound level.

When we share our personal experiences, we create a space for connection and empathy. We allow others to see themselves reflected in our struggles, to find solace in our shared vulnerabilities, and to find strength in our shared triumphs. This shared vulnerability fosters a sense of community, bridging the gap between individual experiences and creating a sense of collective understanding.

The act of sharing a personal experience, however, requires more than just recounting events. It requires authenticity, transparency, and a willingness to delve into the raw emotions that lie beneath the surface. It requires us to be honest with ourselves and with others, to acknowledge our mistakes, and to embrace the imperfections that make us human. This vulnerability, this willingness to expose ourselves, is what resonates with others and creates the potential for real, lasting inspiration.

Inspiring others through personal experience requires a shift in perspective. It's not about emphasizing our successes, but about acknowledging the lessons learned along the way. It's about sharing our struggles, not as a means of seeking pity, but as a testament to our resilience and our ability to overcome adversity. By being transparent about our challenges, we create space for others to recognize their own struggles, to validate their own experiences, and to find strength in the knowledge that they are not alone.

This approach to sharing personal experiences fosters a sense of shared humanity, creating a space for empathy and understanding.

It allows others to see themselves in our stories, to find comfort in our shared vulnerabilities, and to feel empowered by our shared triumphs. By sharing our stories, we create a ripple effect of inspiration, encouraging others to embrace their own vulnerabilities, to seek growth through their own challenges, and to ultimately find their own unique paths to personal transformation.

The Power of Vulnerability

The concept of vulnerability is often misunderstood, misrepresented as weakness. However, vulnerability is the foundation of authentic connection. It is the courage to be seen, to be heard, and to be understood, imperfections and all. When we embrace vulnerability, we create a space for genuine connection, inviting others to do the same.

In the context of inspiring others through personal experiences, vulnerability plays a crucial role. It allows us to connect with others on a deeper level, to build trust, and to create a sense of shared humanity. By acknowledging our own flaws, our own struggles, and our own insecurities, we create a space for others to do the same, to feel seen, and to feel understood.

Imagine a speaker sharing a story of overcoming a debilitating fear. By being vulnerable about their struggle, they not only inspire others who may be facing similar challenges but also create a space for dialogue and support. Their vulnerability becomes a catalyst for positive change, offering a tangible example of how to navigate difficult emotions and achieve personal growth.

The Art of Storytelling

Sharing personal experiences is not simply a matter of recounting events. It is an art form, a skillful weaving of narrative and emotion that resonates deeply with the listener. The art of storytelling lies in the ability to connect with others on an emotional level, to paint vivid pictures with words, and to evoke a sense of shared experience.

Effective storytelling involves more than just the facts. It involves weaving in personal reflections, emotional insights, and lessons learned. It involves using language that is both powerful and accessible, creating a sense of immediacy and immersion. It requires a willingness to be vulnerable, to share our raw emotions, and to connect with the audience on a deeply human level.

Consider the impact of a speaker sharing their story of navigating a difficult career transition. By using vivid language, emotional depth, and a clear narrative arc, they can capture the listener's attention, elicit empathy, and ultimately inspire them to embrace their own challenges with newfound courage.

The Transformative Power of Shared Experiences

Inspiring others through personal experiences has a profound transformative power. When we share our stories, we not only offer a glimpse into our own journeys, but we also inspire others to embark on their own paths of growth and transformation.

Shared experiences create a sense of community, fostering a sense of belonging and connection. They challenge our perspectives, broaden our understanding of the human condition, and ultimately empower us to make a positive impact on the world. They offer a sense of hope, reminding us that even in our darkest moments, there is potential for healing, growth, and renewal.

Consider the impact of a speaker sharing their story of overcoming a personal trauma. Their story, shared with authenticity and vulnerability, can inspire others who may be struggling with similar experiences, offering a tangible example of resilience, healing, and the potential for a brighter future.

Examples of Inspiring Others Through Personal Experiences

Throughout history, countless individuals have used their personal experiences to inspire others. From the powerful narratives of Holocaust survivors to the heartfelt accounts of social justice activists, these stories serve as a testament to the transformative power of sharing our stories.

Malala Yousafzai: Malala's story of fighting for girls' education in the face of violence and oppression has inspired millions around the world. Her courage and resilience, shared through her own words and actions, have empowered countless individuals to fight for justice, equality, and a brighter future.

Nelson Mandela: Mandela's life story, a testament to his unwavering commitment to social justice and human rights, has resonated with people across the globe. His struggles against apartheid, his unwavering belief in forgiveness, and his ultimate triumph over adversity have inspired generations to fight for a more just and equitable world.

Oprah Winfrey: Oprah's journey from poverty to becoming a global media mogul is a testament to the power of resilience, perseverance, and self-belief. Her story, shared through her own experiences and through the stories of others, has empowered countless individuals to overcome adversity and achieve their dreams.

Conclusion

Inspiring others through personal experiences is a powerful force for positive change. By embracing vulnerability, honing our storytelling skills, and sharing our journeys with authenticity, we can create a space for connection, empathy, and growth. These stories, shared with intention and compassion, have the power to transform lives, to build communities, and to ultimately make the world a better place.

In an increasingly interconnected world, the power of shared experiences has never been more relevant. As we navigate the complexities of our modern lives, the stories we share, the vulnerabilities we embrace, and the connections we forge through our shared experiences will ultimately shape the future of our world.

Demonstrating the Impact of Messianic Judaism

Internal Dynamics: Theological Innovation and Communal Identity

The very existence of Messianic Judaism challenges traditional understandings of Judaism and Christianity. At its core lies a theological innovation: the integration of Jesus Christ into the Jewish narrative. This move, while controversial, allows Messianic Jews to claim both Jewish identity and faith in Jesus. This inherent tension creates a unique theological landscape within the movement.

One prominent aspect of this internal debate revolves around the concept of "replacement theology. " Critics argue that Messianic Judaism, by embracing Jesus as the Messiah, inadvertently replaces Judaism with Christianity, effectively negating the unique role of the Jewish people in God's plan. This argument is often countered by emphasizing the continuity of Jewish traditions within Messianic Judaism, highlighting practices like Sabbath observance, dietary laws, and the celebration of Jewish holidays. This emphasis on continuity aims to distinguish Messianic Judaism from evangelical Christianity, emphasizing its distinctively Jewish character.

The ongoing debate about theological boundaries within Messianic Judaism also manifests in various communal practices. For instance, the role of the Hebrew Bible (Tanakh) as the central religious text is often a point of contention. Some congregations interpret the Tanakh literally, while others adopt a more nuanced approach, integrating both the Old and New Testaments into their theological framework. This difference in biblical interpretation can significantly impact worship practices and theological teachings, shaping the internal landscape of Messianic Judaism.

The influence of Jewish tradition is further evident in the emphasis on Hebrew language and culture within many Messianic Jewish communities. The use of Hebrew in worship services, the study of Jewish texts and traditions, and the celebration of cultural holidays like Hanukkah and Passover all contribute to a strong sense of Jewish identity within the movement. This focus on cultural continuity helps to bridge the gap between Jewish tradition and Christian beliefs, fostering a unique communal identity.

External Influence: Dialogue, Debate, and Transformation

The impact of Messianic Judaism extends beyond its internal dynamics, influencing the broader Jewish and Christian communities. One prominent area of influence lies in the realm of interfaith dialogue. The very existence of Messianic Judaism challenges traditional assumptions about Judaism and Christianity, forcing both communities to re-examine their theological positions and engage in dialogue regarding shared beliefs and divergent interpretations.

This dialogue, however, is often fraught with tension. While some Jewish groups engage in constructive dialogue with Messianic Jewish communities, others perceive them as a threat to Jewish identity, actively opposing their inclusion in Jewish spaces. This resistance stems from concerns about Messianic Judaism's potential to dilute Jewish tradition, and from the perception of Messianic Judaism as a proselytizing force seeking to convert Jews to Christianity.

The debate surrounding Messianic Judaism also extends to the Christian world. Some Christian denominations embrace Messianic Judaism as a valuable example of Jewish expression of faith in Jesus, seeing it as a bridge between Judaism and Christianity. Others, however, remain skeptical, viewing Messianic Judaism as a hybrid religion that blurs the lines between Jewish and Christian beliefs.

This multifaceted interaction between Messianic Judaism and other communities has led to significant transformations within both Judaism and Christianity. On the one hand, Messianic Judaism has contributed to a more nuanced understanding of Jewish identity, challenging the monolithic view of Judaism as a purely secular religion. On the other hand, the movement has prompted a reassessment of the relationship between Judaism and Christianity, encouraging a more inclusive understanding of Christian faith that acknowledges the Jewish roots of Christianity.

Challenges and Prospects: Navigating the Future

Messianic Judaism, despite its impact, faces ongoing challenges. The internal debate surrounding theological boundaries and communal practices continues to shape the movement's trajectory. Externally, Messianic Judaism confronts criticism and resistance from both Jewish and Christian communities, navigating the complex terrain of interfaith relations.

Despite these challenges, Messianic Judaism continues to flourish, with growing congregations and a vibrant theological and cultural landscape. The movement's future likely hinges on its ability to navigate the ongoing dialogue with other religious communities, fostering understanding and dialogue while maintaining its distinctive identity. It is a movement in motion, constantly evolving, challenging preconceived notions, and shaping the religious landscape of both Judaism and Christianity. Understanding its influence requires a multifaceted approach that considers its internal dynamics, its external interactions, and its ongoing journey towards a more inclusive and nuanced understanding of faith and identity. As Messianic Judaism continues to evolve, its impact on religious thought and practice will undoubtedly continue to shape the future of Jewish-Christian relations and religious expression in the 21st century.

Connecting with a Community of Believers

The allure of community lies in its ability to provide a sense of identity, belonging, and support. As individuals, we often navigate the world feeling alone, facing challenges that seem insurmountable. A community of believers, however, offers a haven of shared values, beliefs, and experiences that can provide solace and strength. By connecting with others who share our faith, we find ourselves enveloped in a network of support, where our joys are celebrated and our struggles are shared. This sense of shared purpose and collective effort fosters a sense of belonging that transcends the boundaries of individual struggles, providing a sense of community and kinship that is profoundly enriching.

Moreover, connecting with a community of believers fosters a deeper understanding and exploration of our faith. Through shared discussions, communal worship, and service projects, we engage with the intricacies of our faith in a dynamic and interactive manner. Our understanding of the scriptures, the nuances of theological concepts, and the practical application of our beliefs become enriched through the interplay of diverse perspectives and lived experiences. This collective exploration of faith allows us to grapple with complex theological questions, delve into the depths of spiritual practice, and cultivate a more profound understanding of our faith's tenets.

Beyond the intellectual and spiritual benefits, connecting with a community of believers also provides opportunities for personal growth and development. The shared experiences of joy, sorrow, and service within a community foster empathy, compassion, and a sense of responsibility towards others. We learn to embrace the diversity of perspectives within our faith community, fostering tolerance, understanding, and a commitment to inclusivity. Through service projects and acts of kindness, we put our faith into action, translating our beliefs into tangible expressions of love and compassion. This active engagement in our community not only enriches the lives of others but also contributes to our own personal growth and spiritual development.

The journey of connecting with a community of believers is often multifaceted and nuanced. It requires an openness to engage with others, a willingness to learn and grow, and a commitment to actively participate in the life of the community. Finding the right community can be a process of exploration, involving trying different congregations, attending various events, and engaging in conversations with individuals who share our faith. This process of discovery can be both exciting and challenging, requiring us to be patient, persistent, and open to embracing the diversity within our faith tradition.

Ultimately, connecting with a community of believers is an act of faith, an affirmation of our shared belief system and a commitment to living out our faith in a meaningful and enriching way. It is through these connections that we find solace, strength, and purpose in our spiritual journeys, enriching our lives and contributing to the larger tapestry of our shared faith tradition.

Navigating the Landscape of Community

Connecting with a community of believers, however, is not a singular act but an ongoing process, a dynamic interaction between the individual and the collective. It involves navigating the intricacies of communal life, engaging with diverse perspectives, and understanding the ebb and flow of relationships within the community.

One important aspect of navigating this landscape is recognizing the diversity within our faith tradition. Just as individuals hold unique perspectives and experiences, so too do faith communities. Different congregations emphasize different aspects of faith, adopt varying worship styles, and foster unique communal dynamics. This diversity, while enriching, can also pose challenges, requiring us to be sensitive to the nuances of different communities and to engage with them with respect and understanding.

A key aspect of navigating this diversity is embracing the concept of interfaith dialogue. As the world becomes increasingly interconnected, understanding and respecting other faith traditions becomes crucial. Engaging in interfaith dialogue provides a platform for fostering mutual understanding, identifying commonalities, and dispelling misconceptions. By engaging with individuals from different faith backgrounds, we expand our horizons, broaden our understanding of diverse perspectives, and cultivate a spirit of interfaith harmony.

In addition to navigating interfaith dialogue, we also need to understand the dynamics of power and privilege within our own communities. Faith communities, like any social group, can be susceptible to systemic inequalities and hierarchical structures. It is important to acknowledge these dynamics and work towards creating a more inclusive and equitable environment. This involves challenging ingrained biases, advocating for marginalized voices, and promoting a culture of respect and understanding.

In brief, navigating the landscape of community requires a commitment to ongoing learning and growth. As individuals and as a community, we need to constantly engage with new perspectives, challenge our assumptions, and adapt to evolving social and theological landscapes. This requires a spirit of humility, a willingness to listen, and a commitment to continuous learning.

Cultivating Meaningful Connections

Connecting with a community of believers is not merely about joining a group; it is about forging meaningful connections that enrich our lives and deepen our faith. This process of cultivating meaningful connections involves several key components:

1. Active Participation: Merely attending services or events is not enough; active participation is crucial. This involves engaging in conversations, volunteering for service projects, contributing to discussions, and actively participating in the life of the community. Through active participation, we demonstrate our commitment to the community and foster deeper connections with others.

2. Building Relationships: Community is not solely about shared beliefs; it is also about building relationships with individuals. This involves taking the time to get to know others, engaging in meaningful conversations, supporting each other through challenges, and celebrating successes together. Building strong relationships fosters a sense of belonging and creates a network of support within the community.

3. Seeking Shared Purpose: Finding a community that aligns with our values and goals is essential for fostering meaningful connections. This involves exploring different communities, participating in various activities, and finding a group that shares our sense of purpose and mission. Connecting with others who share our vision and commitment strengthens our resolve and empowers us to make a meaningful impact in the world.

4. Serving Others: A community of believers is not just a social group; it is a body of people called to serve others. Engaging in service projects, extending a helping hand, and demonstrating compassion for those in need are essential aspects of connecting with a community of believers. Service, in its many forms, allows us to translate our faith into action, enriching the lives of others and deepening our own spiritual journey.

The Transformative Power of Community

Connecting with a community of believers is not merely a social act; it is a transformative journey that enriches our lives, strengthens our faith, and empowers us to make a positive impact on the world. The power of community lies in its ability to:

Provide a Sense of Belonging: In a world often characterized by isolation and fragmentation, community offers a sense of belonging, kinship, and shared purpose. It creates a space where individuals feel valued, supported, and connected to a larger whole.

Foster Spiritual Growth: Engaging in shared worship, discussions, and service projects within a community fosters a deeper understanding and appreciation of our faith. It provides a platform for exploring theological concepts, grappling with complex questions, and deepening our spiritual practice.

Promote Personal Growth: The shared experiences of joy, sorrow, and service within a community cultivate empathy, compassion, and a sense of responsibility towards others. It challenges us to step outside of ourselves, to embrace diversity, and to contribute to the well-being of others.

Empower Action: By connecting with others who share our values and goals, we gain the strength and support to translate our faith into action. Whether it be through service projects, advocacy efforts, or social justice initiatives, community provides a platform for making a tangible difference in the world. It is through these connections, through the shared experiences of joy, sorrow, and service, that we discover the true meaning of community and the profound power of faith in action.

Chapter 18: Engaging with Technology and the Digital World

Utilizing Social Media for Outreach

The Power of Social Media for Outreach

Social media has emerged as a powerful tool for outreach due to its inherent capacity to transcend geographical boundaries, connect with diverse audiences, and facilitate two-way communication. Unlike traditional media, which often operates in a one-way broadcast model, social media platforms foster interactive dialogue, allowing individuals and organizations to engage directly with their target audiences. This interactive nature cultivates a sense of community and fosters a deeper understanding between the outreach entity and its audience.

Key Benefits of Social Media Outreach:

1. Increased Reach and Visibility: Social media platforms offer a vast and ever-expanding network of users, enabling organizations to broaden their reach beyond traditional communication channels. This expanded reach allows them to connect with new audiences and raise awareness for their initiatives, products, or services.

2. Targeted Audience Engagement: Social media platforms provide sophisticated tools for audience segmentation and targeting, allowing outreach efforts to be tailored to specific demographics, interests, and behaviors. This targeted approach ensures that outreach messages are relevant and resonate with the intended

audience, maximizing engagement and impact.

3. Cost-Effectiveness: Compared to traditional outreach methods like print advertising or television commercials, social media outreach offers a more cost-effective alternative. The ability to reach a vast audience at a fraction of the cost makes it an attractive option for organizations with limited budgets.

4. Real-Time Communication and Feedback: Social media enables real-time communication, allowing organizations to respond to inquiries, address concerns, and engage in dynamic conversations with their audiences. This immediacy fosters transparency and trust, strengthening the relationship between the outreach entity and its stakeholders.

5. Content Diversification and Multimedia Integration: Social media platforms support a wide range of content formats, from text-based posts to images, videos, and interactive polls. This versatility allows organizations to present their message in engaging and accessible ways, catering to diverse learning styles and preferences within their target audiences.

Strategies for Effective Social Media Outreach

To maximize the potential of social media for outreach, it is essential to adopt a strategic and thoughtful approach. This involves identifying target audiences, understanding their needs and interests, and creating relevant content that resonates with them.

1. Define Your Audience: Before embarking on any social media outreach campaign, it is crucial to define your target audience. Who are you trying to reach. What are their demographics, interests, and motivations. Understanding your audience will inform your content strategy and ensure that your messages are relevant and engaging.

2. Choose the Right Platforms: Different social media platforms

cater to distinct audiences and offer different functionalities. For instance, Facebook is known for its broad reach and diverse user base, while Twitter is favored for its real-time news and discussion capabilities. LinkedIn focuses on professional networking, while Instagram excels at visual content and brand storytelling. Selecting the appropriate platforms for your outreach efforts is essential for maximizing impact.

3. Develop Engaging Content: Content is king on social media. Create compelling and shareable content that informs, educates, entertains, and inspires your audience. Employ a variety of formats, including text, images, videos, infographics, and interactive polls, to keep your audience engaged and diversify your outreach strategy.

4. Use Visual Storytelling: Visual content has a powerful impact on social media. Images, videos, and infographics capture attention and convey information more effectively than text alone. Invest in high-quality visual assets that complement your message and enhance its appeal.

5. Build Community and Interaction: Social media is not just about broadcasting messages; it's about building relationships and fostering community. Encourage interaction by asking questions, responding to comments, and engaging in conversations with your audience. This interactive approach will build trust and strengthen your connection with your stakeholders.

6. Embrace Social Listening: Social listening is the practice of monitoring social media conversations related to your industry, brand, or cause. By paying attention to what people are saying about you and your competitors, you can gain valuable insights into their needs, concerns, and perceptions. This information can be used to refine your outreach strategy and ensure that your messages resonate with your target audience.

7. Measure and Evaluate Your Efforts: Social media platforms offer a

range of analytics tools that allow you to track the performance of your outreach campaigns. Monitor metrics like reach, engagement, website traffic, and conversions to assess the effectiveness of your strategy. This data can be used to refine your approach and optimize your outreach efforts for maximum impact.

Ethical Considerations in Social Media Outreach

As social media outreach becomes increasingly prevalent, it is important to consider the ethical implications of this form of communication. Transparency, authenticity, and respect for privacy are crucial principles to uphold.

1. Transparency: Be transparent about your identity and your motivations for engaging with your audience. Avoid misleading or deceptive practices that could erode trust and credibility.

2. Authenticity: Be genuine and authentic in your communication. Don't try to be someone you're not or present a distorted version of your message.

3. Privacy: Respect the privacy of your audience. Avoid collecting or sharing personal information without consent.

4. Responsible Use: Use social media responsibly and avoid spreading misinformation, hate speech, or harmful content.

Conclusion

Social media has become an indispensable tool for outreach, providing organizations and individuals with a powerful platform for connecting with diverse audiences and promoting their causes, initiatives, and ideas. By embracing a strategic approach, prioritizing ethical considerations, and continuously adapting to the evolving landscape of social media, individuals and organizations can leverage these platforms to build meaningful connections, foster engagement, and achieve their outreach goals. As the digital world continues to evolve, it is essential to remain informed, adapt our strategies, and harness the power of social media for positive impact.

Building Online Communities

Understanding the Essence of Online Communities

At their core, online communities revolve around shared values, interests, or goals that unite individuals with a common purpose. They provide a platform for meaningful interactions, knowledge sharing, and mutual support. The success of any online community hinges on its ability to foster a sense of belonging, encourage active engagement, and cultivate a vibrant ecosystem of diverse voices.

Key Pillars of a Successful Online Community:

Shared Purpose and Values: A clear understanding of the community's purpose and underlying values acts as a guiding principle, attracting members who resonate with its core ethos.
Active Engagement: Encouraging active participation through regular discussions, collaborative projects, and interactive events is crucial for community vitality.
Inclusiveness and Diversity: Creating a welcoming environment that embraces diverse perspectives and experiences fosters a richer and more dynamic community.
Trust and Authenticity: Building trust through open communication, transparency, and genuine interactions is paramount for fostering a sense of security and belonging.
Effective Moderation and Governance: Establishing clear guidelines and implementing effective moderation practices ensure a safe and positive environment for all members.

Strategies for Building a Thriving Online Community

Building a successful online community requires a strategic approach, taking into consideration the unique characteristics of the target audience and the overall goals of the community. The following strategies can serve as a roadmap for cultivating a vibrant and engaged online space:

1. Define Your Community's Identity and Purpose:

Mission Statement: Craft a concise and compelling mission statement that encapsulates the community's purpose and values. This serves as a guiding light for both members and community leaders.
Target Audience: Identify the specific group of individuals you aim to attract, considering their interests, demographics, and online behavior.
Unique Value Proposition: Articulate what makes your community distinct and valuable, offering a compelling reason for individuals to join and actively participate.

2. Choose the Right Platform and Tools:

Platform Selection: Consider the platform's functionality, target audience, and ease of use when choosing the best platform for your community. Options range from dedicated forums and social media groups to specialized platforms for niche communities.
Essential Tools: Implement tools that facilitate communication, collaboration, and content creation. Examples include forums for discussion, chat features for real-time interactions, and project management tools for collaborative efforts.
Customization and Branding: Tailor the platform's appearance and branding to reflect the community's identity, creating a visually appealing and cohesive experience.

3. Foster a Welcoming and Engaging Environment:

Onboarding and Welcome Process: Create a smooth onboarding experience that welcomes new members and guides them through the community's norms and expectations.
Interactive Content: Engage members through diverse content formats such as blog posts, polls, quizzes, and interactive discussions.
Community Events and Activities: Organize regular events, challenges, or virtual meetups to encourage interaction, collaboration, and shared experiences.
Member Recognition and Appreciation: Acknowledge and celebrate active members, showcasing their contributions and fostering a sense of belonging.

4. Promote and Grow Your Community:

Strategic Outreach: Target potential members through relevant online channels, including social media, online communities, and industry publications.
Content Marketing: Create compelling and shareable content that attracts new members and fosters engagement within the existing community.
Partner with Influencers: Collaborate with relevant influencers or thought leaders to reach a wider audience and generate interest in your community.
Cross-Promotion: Leverage existing networks and platforms to cross-promote your community, reaching new potential members.

5. Effective Moderation and Governance:

Community Guidelines: Establish clear guidelines that outline acceptable behavior and prohibit harmful content, ensuring a safe and respectful environment for all members.
Active Moderation: Implement effective moderation practices to monitor discussions, address issues promptly, and enforce community guidelines.
Member Feedback and Input: Encourage member feedback and

suggestions for improvement, ensuring the community remains responsive and adapts to the needs of its members.

6. Data Analysis and Measurement:

Community Analytics: Track key metrics such as member growth, engagement levels, and content performance to assess the community's health and identify areas for improvement.
Member Feedback Surveys: Regularly gather feedback from members to understand their needs, satisfaction levels, and suggestions for improvement.

Challenges and Considerations in Building Online Communities

Building and maintaining a thriving online community is an ongoing process that requires continuous effort and attention. Here are some common challenges and considerations:

1. Maintaining Engagement and Preventing Stagnation:

Content Freshness and Variety: Continuously provide fresh and diverse content that keeps members engaged and prevents them from becoming bored or disengaged.
Member Incentives and Recognition: Offer incentives, rewards, or recognition for active participation, encouraging members to contribute and remain engaged.
Dynamic Content Formats: Explore diverse content formats beyond text-based discussions, incorporating video, audio, and interactive elements to keep members interested.

2. Combating Trolls and Negative Behavior:

Proactive Moderation: Implement robust moderation practices to prevent trolling, spam, and harmful content from impacting the community's atmosphere.
Clear Guidelines and Enforcement: Establish clear community

guidelines outlining unacceptable behavior and enforce them consistently, deterring negative behavior.
Community Support: Encourage positive interactions and foster a sense of community support to counter negative behavior and promote constructive dialogue.

3. Scaling and Sustainability:

Community Structure and Governance: Develop a scalable community structure and governance system to manage growth effectively and ensure long-term sustainability.
Funding and Resources: Explore potential sources of funding or resources to support the community's continued operation and expansion.
Partnerships and Collaborations: Collaborate with other communities or organizations to expand reach, resources, and opportunities for growth.

4. Data Privacy and Security:

Data Protection: Implement measures to protect member data and comply with relevant privacy regulations, building trust and ensuring user security.
Secure Platform: Choose a platform that offers robust security features and follows industry best practices for data protection.
Transparency and Communication: Be transparent about data usage and security measures, fostering trust and open communication with community members.

Examples of Successful Online Communities

Reddit: A vast online community platform with thousands of dedicated forums (subreddits) covering a wide range of interests and topics, fostering discussion, knowledge sharing, and entertainment.
Discord: A popular platform for gamers and other online

communities, offering voice and text chat, group messaging, and community management features.

LinkedIn: A professional networking platform that connects individuals in their respective industries, facilitating professional development, job searching, and networking opportunities.

Stack Overflow: A question-and-answer site dedicated to programming and software development, offering a collaborative space for technical knowledge sharing and problem-solving.

5. The Future of Online Communities

The future of online communities is brimming with exciting possibilities, driven by advancements in technology and the evolving landscape of social interaction. Here are some key trends:

The Rise of Virtual Reality and Augmented Reality: VR and AR technologies are opening new avenues for immersive and interactive community experiences, fostering deeper connection and engagement.

Increased Personalization and Customization: Tailored experiences and personalized content will play an increasingly important role in attracting and retaining members.

The Importance of Data-Driven Insights: Data analysis and insights will be crucial for understanding member behavior, optimizing community engagement, and driving growth.

The Intersection of Online and Offline Experiences: Bridging the gap between online and offline experiences through hybrid events and virtual meetups will enhance community engagement and foster deeper connections. By embracing the key principles outlined in this guide, incorporating effective strategies, and continuously adapting to the evolving digital landscape, communities can cultivate a strong sense of belonging, foster active engagement, and thrive as vibrant hubs for connection, learning, and growth.

The journey of building an online community is one of continuous learning, experimentation, and adaptation. By fostering a culture of collaboration, innovation, and genuine connection, online communities can become powerful forces for positive change, enriching the lives of their members and shaping a more connected and inclusive digital world.

Sharing Resources and Information

The Foundation of Collaboration:

At its core, sharing resources and information is the bedrock of collaboration. It dismantles silos, bridges gaps, and creates fertile ground for joint endeavors. Imagine a research team working on a groundbreaking discovery, each member possessing a unique piece of the puzzle. By sharing their findings, their knowledge, and their expertise, they weave a tapestry of understanding, propelling their work towards a shared goal.

This principle transcends the realm of science. In business, sharing market research, best practices, and customer insights can help companies streamline operations, identify new opportunities, and navigate evolving landscapes. Within communities, sharing resources like tools, equipment, and knowledge can empower individuals to pursue their passions, tackle challenges, and contribute to collective well-being.

The Fuel of Innovation:

Beyond mere collaboration, resource and information sharing is the catalyst for innovation. By exposing ourselves to diverse perspectives, unfamiliar ideas, and fresh approaches, we spark the creative process. The cross-pollination of knowledge generates new insights, challenges assumptions, and fuels the birth of groundbreaking solutions.

Consider the rise of open-source software. By sharing code,

developers collaborate globally, building upon each other's work, and fostering rapid innovation. This collaborative spirit has revolutionized industries, creating new possibilities and democratizing access to technology. Similarly, the open exchange of research data has accelerated scientific discovery, unlocking new avenues for understanding the universe and tackling global challenges.

Navigating the Challenges:

While the benefits of resource and information sharing are undeniable, the process is not without its challenges. Trust, transparency, and ethical considerations must be carefully navigated to ensure a positive and productive outcome.

One key hurdle is the fear of losing control or giving away intellectual property. This fear can stifle collaboration and innovation, as individuals and organizations cling tightly to their resources, unwilling to share for fear of being disadvantaged. Building a culture of trust, where sharing is seen as a mutually beneficial exchange rather than a loss, is essential for overcoming this barrier.

Another challenge lies in ensuring equitable access to information. Resources and knowledge are not evenly distributed, and disparities in access can exacerbate existing inequalities. Bridging this digital divide through initiatives that promote digital literacy, provide access to technology, and support the creation of open and accessible resources is crucial for realizing the full potential of knowledge sharing.

Strategies for Success:

Overcoming these challenges requires a deliberate and strategic approach. Creating a culture that values collaboration and knowledge sharing is paramount. This can be achieved through:

Clear communication: Establishing clear protocols for sharing information, including guidelines on confidentiality, attribution, and intellectual property rights, helps build trust and transparency.
Incentivizing participation: Recognizing and rewarding contributions to knowledge sharing can encourage individuals and organizations to actively participate in the process.
Creating platforms for exchange: Developing online and offline platforms for sharing resources and information facilitates connection and collaboration, breaking down barriers and promoting cross-sector interaction.
Promoting digital literacy: Investing in digital literacy programs equips individuals with the skills and knowledge necessary to access, evaluate, and utilize information effectively.
Advocating for open access: Supporting initiatives that promote open access to research, data, and educational resources ensures greater equity and accessibility, democratizing knowledge and fostering innovation.

The Future of Sharing:

As we navigate the ever-evolving information landscape, the importance of sharing resources and information will only intensify. Technology continues to break down barriers, connecting individuals and organizations across continents and fostering a global community of knowledge.

This global interconnectedness presents both opportunities and challenges. It requires us to think critically about the ethics of information sharing, ensuring equitable access, and navigating the complexities of data privacy and security. It also compels us to develop new tools and strategies for managing the ever-growing volume of information, ensuring its accuracy, relevance, and accessibility. By embracing the spirit of shared knowledge, we can unlock the full potential of human ingenuity, tackling global challenges and creating a brighter future for all.

Connecting with a Wider Audience

Understanding the Landscape: Deciphering Your Audience

The first step in connecting with a wider audience is to gain a comprehensive understanding of your intended recipients. This requires a deep dive into their demographics, interests, values, and communication preferences. Are you aiming to engage with a specific age group, cultural background, or professional sector. What are their key motivations and pain points. What platforms do they frequent, and how do they consume information.

Data and Analysis: Unlocking Audience Insights

To gain concrete insights into your audience, utilize data analysis tools and techniques. Social media analytics can reveal audience demographics, engagement patterns, and content preferences. Surveys and questionnaires can gather valuable feedback on their needs, interests, and perceptions. By analyzing website traffic data, you can identify popular content, user behavior patterns, and areas for improvement.

Persona Development: Crafting Ideal Audience Profiles

Based on your research, develop detailed audience personas. These fictional representations of your ideal audience members should encompass their personal and professional backgrounds, interests, goals, and communication styles. By creating these detailed profiles, you can tailor your message and content to resonate with their specific needs and aspirations.

Empathy and Sensitivity: Building Authentic Connections

Beyond data and analysis, empathy plays a critical role in

connecting with your audience. Put yourself in their shoes, understand their perspectives, and tailor your message to address their concerns and aspirations. This requires sensitivity to cultural nuances, diverse experiences, and potential biases.

Crafting Compelling Narratives: Engaging the Mind and Heart

Once you understand your audience, the next step is to craft narratives that resonate with their interests and values. Think beyond simply conveying information; instead, focus on telling stories that engage their emotions and leave a lasting impression.

Storytelling Techniques: Weaving Powerful Narratives

Effective storytelling involves crafting compelling narratives that connect with your audience on a personal level. Employ techniques such as:

Character Development: Create relatable and engaging characters that embody your message and resonate with your audience.
Conflict and Resolution: Introduce challenges and obstacles faced by your characters, and showcase their journey towards overcoming these difficulties.
Emotional Resonance: Evoke emotions in your audience through the use of vivid language, relatable experiences, and evocative imagery.
Themes and Messages: Embed meaningful themes and messages within your narratives that resonate with your audience's values and aspirations.

Visual Storytelling: Engaging the Eyes and Mind

Visual communication, such as images, videos, and infographics, plays a crucial role in conveying complex information in a digestible and engaging manner. Leverage powerful imagery to evoke emotions, illustrate concepts, and enhance your storytelling.

The Power of Visuals:

Visual Appeal: Use high-quality visuals that are aesthetically pleasing and relevant to your message.
Clear and Concise: Ensure your visuals are easy to understand and interpret, effectively conveying your key points.
Emotional Impact: Choose visuals that evoke specific emotions, such as joy, inspiration, or empathy, to create a lasting impression.

Leveraging Effective Communication Channels: Reaching the Right Audience at the Right Time

The choice of communication channels is critical for reaching your target audience effectively. Consider their preferred platforms, consumption habits, and the nature of your message.

Social Media: Building Online Communities

Social media platforms offer valuable opportunities for connecting with a wide and diverse audience. Utilize platforms like Facebook, Twitter, Instagram, LinkedIn, and YouTube to share your content, engage with followers, and build online communities.

Content Marketing: Creating Valuable Content

Content marketing involves creating and sharing valuable, relevant, and consistent content to attract and engage a clearly defined audience. This can include blog posts, articles, infographics, videos, podcasts, and more.

Email Marketing: Cultivating Direct Relationships

Email marketing provides a powerful avenue for building direct relationships with your audience. Utilize email campaigns to share updates, announcements, exclusive content, and personalized offers.

Public Relations and Media Outreach: Amplifying Your Message

Public relations and media outreach involve building relationships with journalists, bloggers, and influencers to generate positive media coverage and amplify your message.

Events and Workshops: Fostering In-Person Connections

In-person events, such as conferences, workshops, and seminars, provide opportunities for face-to-face interactions and fostering meaningful connections with your audience.

Measuring Impact and Adapting Strategies: Continuously Improving

Connecting with a wider audience is an ongoing process that requires continuous monitoring and adaptation. Utilize analytics tools to track key metrics, such as engagement, reach, and conversion rates. Based on your data, analyze your performance, identify areas for improvement, and refine your strategies to enhance your effectiveness.

Embracing Feedback: Learning and Growing

Embrace feedback from your audience, whether positive or negative. This provides valuable insights into their needs, preferences, and perceptions. Use this feedback to inform your future content creation, communication strategies, and overall approach. By understanding your target audience, crafting compelling narratives, leveraging effective communication channels, and embracing feedback, you can foster meaningful connections, amplify your message, and achieve impactful results. Remember, the key to success lies in building authentic relationships, engaging your audience on a personal level, and continuously evolving your approach to stay relevant and impactful in the ever-changing communication landscape.

Chapter 19: Finding a Place to Belong

Identifying with a Specific Messianic Jewish Congregation

Within the umbrella of Messianic Judaism, a variety of congregations exist, each with its own distinct character, practices, and theological nuances. This diverse landscape can be both exhilarating and overwhelming for someone seeking to connect. The journey of identifying with a specific Messianic Jewish congregation is a deeply personal one, guided by individual needs, values, and spiritual aspirations.

Understanding the Landscape: A Multifaceted Mosaic

Before diving into the process of identification, it's essential to understand the tapestry of Messianic Jewish congregations. These communities are not monolithic; they are shaped by a multitude of factors, including:

Theological Emphasis: Some congregations may focus heavily on the teachings of the Old Testament, drawing deeply from the rich heritage of Jewish tradition. Others might emphasize the New Testament, highlighting the role of Jesus in the Jewish faith. Still others strive to find a harmonious balance between these two pillars.
Liturgical Practices: Messianic Jewish congregations often integrate elements of traditional Jewish worship, such as Hebrew prayers, Torah readings, and the use of the Hebrew language. However, the

extent of these practices can vary significantly, with some congregations embracing a more traditional approach while others opt for a more contemporary style.

Cultural Identity: Some congregations place a strong emphasis on Jewish cultural traditions, celebrating holidays like Passover and Hanukkah with reverence and authenticity. Others may have a more universal focus, seeking to bridge the gap between Jewish and non-Jewish believers.

Congregational Dynamics: The overall atmosphere and dynamics within a congregation can be a major factor in determining a sense of belonging. Some congregations may be more formal and structured, while others are more informal and interactive. The size and composition of the congregation, as well as the leadership style, can also influence the overall experience.

Navigating the Journey: A Multi-Step Approach

Identifying with a Messianic Jewish congregation is not a passive process; it involves active exploration and self-reflection. Here's a multi-step approach that can guide individuals on this journey:

1. Self-Assessment: Begin by reflecting on your own beliefs and values. What aspects of Judaism and Christianity resonate most with you. What kind of spiritual community do you envision. Are there specific teachings, practices, or cultural elements that are particularly important to you.

2. Research and Exploration: Utilize resources like websites, books, and articles to learn about the different branches of Messianic Judaism. Explore the websites of various congregations, attend online events, and engage in conversations with members of different communities.

3. Visiting and Observing: Once you've identified some congregations that seem promising, schedule visits to attend services and events. Observe the worship style, the sermons, and

the interaction among congregants. Take note of the atmosphere and see if you feel a sense of connection and belonging.

4. Engaging with Members: Connect with members of the congregation, both formally and informally. Engage in conversations about their experiences, their understanding of Messianic Judaism, and the community's values. This interaction can provide invaluable insights and help you gauge whether you resonate with the congregation's ethos.

5. Seeking Guidance: Don't hesitate to seek guidance from trusted mentors, pastors, or rabbis. They can offer valuable perspectives, provide insights into different congregations, and help you discern which community aligns best with your spiritual journey.

Beyond the Search: Cultivating Belonging

Finding a Messianic Jewish congregation is just the beginning; it's the starting point of a journey that involves active participation, growth, and the cultivation of meaningful relationships. This journey can be both challenging and rewarding, fostering a sense of identity, purpose, and spiritual connection.

Building a Community:

Active Participation: Engage in congregational activities, such as worship services, study groups, social events, and outreach programs. This active participation strengthens your connection to the community and fosters a sense of belonging.
Meaningful Relationships: Build relationships with fellow congregants. Seek opportunities to connect beyond worship services, engaging in meaningful conversations, sharing experiences, and offering support.
Contribute and Serve: Identify ways to contribute to the community, whether through volunteering, leading a small group, or offering your skills and talents. Serving others helps build a sense of purpose and

strengthens your bond with the congregation.

Embracing the Journey:

Identifying with a specific Messianic Jewish congregation is not a one-time event; it's an ongoing process of discovery, growth, and connection. Be open to the evolving nature of your faith, your understanding of Judaism, and your relationship with the community. Embrace the challenges and joys of this journey, and allow it to shape you into the best version of yourself.

Navigating Challenges:

While finding a spiritual home can be immensely rewarding, it's essential to acknowledge that there may be challenges along the way.

Theological Differences: You might encounter theological perspectives that differ from your own. Approach these differences with respect and an open mind, engaging in constructive dialogue and seeking understanding.
Cultural Adjustments: Integrating into a new community, especially one with a distinct cultural heritage, can require adjustments. Be patient with yourself and the process, allowing time to acclimate and embrace the nuances of the culture.
Finding Your Place: It may take time to find your niche within the congregation and develop meaningful connections. Be proactive in reaching out, engaging in activities, and seeking to build relationships.

A Journey of Enrichment:

The journey of identifying with a specific Messianic Jewish congregation is an opportunity for personal and spiritual growth. It's a chance to delve deeper into your understanding of faith, engage with a vibrant community, and cultivate meaningful relationships that enrich your life. Embrace the journey with an open heart, a curious mind, and a willingness to learn and grow. Your search for a spiritual home can lead you to a place of profound connection, purpose, and belonging.

Building Relationships and Connections

Understanding the Essence of Connection:

At its core, building relationships is a multifaceted process that involves establishing a shared understanding, fostering mutual respect, and developing a sense of emotional connection. It's about creating a space where individuals feel heard, valued, and understood. This process requires active participation, genuine interest, and a willingness to invest time and effort.

The Building Blocks of Relationships:

Building strong relationships is akin to constructing a sturdy edifice, requiring careful attention to the foundational elements.

Communication: Effective communication forms the cornerstone of any relationship. This involves expressing ourselves clearly and respectfully, actively listening to others, and seeking to understand different perspectives. Open and honest communication fosters trust, transparency, and a shared understanding, paving the way for deeper connection.

Empathy: The ability to understand and share the feelings of others is a powerful tool for building rapport. By putting ourselves in another person's shoes, we demonstrate genuine concern and create a space for emotional connection. Empathy allows us to connect on a deeper level, fostering understanding and compassion.

Trust: Trust is the bedrock of any successful relationship. It is built upon a foundation of reliability, honesty, and consistency. When we trust someone, we feel safe and secure, allowing us to open ourselves up and develop a deeper bond.

Shared Interests and Values: Finding common ground is crucial for establishing a sense of connection. Shared interests, hobbies, beliefs, or goals provide a platform for engaging conversation, shared experiences, and mutual understanding.

Respect: Respect is the foundation of healthy relationships. It involves acknowledging and valuing the thoughts, feelings, and boundaries of others. Treating others with respect fosters a positive environment, promoting mutual understanding and appreciation.

Navigating the Dynamics of Relationships:

Building relationships is not a linear process. It involves navigating various dynamics, including:

Conflict Resolution: Disagreements and conflicts are inevitable in any relationship. Effective conflict resolution skills are essential for navigating these challenges constructively. Open and honest communication, active listening, and a willingness to compromise can help resolve conflicts amicably, strengthening the bond between individuals.

Boundaries: Setting healthy boundaries is crucial for maintaining our personal integrity and ensuring healthy relationships. Clear boundaries define our limits and expectations, allowing us to protect our emotional well-being while fostering mutual respect.

Time and Effort: Building strong relationships requires a conscious investment of time and effort. Making time for meaningful conversations, shared experiences, and expressing our appreciation for others demonstrates our commitment to the relationship.

Strategies for Building Stronger Connections:

Building meaningful connections requires a proactive approach. Here are some practical strategies:

Actively Listen: Practice attentive listening, focusing on understanding the speaker's perspective, emotions, and unspoken messages. Ask clarifying questions, demonstrate empathy, and avoid interrupting.

Be Authentic: Embrace your true self, expressing your thoughts and feelings honestly and genuinely. Authenticity fosters trust and allows others to connect with you on a deeper level.

Show Appreciation: Express gratitude for the people in your life. Words of affirmation, acts of kindness, and thoughtful gestures can strengthen bonds and create a sense of value.

Invest in Shared Experiences: Engage in activities that foster connection, such as volunteering together, pursuing shared hobbies, or simply enjoying a meal together.

Seek Out New Connections: Be open to meeting new people and expanding your social circle. Attend events, join clubs, or engage in online communities that align with your interests.

Practice Forgiveness: Holding onto resentment and anger can damage relationships. Practicing forgiveness, while challenging, can be liberating and contribute to a healthier dynamic.

The Power of Building Relationships:

The benefits of strong relationships extend far beyond personal satisfaction. They contribute to:

Increased Happiness and Well-being: Strong relationships provide a sense of belonging, support, and purpose, contributing to our overall happiness and well-being.

Enhanced Emotional Resilience: Having a strong support network can provide a buffer against life's challenges, helping us cope with stress and adversity.

Increased Productivity and Success: Positive relationships in the workplace can foster collaboration, creativity, and innovation, leading to increased productivity and professional success.

Stronger Communities: Healthy relationships contribute to a sense of community and connection, strengthening social bonds and fostering a sense of belonging.

Building relationships is a lifelong journey of growth, learning, and connection. By embracing these principles and strategies, we can cultivate meaningful bonds that enrich our lives, foster personal and professional growth, and create a more connected and compassionate world.

Finding Mentorship and Support

The Power of Mentorship: A Catalyst for Transformation

Mentorship, in its essence, is a relationship built on trust, respect, and a shared commitment to personal and professional growth. It is a journey of learning, where a seasoned individual, the mentor, provides invaluable knowledge, guidance, and encouragement to a less experienced individual, the mentee. This dynamic exchange fosters a symbiotic relationship, enriching the lives of both parties.

Mentors serve as invaluable guides, illuminating the path ahead with their wisdom and experience. They offer a unique perspective, helping mentees navigate the complexities of their chosen field, offering insights into industry trends, best practices, and potential pitfalls. Beyond technical expertise, mentors cultivate critical thinking skills, encouraging mentees to question assumptions, analyze challenges, and develop innovative solutions. They become trusted advisors, providing honest feedback, challenging preconceived notions, and fostering self-awareness.

Mentorship transcends the realm of knowledge acquisition; it fosters personal growth and resilience. By serving as role models, mentors inspire mentees to embrace their aspirations and strive for excellence. They instill a belief in one's abilities, encouraging mentees to step outside their comfort zones and take calculated risks. This process of self-discovery and growth fosters a sense of agency, empowering individuals to navigate challenges with confidence and determination.

Cultivating Supportive Networks: Building Bridges of Belonging

While mentorship offers a focused, one-on-one relationship, cultivating supportive networks expands the circle of guidance and encouragement, creating a tapestry of interconnected relationships that provide strength and resilience. These networks comprise individuals who share similar interests, values, or goals, fostering a sense of belonging and shared purpose.

Supportive networks serve as vital sources of encouragement, offering a safe space for sharing ideas, celebrating successes, and navigating setbacks. They provide a platform for peer learning, fostering collaboration, and promoting collective growth. Members of these networks can offer invaluable perspectives, challenge assumptions, and provide constructive feedback, enriching the experiences and decision-making processes of each individual.

Within these supportive networks, individuals can find solace and understanding during times of difficulty. The shared experiences of navigating challenges, celebrating triumphs, and offering empathy create a sense of connection, reminding individuals that they are not alone in their journey. This collective support system provides emotional resilience, fostering a sense of belonging and purpose amidst the ebb and flow of life.

Navigating the Search for Mentorship and Support:

The journey of finding mentorship and cultivating supportive networks requires intentionality, proactive engagement, and a willingness to embrace the transformative power of human connection. Here are some key strategies to guide this exploration:

Identify your goals and aspirations: Begin by clearly defining your personal and professional goals, identifying the skills, knowledge, and experiences you seek to acquire. This clarity will help guide your search for mentors and supportive networks aligned with your aspirations.

Seek out mentors and connections: Actively seek out individuals who resonate with your values and aspirations. Attend industry events, workshops, and conferences, engaging in conversations with individuals who inspire you. Leverage online platforms and professional networks to connect with individuals working in your field or pursuing similar interests.

Be proactive and demonstrate your commitment: Reach out to individuals you admire, expressing your interest in learning from them. Be prepared to articulate your goals, demonstrate your willingness to learn, and actively engage in the mentorship relationship. Offer to contribute to the mentor's work or initiatives, demonstrating your commitment to mutual growth.

Cultivate reciprocity and value-based relationships: Mentorship and support are not transactional exchanges but rather reciprocal relationships built on shared values and mutual growth.

Acknowledge the contributions of your mentor and support network members, expressing gratitude for their guidance and encouragement. Offer your own expertise and support when the opportunity arises, fostering a culture of collaboration and mutual respect.

The Transformative Power of Mentorship and Support

The journey of finding mentorship and cultivating supportive networks is an ongoing process of discovery, growth, and connection. It is an investment in oneself, a commitment to personal and professional development. As we embrace the guidance of mentors and the strength of supportive networks, we unlock our potential, navigate challenges with greater resilience, and create a meaningful impact on the world around us.

Beyond the Book:

Seek out mentorship programs: Many organizations, institutions, and professional groups offer mentorship programs designed to connect individuals with experienced professionals.

Join online communities and professional networks: Utilize online platforms like LinkedIn, professional association websites, and online forums to connect with individuals in your field.

Engage in volunteer activities: Volunteering offers opportunities to connect with individuals from diverse backgrounds, learn new skills, and contribute to causes you care about.

Final Thoughts:

Finding mentorship and support is not a passive pursuit but an active journey of self-discovery and connection. It requires intentionality, proactive engagement, and a willingness to embrace the transformative power of human relationships. By fostering these connections, we empower ourselves to navigate the complexities of life, achieve our aspirations, and create a lasting impact on the world around us.

Creating a Sense of Community

The Nature of Community:

Community is more than just a geographical location or a shared physical space. It transcends physical boundaries and can be found in online forums, interest groups, and even shared passions. At its core, community represents a group of individuals who share common values, interests, and experiences. These shared elements create a sense of connection, fostering a feeling of belonging and mutual support.

The Benefits of Belonging:

The benefits of fostering a sense of community are manifold and extend far beyond mere social interaction. A strong sense of community can contribute significantly to individual and collective well-being. Studies have consistently shown that individuals who feel connected to a community experience:

Increased Well-being: Strong social connections are linked to improved mental and physical health, leading to lower rates of depression, anxiety, and even chronic diseases.
Enhanced Resilience: Individuals within a strong community are better equipped to navigate life's challenges, finding solace and support in shared experiences and collective action.
Greater Civic Engagement: A sense of belonging often translates into active participation in community affairs, fostering a stronger sense of responsibility and promoting collective action for the greater good.
Improved Social Cohesion: A shared sense of identity and purpose

strengthens social bonds, reducing prejudice and fostering understanding and cooperation between different groups.

Building Blocks of Community:

Creating a sense of community is not a spontaneous event. It requires deliberate effort and a commitment to nurturing shared values and experiences. Building a strong community involves weaving together various threads:

Shared Values and Beliefs: Common values, beliefs, and aspirations act as the foundation for any community. Identifying and celebrating these shared ideals fosters a sense of unity and purpose.
Shared Experiences and Activities: Engaging in shared activities, whether it be volunteering, attending local events, or participating in group projects, creates common memories and strengthens bonds.
Open Communication and Dialogue: Open and honest communication is crucial for fostering understanding, resolving conflicts, and building trust within a community.
Mutual Support and Trust: A sense of belonging thrives on the knowledge that one can rely on others for help and support. This mutual trust fosters a sense of safety and security.

Creating a Sense of Community: Practical Strategies

While the concept of community might seem abstract, its creation involves practical steps that individuals and organizations can take to cultivate a sense of belonging and connection:

1. Encourage Participation and Engagement:

Organize Community Events: Host regular events that cater to diverse interests, promoting opportunities for social interaction and shared experiences. These events can range from potlucks and movie nights to workshops and volunteer projects.
Establish Community Spaces: Create designated physical spaces

that serve as gathering points for residents, fostering informal interactions and casual conversations. These could include community centers, libraries, parks, or even designated areas within workplaces.

Promote Volunteerism: Encourage community members to participate in volunteer activities, promoting a sense of purpose and collective action while building relationships with fellow volunteers.

2. Facilitate Communication and Dialogue:

Create Online Forums: Establish online platforms where community members can connect, share information, and engage in discussions on topics of common interest.

Organize Town Hall Meetings: Host regular town hall meetings to address community concerns, gather feedback, and foster open dialogue between residents and local authorities.

Develop Local Newsletters: Create informative newsletters that keep residents updated on community events, local initiatives, and important news, promoting a sense of shared awareness and involvement.

3. Nurture Shared Identity and Belonging:

Celebrate Local History and Culture: Organize events and activities that celebrate the unique history and culture of the community, fostering a sense of pride and shared identity.

Support Local Businesses: Encourage residents to patronize local businesses, promoting a sense of community ownership and contributing to the local economy.

Promote Arts and Culture: Support local arts organizations and initiatives, providing opportunities for creative expression and community engagement.

4. Address Barriers and Promote Inclusivity:

Identify and Challenge Barriers: Recognize and address existing

barriers to participation and inclusivity within the community, ensuring all residents feel welcomed and valued. This might involve addressing issues of socioeconomic disparities, language barriers, or cultural differences.
Foster Dialogue and Understanding: Promote cross-cultural communication and understanding through workshops, community events, and interfaith initiatives.

Building a Strong Sense of Community: A Collective Effort

Creating a strong sense of community is a collective effort that requires the commitment and participation of individuals, organizations, and local authorities. By fostering shared values, promoting meaningful interactions, and addressing barriers to inclusion, we can weave together the threads of belonging and create vibrant communities where everyone feels connected, supported, and empowered.

The journey of building a sense of community is ongoing and requires continuous effort. It involves not only actively participating in community activities but also being mindful of the needs and perspectives of those around us. By embracing the shared responsibility of nurturing a sense of belonging, we can create communities that are not just places to live but places to truly thrive.

Chapter 20: Conclusion

The Promise of Hope and Transformation

Hope, a beacon in the darkest of nights, is not merely a wishful sentiment but a powerful catalyst for action. It is the belief that despite the present struggles, a better tomorrow is attainable. This belief, rooted in our deepest convictions and fueled by our experiences, inspires us to persevere, to strive for a more fulfilling life, and to contribute to a more just and equitable world. It is the unwavering conviction that our efforts, however small, can make a difference, that our voices, however quiet, can be heard, and that our actions, however insignificant they may seem, can contribute to a brighter future.

Transformation, the process of becoming something new, is a journey of profound personal growth and societal evolution. It is the process of shedding old patterns, embracing new perspectives, and evolving into our best selves. This journey is often arduous, demanding a willingness to confront our limitations, to challenge our beliefs, and to embrace discomfort as a steppingstone towards growth. It requires courage, vulnerability, and a relentless pursuit of self-understanding, a willingness to be transformed by our experiences and to use our vulnerabilities as catalysts for positive change.

The promise of hope and transformation lies in the intersection of these two powerful forces. Hope provides the fuel, the unwavering belief in a better tomorrow, while transformation provides the direction, the path towards achieving that brighter future. It is a journey that requires us to embrace both the light and the darkness within ourselves, to acknowledge our strengths and our weaknesses, and to use our experiences as stepping stones towards growth.

This journey begins with a conscious choice, a commitment to personal growth and societal progress. It is a journey that requires us to actively cultivate hope, to nurture our capacity for resilience, and to embrace the transformative power of change. It is a journey that calls upon us to confront our fears, to challenge our preconceived notions, and to embrace the unknown with courage and conviction.

The promise of hope and transformation is not a guarantee, but a possibility, a potential that lies within each of us. It is a potential that we can realize by embracing our capacity for change, by nurturing our unwavering belief in a better future, and by taking the steps necessary to make that future a reality.

Hope as a Catalyst for Action

Hope is not merely a passive sentiment; it is a potent catalyst for action. It fuels our resilience, empowers our efforts, and inspires us to strive for a better world. It is the unwavering belief that change is possible, that our voices can be heard, and that our actions can make a difference. This belief, rooted in our deepest convictions and informed by our experiences, motivates us to take the necessary steps towards achieving our aspirations.

Hope is not about ignoring the challenges we face; it is about facing them with the conviction that we can overcome them. It is about acknowledging the darkness, but also recognizing the flicker of light within ourselves, the potential for growth, and the possibility of a brighter future. This hope is not blind optimism, but a calculated risk, a bet on ourselves and our collective capacity for change.

Hope is the driving force behind countless social movements, from the civil rights movement to the environmental movement. It is the fuel that drives activists to fight for justice, to advocate for change, and to challenge the status quo. It is the belief that collective action can create a more just and equitable world, that our voices can be heard, and that our efforts can make a difference.

Hope is not merely a collective sentiment; it is also a deeply personal experience. It is the belief that we can overcome adversity, that we can heal from trauma, and that we can achieve our goals. This belief, nurtured by our own resilience and guided by our aspirations, empowers us to confront our challenges with courage and determination.

In the face of overwhelming odds, hope can be a lifeline, a source of strength and resilience. It is the belief that we are not defined by our past, that we have the capacity to grow and to change, and that we have the power to shape our own future.

Transformation as a Journey of Self-Discovery

Transformation is not simply a change in external circumstances; it is a profound journey of self-discovery. It is a process of shedding old patterns, embracing new perspectives, and evolving into our best selves. This journey is often challenging, requiring us to confront our limitations, to challenge our beliefs, and to embrace discomfort as a steppingstone towards growth.

The process of transformation begins with self-awareness, with a willingness to honestly examine our beliefs, our values, and our behaviors. It requires us to acknowledge our strengths and our weaknesses, our vulnerabilities and our resilience. This self-reflection is not about self-criticism, but about self-understanding, about recognizing our potential for growth and the areas where we can make positive changes.

Transformation is often fueled by experiences that challenge our perspectives, that force us to confront our limitations, and that push us to grow beyond our comfort zones. It is through these challenges that we discover our resilience, our capacity for adaptation, and our potential for transformation.

The journey of transformation is not linear; it is often characterized by setbacks, doubts, and moments of uncertainty. It requires us to be patient with ourselves, to embrace the process of growth, and to celebrate our progress, no matter how small. It is a journey that demands courage, vulnerability, and a relentless pursuit of self-understanding.

Transformation is not just a personal journey; it is also a societal process. It is the recognition that our systems, our institutions, and our cultures can evolve to better reflect our values and our aspirations. This societal transformation requires collective action, a shared commitment to progress, and a willingness to challenge the status quo.

The promise of transformation lies in the potential for growth, both individually and collectively. It is the belief that we can create a more just, equitable, and sustainable world, by embracing our capacity for change and by working together to build a brighter future.

Embracing the Power of Hope and Transformation

The journey of hope and transformation is not a passive experience; it is an active pursuit, a conscious choice to embrace the potential for growth and to strive for a better future. It requires us to cultivate hope, to nurture our resilience, and to embrace the transformative power of change.

This journey begins with a commitment to self-awareness, to recognizing our strengths and our weaknesses, and to acknowledging our capacity for growth. It requires us to be honest with ourselves, to confront our limitations, and to challenge our beliefs.

Embracing the power of hope and transformation means believing in our own potential for change, in our capacity to overcome adversity, and in our ability to contribute to a better world. It requires us to nurture our inner strength, to cultivate a positive mindset, and to surround ourselves with people who inspire and support us.

This journey also demands a willingness to engage in our communities, to advocate for change, and to contribute to the collective effort to create a more just and equitable world. It requires us to challenge injustice, to stand up for what we believe in, and to work towards a future where everyone has the opportunity to thrive.

The promise of hope and transformation is not a guarantee, but a possibility, a potential that lies within each of us. It is a potential that we can realize by embracing our capacity for change, by nurturing our unwavering belief in a better future, and by taking the steps necessary to make that future a reality.

This journey is not always easy, but it is ultimately a rewarding one. It is a journey that leads to personal growth, societal progress, and the fulfillment of our potential as individuals and as a collective. It is a journey worth taking, a journey that offers the promise of a brighter future, a future filled with hope and transformation.

Embracing a Life of Faith and Meaning

The path to embracing a life of faith and meaning is rarely linear or predictable. It is a journey marked by both moments of profound clarity and periods of doubt and uncertainty. It requires a willingness to question, explore, and engage with the complexities of life and the depths of our own hearts. It demands an open mind, a curious spirit, and a commitment to ongoing growth and evolution.

Finding Your Path: The Journey Begins with Self-Reflection

The first step on this journey is often an inward one. It begins with self-reflection, a willingness to examine our own beliefs, values, and motivations. We must ask ourselves: What do I truly believe. What are the core values that guide my life. What gives my life meaning. What kind of legacy do I want to leave behind.

These questions are not meant to be answered definitively in a single moment. They are invitations to embark on a lifelong process of inquiry and discovery. They are the seeds that, when planted in the fertile ground of our hearts, can sprout into a vibrant and meaningful life.

The answers to these questions are often found not through logical deduction but through lived experience. It is through engaging with the world, with others, and with ourselves that we begin to discern the threads of meaning that weave through our lives.

The Role of Faith in Finding Meaning:

Faith, in its broadest sense, can be understood as a belief in something larger than oneself. It is the act of trusting in something beyond our immediate grasp, something that gives our lives a sense of purpose and direction. Faith can be expressed through a variety of avenues, including religious traditions, spiritual practices, or even personal philosophies.

A life of faith, whether grounded in a specific religion or not, offers a unique framework for finding meaning. It provides a sense of belonging, a community of like-minded individuals who share a common belief system. It offers a set of ethical guidelines, principles to live by that can help navigate the complexities of life. It provides a source of comfort and hope, a belief that there is something greater at work in the world, something that transcends our own limitations.

Exploring the Landscape of Faith: Traditions and Beyond

The world of faith is vast and diverse. From the ancient wisdom of Eastern traditions like Hinduism, Buddhism, and Taoism to the monotheistic religions of Christianity, Judaism, and Islam, each faith offers a unique perspective on the nature of reality, the human condition, and the divine.

Exploring these traditions, not with a focus on converting to one but with a spirit of curiosity and open-mindedness, can be a profoundly enlightening experience. It allows us to encounter different ways of seeing the world, different lenses through which to interpret the human experience. It can challenge our preconceptions and broaden our understanding of the tapestry of human spirituality.

Beyond established religious traditions, many find meaning in spiritual practices such as meditation, yoga, mindfulness, or nature-based rituals. These practices, often rooted in ancient traditions, offer ways to cultivate inner peace, connect with the divine, and deepen our understanding of ourselves and our place in the universe.

Embracing the Journey of Faith and Meaning:

The pursuit of faith and meaning is an ongoing journey, not a destination. It is a process of constant growth, exploration, and transformation. It requires a willingness to be open to new experiences, to challenge our own beliefs, and to embrace the uncertainties and complexities of life.

This journey may be marked by moments of doubt, questioning, and even periods of disillusionment. But it is within these challenges that we can discover the true depth of our faith and the resilience of our spirits. It is through embracing the full spectrum of human experience, the joys and sorrows, the triumphs and failures, that we can find a life imbued with meaning and purpose.

Living a Life of Faith and Meaning in the World:

The pursuit of faith and meaning is not an inward endeavor alone. It also calls us to engage with the world around us, to act on our beliefs, and to make a positive difference in the lives of others. It is through service, compassion, and a commitment to justice that we bring our faith to life.

Faith can inspire us to act with empathy and understanding towards those who are different from us. It can guide us to advocate for the vulnerable and marginalized. It can empower us to fight for a more just and equitable world. It is a journey that begins within ourselves, unfolds through our encounters with the world, and finds expression in how we live our lives. Embracing a life of faith, whether through religious tradition, spiritual practices, or personal philosophies, can provide a framework for finding purpose, connection, and meaning in a world that can sometimes feel overwhelming and chaotic.

This journey is not about achieving some predetermined state of perfection; it is about embracing the dynamic process of growth, exploration, and transformation. It is about discovering the unique spark of meaning that resides within each of us and allowing it to shine brightly in the world. It is about finding our place in the grand tapestry of life, contributing our own unique threads to the intricate design, and leaving a legacy that transcends our time on Earth.

Living a Life of Purpose and Impact

This journey begins with self-discovery, a process of introspection and exploration that helps us understand our values, passions, and talents. It is about identifying the areas where our unique skills and experiences intersect with our deepest desires to make a positive impact. This may involve delving into our personal histories, exploring our interests, and engaging in activities that ignite our curiosity and inspire us. The key is to be open to new possibilities, to embrace the unknown, and to allow ourselves to be guided by our intuition and our innate sense of purpose.

Once we have a clearer understanding of ourselves and our aspirations, we can begin to identify the specific ways in which we can contribute to the world. This may involve pursuing a career that aligns with our values, volunteering our time and resources to causes we care about, or simply engaging in acts of kindness and compassion in our daily lives. The act of giving, whether it be through our time, skills, or resources, is a powerful force for positive change, not only in the lives of others but also in our own.

It is important to recognize that living a life of purpose and impact is not a linear path. There will be challenges, setbacks, and moments of doubt along the way. It is in these moments that we must draw upon our resilience, our unwavering belief in ourselves and our purpose. Remember that failure is not the opposite of success, but rather a necessary part of the journey. Every obstacle, every mistake, is an opportunity to learn, to grow, and to refine our path.

Furthermore, living a life of purpose is not about achieving a specific outcome, but rather about embracing the process of continuous growth and learning. It is about embracing the journey, the constant evolution of our values, beliefs, and aspirations. It is about remaining open to new possibilities, to new ways of contributing and making a difference in the world.

Building a Foundation: The Pillars of Purposeful Living

Several key principles provide a solid foundation for living a life of purpose and impact:

1. Self-Awareness: The journey begins with understanding ourselves. This involves a deep exploration of our values, beliefs, passions,

skills, and experiences. It is about identifying what truly matters to us, what motivates us, and what we are truly passionate about. Self-awareness allows us to align our actions with our deepest desires, leading to a more fulfilling and purposeful life.

2. Authenticity: Authenticity is about being true to ourselves, living in alignment with our values and beliefs. It is about embracing our unique qualities, strengths, and weaknesses, and expressing them freely and honestly in the world. Living authentically allows us to connect with others on a deeper level, build meaningful relationships, and create a positive impact that resonates with our true selves.

3. Contribution: Purpose is not a passive concept; it is about actively contributing to something bigger than ourselves. This can take many forms, from pursuing a career that aligns with our values to volunteering our time and resources to causes we care about. The act of giving, whether it be through our time, skills, or resources, is a powerful force for positive change, both in the lives of others and in our own.

4. Resilience: The path to purpose is not always smooth. There will be challenges, setbacks, and moments of doubt. Resilience is the ability to bounce back from adversity, to learn from our mistakes, and to persevere in the face of obstacles. It is about maintaining our focus on our goals, believing in ourselves and our ability to make a difference, even when things get tough.

5. Growth Mindset: Living a life of purpose is a continuous journey of growth and learning. It requires a growth mindset, a belief that our abilities and skills can be developed through effort and dedication. This mindset allows us to embrace new challenges, learn from our experiences, and constantly evolve as individuals.

Cultivating Purposeful Habits: Building a Life of Impact

While the pursuit of purpose is a lifelong journey, there are specific habits and practices we can cultivate to foster a life of impact:

1. Mindful Reflection: Regularly taking time for introspection and reflection allows us to connect with our values, assess our progress, and identify areas for growth. This can involve journaling, meditation, or simply spending time in nature, allowing our thoughts to wander and our intuition to guide us.

2. Goal Setting: Setting clear, specific goals that align with our purpose provides direction and motivation. It is important to set goals that are challenging but achievable, and to break down larger goals into smaller, manageable steps.

3. Continuous Learning: Staying curious, open to new experiences, and continuously seeking knowledge is essential for personal and professional growth. This can involve reading books, attending workshops, engaging in meaningful conversations, and embracing opportunities for learning and development.

4. Building Meaningful Relationships: Strong, supportive relationships with family, friends, and mentors play a vital role in our journey of purpose. These relationships provide encouragement, support, and guidance, helping us stay motivated and focused on our goals.

5. Giving Back: Engaging in acts of service and generosity, whether through volunteering, donating to charity, or simply offering a helping hand to those in need, not only benefits others but also deepens our sense of purpose and fulfillment.

Finding Your Unique Path: A Personal Journey

Living a life of purpose and impact is not a one-size-fits-all approach. It is a deeply personal journey that unfolds uniquely for each individual. There is no right or wrong way to find your purpose;

it is about listening to your inner voice, exploring your passions, and embracing your own unique path.

Some may find purpose through creative pursuits, while others may be driven by a desire to serve their community or make a difference in the world. There are countless ways to live a life of purpose and impact, and it is a journey that evolves and transforms over time.

Embrace the Journey: A Life of Endless Possibilities

Living a life of purpose and impact is not a destination but a continuous journey of exploration, contribution, and growth. It is about embracing the unknown, embracing our unique gifts and talents, and using them to make a positive difference in the world. It is about being true to ourselves, living authentically, and connecting with others in meaningful ways.

The path to purpose is paved with challenges, setbacks, and moments of doubt. But it is also filled with moments of joy, fulfillment, and the deep satisfaction of knowing that we are making a difference in the world. Embrace the journey, and you will discover a life that is truly meaningful and impactful.

Connecting with the Messianic Jewish Community

Understanding Messianic Judaism: A Spectrum of Belief

Messianic Judaism, often referred to as "Hebrew Roots" or "Torah Observant Messianic Judaism," is a multifaceted movement within Judaism. Its core belief revolves around the acceptance of Jesus as the Jewish Messiah, fulfilling the ancient prophecies and bringing about the ultimate redemption. While acknowledging Jesus' divinity, Messianic Jews maintain their Jewish identity, observing traditional Jewish practices and adhering to the Torah's teachings.

The Messianic Jewish community presents a spectrum of beliefs and practices. Some groups emphasize a stricter adherence to traditional Jewish law, while others embrace a more liberal approach. Within this diverse landscape, it's crucial to recognize the heterogeneity of beliefs and practices, avoiding generalizations that might misrepresent the nuances of this dynamic community.

Bridging the Gap: A Path of Respect and Sensitivity

Building meaningful connections with Messianic Jews requires acknowledging their unique perspective on faith and identity. This involves respecting their Jewish heritage and recognizing their commitment to both Jewish tradition and Christian faith. Open communication and a willingness to listen are paramount. Avoid imposing external perspectives or judgment, instead fostering an environment of mutual respect and understanding.

The Challenge of Terminology: Navigating Sensitive Language

Language plays a pivotal role in fostering meaningful connections. It's crucial to understand and utilize respectful terminology when interacting with Messianic Jews. Avoid language that might be perceived as offensive or disrespectful. For instance, using the term "Jewish Christians" might be viewed as minimizing the distinctiveness of Messianic Judaism. Instead, acknowledge their identity as "Messianic Jews," respecting their commitment to both Jewish tradition and belief in Jesus as the Messiah.

Engaging in Dialogue: A Foundation for Understanding

Engaging in open and respectful dialogue is key to building meaningful connections. Avoid approaching conversations with predetermined conclusions or agendas. Instead, listen attentively to their perspective, seeking to understand their beliefs, experiences, and motivations. Engage in dialogue with genuine curiosity, demonstrating a desire to learn and appreciate their unique perspective.

Navigating Differences: Cultivating Respectful Exchange

Differences in belief and practice are inevitable within any community, and the Messianic Jewish community is no exception. Approaching differences with humility and respect is paramount. Avoid using these differences as a basis for judgment or dismissal. Instead, recognize that diversity strengthens the community and promotes a vibrant and multifaceted dialogue.

The Role of Common Ground: Finding Shared Values

While differences in belief may be present, it's crucial to recognize and appreciate areas of shared values. Many Messianic Jews value traditional Jewish practices, such as Sabbath observance, dietary laws, and holidays. Sharing these commonalities provides a platform for building connections and fostering deeper understanding.

Building Relationships: A Journey of Mutual Respect

Connecting with the Messianic Jewish community is not a one-time event but an ongoing journey. It involves nurturing relationships based on mutual respect, understanding, and a genuine desire to learn from each other. Cultivate friendships, engage in meaningful conversations, and participate in community events to build deeper connections.

The Importance of Resources: Embracing Knowledge and Understanding

Engaging with the Messianic Jewish community requires an understanding of their history, beliefs, and practices. Explore resources such as books, articles, websites, and documentaries to gain a comprehensive understanding of their perspectives and experiences. Seek out opportunities to learn from Messianic Jewish leaders and scholars, appreciating their insights and expertise.

Building Bridges: A Path of Reciprocal Learning

Connecting with the Messianic Jewish community is not merely a process of receiving information but a reciprocal journey of learning. Be open to sharing your own experiences and perspectives, acknowledging the value of diverse viewpoints. Encourage open dialogue and constructive exchange, building bridges of understanding and mutual respect.

Cultivating Compassion: Recognizing Shared Humanity

Ultimately, connecting with the Messianic Jewish community transcends theological or religious boundaries. It involves recognizing the shared humanity we all possess, embracing compassion and understanding as the foundation for meaningful relationships. Approach interactions with genuine empathy, recognizing the unique challenges and triumphs faced by every individual within this community.

Moving Forward: Embracing Growth and Understanding

Connecting with the Messianic Jewish community is an ongoing process of learning and growth. Be prepared to adjust your understanding as you encounter new perspectives and engage in deeper dialogue. Embrace this ongoing journey of discovery, recognizing that true understanding requires continual growth and open-mindedness. It requires respect, sensitivity, and a genuine desire to learn. By embracing open dialogue, fostering meaningful relationships, and appreciating the richness of their traditions and beliefs, we can build bridges of understanding and create a more inclusive and harmonious society.

Printed in Great Britain
by Amazon